On Psychotherapy 2
including the 7-Level Model

On Psychotherapy 2
including the 7-Level Model

PETRŪSKA CLARKSON

With contributions from
Geoffrey Lindsay and John Nuttall

W
WHURR PUBLISHERS
LONDON AND PHILADELPHIA

First published 2002 by Whurr Publishers Ltd
19b Compton Terrace, London N1 2UN, England and
325 Chestnut Street, Philadelphia PA 19106, USA

British Library Cataloguing in Publication Data
A catalogue record for this book is available from the
British Library.

ISBN 1 86156 227 6

Printed and bound in the UK by Athenaeum Press Ltd,
Gateshead, Tyne & Wear

Contents

About the authors

Professor Petrūska Clarkson, PhD, C Psychol., Fellow of the British Association for Counselling and Psychotherapy, and Fellow of the British Psychological Society, is a consultant philosopher, BPS chartered clinical, chartered counselling and chartered occupational and organisational psychologist as well as an accredited research psychologist, UKCP registered individual, child and group psychotherapist, and an accredited and recognised supervisor and management consultant with almost 30 years' international experience, who has more than 150 publications (22 languages) in these fields.

She is a past Chair of the BPsS Counselling Psychology Diploma Examination Board, a Professor of Psychotherapy at the University of Surrey, Roehampton, visiting Professor at Westminster University and at other training institutions and universities in the UK and abroad. She was Honorary Secretary of the Universities Association, has served on many Ethics Boards and founded several nationally and inter-nationally recognised training and accrediting organisations in psychotherapy.

She is the author of the acclaimed *The Therapeutic Relationship*, *The Bystander* and *Ethics: Working with Ethical and Moral Dilemmas in Psychotherapy* which is based on extensive research integrating life, theory and practice. She is also a poet and a parfumier.

Professor Clarkson teaches and supervises clinicians, supervisors, PhD researchers and organisational consultants in the areas of Jungian analysis, psychotherapy, psychology, supervision, ethics, culture and archetype as well as organisational dynamics. She works co-operatively as well as independently at the Centre for Qualitative Research in Training and Supervision at PHYSIS based at 58 Harley Street, London, W1G 9QB, email: petruska.c@dial.pipex.com or www.physis.co.uk.

Geoffrey Lindsay is Director of the Psychology and Special Needs Research Unit and of the Centre for Educational Development, Appraisal and Research in the Institute of Education, University of Warwick, and is a Chartered Psychologist. He is a former President of the British Psychological Society, a former Chair of its Investigatory Committee, and now a member of the Society's Disciplinary Board. He is also convenor of the European Federation of Professional Psychologists' Associations' Standing Committee on Ethics.

John Nuttall is a Chartered Marketer, Certified Management Consultant (IMC), and counsellor. After post-graduate study in organisation theory he followed a career in management and has been a director of a number of well-known companies in the UK and Europe. He has diplomas and an MA in psychotherapy and counselling and is current chair of the West London Centre for Counselling. He continues to study advanced psychotherapy at PHYSIS and Regents College.

Preface

Be patient toward all that is unsolved in your heart and try to love the *questions themselves* like locked rooms and like books that are written in a very foreign tongue. Do not now seek the answers, which cannot be given you because you would not be able to live them. And the point is, to live everything. *Live* the questions now. Perhaps you will then gradually, without noticing it, live along some distant day into the answer.

(Rilke, 1993, p. 35)

I could have called this volume *Meditations on Relationship,* because it is an articulation of my spiritual practice. I could also have called it *Researching the Therapeutic Relationship,* because I (with others such as Richardson, 1994) consider writing as a primary way of both seeing and acting in the world. I was not trying to write a single text in which everything is said to everyone.

Writing is validated as a method of knowing (p. 518). It has even been suggested that this volume is actually the **philosophy of psychology in practice** – as philosophy is the discipline of 'thinking about thinking' (Wittgenstein, 1922, p. 17). Perhaps these aspects cannot and should not be separated.

Important strands of my life's work are represented here. These include a concern with the **relationship between different psychotherapy approaches** ('psycho-languages') and the unity that seems to underlie them. The relationship itself forms the substance of Chapter 1.

Humpty Dumpty took the book, and looked at it carefully. 'That seems to be done right,' he began.
'You're holding it upside down!' Alice interrupted.
'To be sure I was!' Humpty Dumpty said gaily, as she turned it round for him. 'I thought it looked a little queer. As I was saying, that *seems* to be done right – though I haven't time to look it over thoroughly just now – and that shows that there are three hundred and sixty-four days when you might get un-birthday presents.'
'Certainly,' said Alice.

'And only *one* for birthday presents, you know. There's glory for you!'
'I don't know what you mean by "glory",' Alice said.
Humpty Dumpty smiled contemptuously. 'Of course you don't – till I tell you. I meant "there's a nice knock-down argument for you!"'
'But "glory" doesn't mean "a nice knock-down argument",' Alice objected.
'When I use a word,' Humpty Dumpty said in rather a scornful tone, 'it means just what I choose it to mean – neither more nor less.'
'The question is,' said Alice, 'whether you *can* make words mean so many different things.'
'The question is,' said Humpty Dumpty, 'which is to be master – that's all.'

(Carroll, 1994, p. 87)

Chapter 2 is concerned with the value of 'going in search of oneself' (through studying countertransference), only to discover that one 'cannot find the limits of the soul', no matter how far one travels (Heraclitus, in Kahn, 1981).

Chapter 3 explores the five modes of the therapeutic relationship (see, for example, Clarkson, 1995, 1996) in the language of existentialism.

But in the beginning: *logos* as the gathering that makes manifest, and in the same sense being as fitness or *physis,* became the necessary essence of historical man. Thence it takes only a step to understand how *logos,* thus understood, determined the essence of language and how *logos* became a name for discourse.

(Heidegger, 1959, p. 171)

The meanings of **intersubjectivity** and the different levels of human experience of hurting and healing enriched by information from the new sciences are addressed in Chapter 4.

Samuels (1981) was one of the first to say it openly: 'In general, there are three places to start a training – at the beginning, where you're told, or you can look for where the explosion is and start there' (p. 217). The debates around **recovered memories of abuse** are such an explosion.

The epitaph I would like for my life and my education of psychotherapists, psychologists and organisational consultants is: 'I myself hearken to and bring out the **physis** in others'. I can only do this by standing on the shoulders of the pre-Socratic Heraclitus (Guerrière, 1980, p. 87). This is the subject matter of Chapter 5.

The world order speaks to humans as a kind of language they must learn to comprehend. Just as the meaning of what is said is actually 'given' in the sounds which the foreigner hears, but cannot understand, so the direct experience of the *physis* of things [or people] will be like the babbling of an unknown tongue for the soul that does not know how to listen.

(Kahn, 1981, p. 107)

Chapter 6 is concerned with the relationship between the individual and the collective – **individual and social psychology** – particularly as it plays out in the arena of **creativity and excellence**. Wertz (1995) is applying Foucault's approach when he writes:

> Psychology's methods of dealing with persons are structurally no different from those in the areas of medicine, criminal justice, education and industry . . . and yet I do argue that we as individual persons and as psychologists are responsible for our participation in this order and are free to abandon the project of domination and control, to practice a psychology that recognizes, embraces, liberates and empowers the Other through a practice of open dialogue. This entails not eradication but a respectful acknowledgement of the presence of inimicality in others and in ourselves.
>
> (p. 451)

Enhancing our quality of practice for clients in all forms of psychological counselling and psychotherapy through **supervision** – where practitioner and supervisor work together for the benefit of the client – is the subject matter of Chapter 7 (see also Clarkson, 1998).

We can speak of roughly two kinds of training and supervision in psychotherapy. It is good to remember that the root of the word education (*educare*) means 'to lead forth from within'. The thirteenth century Rumi (1988) says it best:

Two Kinds of Intelligence

There are two kinds of intelligence: One acquired,
as a child in school memorizes facts and concepts
from books and from what the teacher says,
collecting information from the traditional sciences
as well as from the new sciences.

With such intelligence you rise in the world.
You get ranked ahead or behind others
in regard to your competence in retaining
information. You stroll with this intelligence
in and out of fields of knowledge, getting always more
marks on your preserving tablets.

There is another kind of tablet, one
already completed and preserved inside you.
A spring overflowing its springbox. A freshness
in the centre of the chest. This other intelligence
does not turn yellow or stagnate. It's fluid,
and it doesn't move from outside to inside
through the conduits of plumbing-learning.

This second knowing is a fountainhead
from within you, moving out.

This chapter includes the Clarkson Invariant Action Sequence – the result of a phenomenological observation of a natural and **invariable sequence in effective human actions** – even supervision – as well as transcultural aspects of our work.

> No, only that man is knowing who understands that he must keep learning over and over again and who above all, on the basis of this understanding, has attained to the point where he is always *able to learn*. This is much more difficult than to possess information. Ability to learn presupposes ability to inquire. Inquiry is the willing-to-know analysed above: the resolve to be able to stand in the openness of the essent [Being or *physis*].
>
> (Heidegger, 1959, p. 22)

The inescapability of ethical and moral concerns investigated through integrating research and practice – particularly **collegial relationships** with their vital implications for clients' welfare and integrity in our professions, is the subject of Chapter 8 (see also Clarkson, 2000). As the 'unexamined life may not be worth living' the unexamined psychotherapy may not be worth doing.

> The postmodern years are bringing, instead of a collapse of morality, a renaissance of searching for principles of life that we variously call morals, ethics, values. And this is not merely a single shift of values but a continual dynamic process of moral discourse and discovery. Morals are not being handed down from the mountaintop on graven tablets; they are being created by people out of the challenges of the times. The morals of today are not the morals of yesterday, and they will not be the morals of tomorrow.
>
> (Anderson, 1990, p. 259)

Chapter 9 on 'the sublime' (Clarkson, 1997) is a reprinting in this book of a much-loved paper first delivered at a Jungian studies day and previously only available in hardback with Harvard style references. Samuels (1993) already said that 'one of the things that depresses me about the UKCP is that we have to listen to men and women of the psyche talking like bloody bankers!' (p. 321). Chapter 9 is a possible antidote.

Finally Chapter 10 is included for its usefulness in applying understandings from epistemology – the discipline of studying knowledge – including what we can know and how **seven different, but co-existing domains of knowledge** involve different kinds of 'truth values'. It has been found helpful in understanding yourself, improving communication between people and managing 'knowledge'. It is in the area of the philosophy of psychology.

All my usual caveats apply. As Jim Hartle said: 'anyone over the age of twelve knows there is no such thing as certainty, right?' (Hawking, 1992, p.

177). This book is only part of an ongoing conversation, which only bears its true fruit when

> In the experience of dialogue, there is constituted between the other person and myself a common ground; my thought and his are interwoven into a single fabric, my words and those of my interlocutor are called forth by the stage of the discussion, and they are inserted into a shared operation of which neither of us is the creator. We have here a dual being, where the other is for me no longer a mere bit of behaviour in my transcendental field, nor I in his; we are collaborators for each other in consummate reciprocity.
>
> (Merleau-Ponty, 1992, p. 354)

This book is dedicated to all those (particularly students, novice and veteran clinicians and other learners) who have privileged me by participating in this consummate reciprocity.

References

Anderson WT (1990) Reality Isn't what it Used to Be. San Francisco: Harper & Row.

Carroll L (1994) Through the Looking Glass. London: Puffin Books. First published 1872.

Clarkson P (1995) The Therapeutic Relationship in Psychoanalysis, Counselling Psychology and Psychotherapy. London: Whurr.

Clarkson P (1996) Researching the 'therapeutic relationship' in psychoanalysis, counselling psychology and psychotherapy – a qualitative inquiry. Counselling Psychology Quarterly 9(2): 143–62.

Clarkson P (ed.) (1997) On the Sublime. London: Whurr.

Clarkson P (ed.) (1998) Counselling Psychology: Integrating Theory, Research and Supervised Practice. London: Routledge.

Clarkson P (ed.) (2000) Ethics: Working with Ethical and Moral Dilemmas in Psychotherapy, London: Whurr.

Guerrière D (1980) Physis, Sophia, Psyche. In Sallis J and Maly K (eds) Heraclitean Fragments: A Companion Volume to the Heidegger/Fink Seminar on Heraclitus. Tuscaloosa, AL: University of Alabama Press, pp. 86–134.

Hawking S (ed.) (1992) Stephen Hawking's 'A Brief History of Time': A Reader's Companion. Prepared by Stone G. London: Bantam Press.

Kahn CH (1981) The Art and Thought of Heraclitus: An Edition of the Fragments with Translation and Commentary. Cambridge: Cambridge University Press.

Merleau-Ponty M (1992) Phenomenology of Perception. Trans. Colin Smith. London: Routledge & Kegan Paul.

Richardson L (1994) Writing – a method of enquiry. In Denzin NK and Lincoln YS (eds) Handbook of Qualitative Research. Thousand Oaks, CA: Sage, pp. 516–29.

Rilke RM (1993) Letters to a Young Poet (trans. Herter Norton MD) (revised edn). New York: WW Norton.

Rumi J (1988) Two kinds of intelligence. In Mathnawi IV, 1960–1968 This Longing. Trans. Barks C and Moyne J. Vermont: Threshold Books, p. 36.

Samuels A (1981) Fragmentary vision: a central training aim. Spring pp. 215–25.

Samuels A (1993) What is a good training? British Journal of Psychotherapy 9(3): 317–23.

Wertz FJ (1995) 'Yerkes' rabbit and career: from trivial to more significant matters. Theory and Psychology 5(3): 451–4.

Wittgenstein L (1922) Tractatus Logico Philosophicus (trans. Pears DF and McGuinness BF). (Reprinted.) London: Routledge, 1961.

Chapter 1
Beyond Schoolism

PETRŪSKA CLARKSON

> Tolstoy: I know that most men, including those at ease with problems of the greatest complexity, can seldom accept even the simplest and most obvious truth if it be such as would oblige them to admit the falsity of conclusions which they have delighted in explaining to colleagues, which they have proudly taught to others, and which they have woven, thread by thread, into the fabric of their lives.
>
> (Gleick, 1988, p. 38)

Introduction

Almost a hundred years after Freud, Moreno and Pavlov birthed the three great lineages of psychotherapy, more than 450 different approaches have been identified (Corsini, 1984). Polkinghorne's (1992) words summarize those of many thinkers since: 'The large number of theories claiming to have grasped the essentials of psychological functioning provide *prima facie* evidence that no one theory is correct' (p. 158).

The contemporary situation in psychotherapy

'Pure' forms of psychotherapy seem to exist only in the minds of people not part of current insider debates, however the orthodox party lines are defended to outsiders (Malcolm, 1981). There is, in any case, substantial evidence to indicate that most schools of psychotherapy or psychoanalysis continue to challenge and integrate within these forms (Hinshelwood, 1990; Gee, 1995).

In the US and in five other countries 'integrative psychotherapy' is now being hailed as the most popular descriptive term of psychotherapists (Norcross, 1997). However this is also leading to another infinite proliferation. In 1984, Dryden estimated that there were about a dozen different

1

forms of integrative psychotherapy and I would think the figure today would be around 28. Unfortunately, integrative approaches are as susceptible to schoolism as any of the others – if they do not descend into a hotchpotch of other people's theories brought together 'eclectically' without coherence or systemization.

So in contemporary psychotherapy we could have the polarization of a defensive fundamentalist orthodoxy on the one hand and an infinitely expanding relativity on the other. (By analogy, Latin died as a spoken language. Esperanto, or Yiddish or Fanagalo, are not gibberish but each has both a structure and a grammar.) Multi-lingualism is a third possibility – the pluralistic or postmodern engagement with the coexistence of many different languages. This will require some patience in the translation. However, there are always structural, utilitarian and aesthetic differences between pidgin and poetry, between superstition and science, whatever one's preferences may be.

Heine (1953) found that it was not possible, from a description of psychotherapist activity, to determine to which theoretical school a psychotherapist belongs. What differentiates between them are, in fact, the names and labels clients attach to the 'fundamental causes' of their troubles. Fiedler (1950) studied the differences between exponents of three different schools of psychotherapy – Freudian, Adlerian and non-directive. He found that the differences in actual practice between experienced practitioners in different schools were considerably smaller than between beginners and their more senior colleagues in the same school. That is, it appears that their practice was more a function of their experience of the therapautic relationship than of their theoretical orientation per se.

Subsequent research has shown that one of the most overriding and influential factors in the outcome of psychotherapy is the **relationship** between psychotherapist and client (Frank, 1979; Hynan, 1981). Theoretical differences between 'schools or approaches' are found to be far less important in terms of successful outcome of counselling or psychotherapy than the quality of the relationship between counsellor and client and certain client characteristics, including motivation for change and the willingness to take responsibility for their part in the process (Norcross, 1986; Beutler and Consoli, 1992; Lambert, 1992).

A wealth of studies (for example, Luborsky, Crits-Christoph, Alexander, Margolis and Cohen, 1983; O'Malley, Suh and Strupp, 1983; Bergin and Lambert, 1978) have demonstrated that it is the relationship between the client and psychotherapist, more than any other factor, which determines the effectiveness of psychotherapy in terms of success as defined by the client or clients. That is, success in psychotherapy can best be predicted by the properties of the patient, psychotherapist and their particular relationship (Norcross and Goldfried, 1992).

More recently, in his paper 'The effectiveness of psychotherapy', which discussed a consumer report study sampling some 3,000 consumers of psychotherapy in the US, Seligman (1995, p. 965) wrote in summary that:

> Long-term treatment did considerably better than short-term treatment . . . No specific modality of psychotherapy did better than any other for any disorder . . . Patients whose length of therapy or choice of therapist was limited by insurance or managed care did worse.

Of course it is also **always** possible to contest or question research results – and the justifications are infinite. They range from methodological criticisms on the one hand to a treasuring of the essentially ineffable mystery of the therapeutic encounter that intrinsically cannot (and, on the other hand, according to some views - for example, Plaut, 1996, p. 8 – should not) be measured. As recently as late 1996 Shapiro (p. ix) wrote:

> Many, if not most, of the cherished beliefs of theorists and practitioners of particular methods of psychotherapy remain largely unsupported by the kinds of evidence preferred by those who control the budgets of health care systems across the globe . . . However, 'head-to-head' comparisons among treatments differing in the strengths of their respective evidential support show surprisingly modest differences. For most of the disorders reviewed here, there is little evidence to take us beyond the paradoxical 'Dodo bird verdict' of equivalent outcomes from very different treatment methods.

There are certainly some leaders in the field who are looking towards the possibilities of 'integration' in terms of the commonalities between different schools of psychotherapy. Storr (1979, p. viii) has prophesied that 'the labels of "Jungian", "Kleinian", "Freudian", will become less and less important as research discloses the common factors which lead to a successful outcome in psychotherapy, which is largely independent of the school to which the psychotherapist belongs.'

Even the 1996 National Health Service document about psychotherapeutic services concluded that: 'it would be premature and unjustified to imagine that certain treatments have been "validated" . . . The NHS Executive will not therefore publish a list of "effective" therapies on which funding decisions should be based' (Parry and Richardson, 1996, p. 42). With even less research evidence for differential effectiveness related to theory, the same is probably true for supervision (see Clarkson, 1998).

In discussing what an expert such as Barkham (1995) has described as 'the pinnacle of research efforts in researching psychotherapy', Elkin (1995, p. 183) concluded that there appears to be no significant difference that can be particularly ascribed to specific differences in approach, and she is now focusing 'on the actual patient–therapist interactions in the videotaped treatment sessions'.

The special issue of the journal *Changes* (Vol. 13, No. 3) on outcome in psychotherapy is also well worth attention. In it Russell (1995) considers the work of Smith and Glass (1977), Lipsey and Wilson (1993), and Strupp (1979, p. 215) and finds that they all seem to point to the conclusion that 'positive change was generally attributable to the healing effects of a benign human relationship'.

In summary, as of today there are thus some six facts that emerge reliably from the research:

- Eysenck's challenge from the 1950s has been met. **There is substantial evidence of various kinds that psychotherapy seems to help many people** (Consumer Reports, 1995; Parry and Richardson, 1996).
- **There is no significant evidence that theoretical approach is relevant to the successful outcome of Eurocentric psychotherapies – no matter how measured** (Heine, 1953; Norcross and Goldfried, 1992; Seligman, 1995; Barkham, 1995; Shapiro, 1996; Elkin, 1995; Roth and Fonagy, 1996; Norcross 1997, Parry and Richardson, 1996; Arundale 1997; Clarkson 1997b. See also Youngson and Alderman, 1994 where a cognitive-behavioural psychologist reports substantial behavioural change without the theoretically required cognitive changes).
- **There is substantial evidence that it is in fact the psychotherapeutic relationship rather than diagnosis or technique that potentiates the beneficial effects of psychotherapy** (see Fiedler, 1950; Norcross, 1997; and Clarkson, 1990, 1995b, 1997b for more detail).
- This finding is consistent with experience and research reporting that (as long as the explanation or 'narrative' is culturally congruent) **experiences of mental and emotional healing have always existed in human societies perhaps for 60,000 years**. Furthermore such healing practices are right now helping many people in distress across the world through what is sometimes referred to as indigenous medicine (for example Moodley, 1998). According to Frank and Frank's (1993) masterly survey, (a) the therapeutic relationship – often a group – always in context of community (cf. de Mare et al.'s 1991 Median Group); (b) a culturally congruent narrative; (c) a dedicated space; and (d) a prescription for some action constitute the four necessary ingredients for all healing practices.
- In addition to the multitude of studies that have testified to the overriding importance of the therapeutic relationships, it has been

found that **there are different kinds of relationship required for different kinds of patients and this factor is more important than diagnosis in predicting effectiveness of psychotherapy** (Norcross, 1997). A major, externally validated study found five different universes of discourse or kinds of psychotherapeutic relationship spanning all approaches: working alliance, transference/countertransference, developmentally needed or reparative, person-to-person, and transpersonal (Clarkson, 1975, 1990, 1996b, 1997b).

- **Evidence exists that there are experiences of psychotherapy by which people feel harmed.** One of the most salient facts here is that the harmfulness seems to have to do with the extent to which a psychotherapist entrenches into a theoretical position when challenged or questioned by their client (see Winter, 1997 for a review).

A puzzle: why are Eurocentric psychotherapists behaving as if theoretical allegiance is all important?

Several psychotherapy organizations and many conferences are organized around the notion of different theoretical approaches – whether 'integrative' or not. Psychotherapy school syllabuses and curricula all specify theory. Few, if any, specify demands for research capability, philosophical understanding or performance. At conference after conference dozens of intelligent people passionately expound on the differences (usually 'theory') and commonalities (usually 'high standards') between their 'schools'. Numerical and geographical popularity arguments abound. There is the semiotically rich use of 'flag' statements as distinguishing emblems of theories. There are even those who still essentially claim that 'mine is better than yours'. Yet **there is no evidence to date that theory is actually relevant to the delivery of effective psychotherapy**.

Upon inspection of the documents it appears that psychotherapy's standards are often judged more by democratic votes – not accountability to internal and external critique. Indeed standards ordinarily applicable to judging academically accountable theories are usually not mentioned – elegance, economy, explanatory power, academic rigour or effort (judging by the number of quality texts), freedom from (or awareness of) presumptive and logical errors, provability, the relationship to research (whether scholarly, quantitative, qualitative, or philosophical), critical self-reflection and freedom of expression, the relationship to other theories – or even to fit with the scientifically proven facts within the contemporary culture and sciences.

Much of psychoanalysis and academic psychology is handicapped by having harnessed itself to exclusively Newtonian and Cartesian models which the hard sciences such as physics substantially relinquished some 70 years ago. The new paradigms of quantum physics, chaos and complexity (Clarkson, 1995b) as well as developments in computer and qualitative methodology (Denzin and Lincoln, 1994) have opened possibilities of research upon which psychotherapy could genuinely thrive with its integrity intact. By using these with conceptual shifts such as Shotter's (1992) meta-methodology, we could make a genuine contribution in the new millennium, rather than attempting to emulate a historically passé ideal of science or religion (exclusively logical positivism or exclusively ideological beliefs).

Tantam, at the 1996 UKCP professional conference (as reported in *The Psychotherapist* by Smith, 1997, p. 6) confirmed that:

> 1. Differences in technique are increasingly trivial and unimportant 2. theoretical knowledge has been over-emphasised and 3. we have overlooked that kind of practical knowledge that the media is interested in, the knowledge of outcomes. We each have our particular myths and rituals of healing; so long as they are valid for us and our patients, which we use does not really matter. This can also be said of theoretical knowledge.

This is consistent with the quantitative and qualitative psychological research evidence reviewed in this chapter and with the psychotherapy values and practice that I have named 'Beyond schoolism' (Clarkson, 1995a, 1997a and 1997b). This is a working title to refer to a situation in psychotherapy where 'schools' or 'orientations' or 'approaches' will be acknowledged as less important than the therapeutic relationship itself, and where a common value commitment to the alleviation of human suffering and the development of human potential will have replaced factionalism, rivalry and one-up-one-down politics. The attendant destructiveness to creativity and innovation of the latter tendencies hardly needs elaboration.

'Schoolism' in psychotherapy is the result of passionately held convictions of being right that fly in the face of the facts. Schoolism outlaws questioning and expels dissidents. Grosskurth (1989, p. 428) for example reported how, in 1950, Bowlby compared the Kleinian group of analysts to a religious sect (Rycroft called it the Ebenezer Church) 'in which, once one had espoused the doctrine, one was welcomed to the fold. If one deviated, if one did not subscribe totally to the doctrine, one faced the terrible threat of excommunication.' Unfortunately recent events in the UK (see Clarkson, 2000) have proved that this is now also true for some UKCP Gestalt organizations such as CPTI.

It is only by stepping outside of this inherited frame of reference that psychotherapy can offer something equivalent or better. It is of course usually in the interstices and liminal spaces where the creative discoveries of any art or science are made (Koestler, 1989; Gleick, 1992).

> The major problem with the notion of 'school' is its relative inflexibility in response to new ideas in psychotherapy. Schools have responded to varying degrees of psychotherapy innovation, but the value of schools has been to preserve good ideas. At this point in psychotherapy's history, these good ideas within schools have been preserved well enough.
>
> (Beitman, 1994, p. 210)

Rationalizations for schoolism

While at a psychotherapy conference in Rome during the summer of 1997 I consulted the Italian dictionary to find the definition of science as 'il resultato delle operazioni del pensiero'. Science is the result of thinking. Independent thinking and unquestioning adherence to ideological statements are not natural bedfellows. Thinking is hard work. It is often lonely work too. It is, of course, often easier to adapt, introject, claim or modify other people's ideas – with or without appropriate academic acknowledgement – as your own 'integration'.

Information in psychotherapy and psychology is being produced at the rate of hundreds of books and thousands of papers and research reports per year – that's a lot of reading. If you are unable or unwilling to read you have a problem. Research of any kind is notoriously difficult. It's far more comfortable to avoid its multiple risks by adherence to ideological statements claiming the status of 'philosophy'. Philosophy is an ancient academic discipline; it is not a gratuitous statement of unquestioned preferences. It is indeed very difficult to make research relevant to practitioners (Morrow-Bradley and Elliott, 1986) but this bridge between the academy and the clinic is precisely what psychotherapy trainers who take research into account are uniquely equipped to sponsor (Lepper, 1996; Clarkson, 1995c). A research practice for psychotherapy may be the only truly accountable way forward for this profession.

Parry's 1997 keynote address to the BAC's annual conference actually recommended that we relinquish the impossible if not unsuitable gold standard of double-blind controlled quantitative outcome research in psychotherapy. In my opinion the research projects of priority (of which I have done some already) should now be (a) qualitative research in terms of exploring the commonalities such as dimensions of the psychotherapeutic relationship between approaches (Clarkson, 1996b), (b) the subjective experiences of what **clients** experience as helpful or harmful across approaches (Clarkson and Winter, in press) and (c) the possibilities of educating novices and continuing to educate experienced professionals and supervisors in methods and attitudes of rigorous philosophical as well as postmodern scientific enquiry (Clarkson, 1997c).

Schoolism is comfortable because it can relieve the existential burdens of thinking, of doubting oneself and of exercising free choice (see the Grand Inquisitor's speech in Dostoevsky's *Brothers Karamazov*). It makes it possible for a professional psychotherapist to say (as was found in recent research, Clarkson and Lindsay, 1997): 'in my 30 years of clinical practice I have never had the misfortune to encounter an ethical dilemma'. As the histories of our world and our professions prove, it is infinitely more comfortable to be 'bystanders' to malpractice and injustice than to risk the responsible engagement with such demanding issues (Clarkson, 1996a).

It is patently uncomfortable to live up to the House of Lords statement that 'professionals, whether in practice or in employment, must be independent in thought and outlook, willing to speak their minds without fear or favour, and not be in the control or dominance of any person or organisation' (Lord Benson, Hansard 618, LD92/93 July 6–11 1207). Historical events such as the judicial review of the UKCP bring this further into question (see Clarkson, 2000). Can one speak of psychotherapy as a profession in this sense? Or is what Szasz said at the 1997 UPA conference true: that psychotherapy organizations exist to protect the professionals from the public?

As the Oxford philosopher of psychology Farrell pointed out in 1979, participants, 'trainees' or clients are usually considered to be 'cured' or 'trained' or 'analysed' or 'qualified' by one single criterion – they have adopted the WOT ('way of talking') of the leaders, governing bodies, examination boards and others of perceived status or power. An empirical study by Silverman (1997, p. 209) from London University also found repeatedly that 'rather than being a deviant case, such adoption by clients of the professionals' rhetoric is common . . . each centre [of counselling] offers an incitement to speak structured according to its own practical theories.'

The frequently heard statement that 'we must give the trainees a secure theoretical base' has enormous face validity. It is perhaps even true at a certain ideological level. However, the epistemological nature of this vaunted security deserves profound investigation, not an unquestioning culture-blind acceptance (Ani, 1994). Every West European psychotherapeutic narrative minimizes the 'radical differences between egocentric Western culture and socio-centric non-Western cultures and disclose that **culture exerts a powerful effect on care**' [emphasis added] (Kleinman quoted in Helman, 1994, p. 279). Helman continues: 'Whether this narrative is short (as in spirit exorcisms) or lengthy (as in psychoanalysis) it summarizes *post hoc* what had happened to them, and why, and how the healer was able to restore them to happiness or health' (p. 280). (See also Gergen, 1994 and Smail, 1987.)

All these perspectives are, of course, in line with the seminal work of Lyotard (1989) and Foucault (1980, 1988) who laid bare the power of social processes to constitute certain kinds of realities and distinctive kinds of human subjects in situations where professional knowledge is used, such as clinics and prisons. Unless psychotherapy training and supervision are done with these considerations in mind, they are likely to suffer from the very defects and destructive consequences entailed by short-sighted ignorance of these issues or adoption of unquestioning compliance with potentially fundamentalist ideologies. Indeed, what research there is, of an acceptable standard, about psychotherapy supervision suggests, for example, that developmental models of supervision are not empirically supportable, but it has been found again that it is the 'quality of the supervisory relationship [which] is paramount to successful supervision' (Watkins, 1997, p. 495).

The time may be ready for a transcultural, transtheoretical, transdisciplinary perspective which is genuinely based on learning by enquiry (*dieratao*). This is research in the widest, most philosophical, objective and most subjective sense of the term, because there is (a) little if any evidence that theory has an appreciable effect on the effectiveness of psychotherapy and (b) an increasing valuing of exploratory process-oriented research; (c) an increasingly felt need for professionals to associate, collaborate, interact and research across disciplines, across orientations and across cultural divides; and (d) although not necessarily wanting to give up specializations and loyalties to specific 'psycholanguages', there is an increasing number of professionals who want instead, or also, to be **independent** of such languages, concentrating on transtheoretical and epistemological aspects as well as fundamental empirical questions and methods (see Clarkson, 1997b, 1997c). This moment might even mean recognizing and celebrating our essential and inescapable **interdependence** on each other (Hahn, 1997). As Stewart (1996, p. 80) pleaded: 'We must get away from the simplex [or even complex] emphasis on the differences between areas of human culture, and begin to construct a multiplex vision founded on their similarities.' Anderson (1990, p. 152) phrases it thus:

> We will have to come to terms, as we stagger into the postmodern era, with the hard-to-avoid evidence that there are many different realities, and different ways of experiencing them, and that people seem to want to keep exploring them, and that there is only a limited amount any society [or psychotherapy organization] can do to ensure that its official reality is installed in the minds of most of its citizens [members] most of the time.

Conclusion

The narratives of psychotherapy theory are located in a different universe of discourse from that of facts or even research. Theory cannot properly substitute for these other universes of discourse nor be conflated with them. Theories are the stories we tell about the facts, about how we constitute the phenomena, about how the observer perceives and co-creates the field of the research. It surely behoves psychotherapy to avoid the simplistic category errors that Gilbert Ryle (1960) pointed out decades ago in his philosophy classes at Oxford. To honour the value of theory appropriately, it should not be abused in the service of work it is ill equipped and perhaps even dangerous to do.

This chapter is not intended as a call to the abandonment of theory. Theory is too important and too necessary to abandon. However **this chapter is an invocation to take philosophical and empirical research seriously** – not as a luxurious special interest but as a depth charge challenge to our foundational assumptions and organizational structures. Each well-developed theory, like each well-developed question, has its own language, grammar, rhetoric and poetry. At the very least theories can be essential, beautiful and useful as tools are to the artist and the craftsman. They can live, die or be improved.

The Greek word **theoreo** (the root of theory) indicates a show, a spectacle or the sacred procession around the temple – a story told or performed for the audience. The concept is closely linked to the ancient idea of theatre. A **theoros** was an ambassador sent by the state to consult the oracle. **Theoria** was the office of such an ambassador (Liddell and Scott, 1996). But we all know how oracles can instruct or deceive. Indeed, contemporary psychotherapy theories could be equated to what we would now understand as their socially constructed narratives or stories (Harré and Gillett, 1994; Winter 1997). As the map is not the territory, so the story is never what actually happened.

When we bridge the academy/clinic divide through research, we find that it is about relationship again – the researched itself with the researcher (Einstein – see Schlipp, 1949). As Jung (1928, p. 361) wrote: 'Learn your theories as well as you can, but put them aside when you touch the miracle of the living soul.' Separating our philosophical universes of discourse for their proper differential uses of theoretical languages, forms of rational research and experientially based beliefs, the mystery remains (Marcel, 1950; Tillich, 1973).

We may refer to this mystery as God, **phusis** or **physis** (the healing force), **élan vital**, **prakriti** from the Hindu tradition, **ikiru-energiea** from the Japanese or **ntu** from Africa (Ani, 1994). It may be called Heisenberg's uncertainty principle (Heisenberg, 1959), entanglement theory, the emergent order in positivistically, scientifically measured chaos and complexity which is auto-poeisis, or Schrödinger's cat (Clarkson, 1993; Black, 1996; Marshall, Zohar and Peat, 1997). But it is very scientific to acknowledge that we don't know, when in truth, we do not know. It is also ethical.

'Whereof one cannot speak, thereof one must be silent' (Wittgenstein, 1922, p. 189).

References

Anderson WT (1990) Reality Is Not What It Used To Be. San Francisco: Harper & Row.

Ani M (1994) Yurugu – an African-centred Critique of European Cultural Thought and Behavior. Trenton, NJ: Africa World Press.

Arundale J (1997) Editorial. British Journal of Psychotherapy 13(3): 305–6.

Barkham M (1995) Editorial: why psychotherapy outcomes are important now. Changes 13(3): 161–3.

Beitman BD (1994) Stop exploring! Start defining the principles of a psychotherapy integration: call for a consensus conference. Journal of Psychotherapy Integration 4(3): 203–28.

Bergin AE and Lambert MJ (1978) The evaluation of therapeutic outcomes. In Garfield SL and Bergin AE (eds) Handbook of Psychotherapy and Behavior Change. 2nd edn. New York: Wiley, pp. 139–89.

Beutler LE, Consoli AJ (1992) Systematic eclectic psychotherapy. In Norcross JC, Goldfried MR (eds) Handbook of Psychotherapy Integration. New York: Basic Books, pp. 264–99.

Black DM (1996) Abiding values and the creative present: psychoanalysis in the spectrum of the sciences. British Journal of Psychotherapy 12(3): 314–21.

Clarkson P (1990) A multiplicity of psychotherapeutic relationships. British Journal of Psychotherapy 7(2): 148–63.

Clarkson P (1993) New perspectives in counselling and psychotherapy (or adrift in a sea of change). In Clarkson P (1993) On Psychotherapy Vol. I. London: Whurr, pp. 209–32.

Clarkson P (1995b) The Therapeutic Relationship. London: Whurr.

Clarkson P (1995c) Counselling psychology in Britain – the next decade. Counselling Psychology Quarterly 8(3): 197–204.

Clarkson P (1996a) The Bystander (An End to Innocence in Human Relationships?). London: Whurr.

Clarkson P (1996b) Researching the 'therapeutic relationship' in psychoanalysis, counselling psychology and psychotherapy. Counselling Psychology Quarterly 9(2): 143–62.

Clarkson P (1997a) Integrative psychotherapy, integrating psychotherapies, or psychotherapy after schoolism? In Feltham C (ed.) Which Psychotherapy? London: Sage, pp. 33–50.

Clarkson P (1997b) The Therapeutic Relationship beyond Schoolism. Post-conference seminar: Psychotherapy in Perspective, 29 June 1997, at the Seventh Annual

Congress of the European Association for Psychotherapy, Rome.

Clarkson P (1997c) Dieratao – learning by inquiry – concerning the education of psychologists, psychotherapists, supervisors and organisational consultants. In Clarkson P (ed.) Counselling Psychology: Integrating Theory, Research and Supervised Practice. London: Routledge, pp. 242–72.

Clarkson P (1998) Supervision in counselling, psychotherapy and health – an intervention priority sequencing model. European Journal of Psychotherapy, Counselling and Health 1(1): 3–20.

Clarkson P (2000) Ethico Working with Ethical Model Dilemmas in Psychotherapy. London: Whurr.

Clarkson P, Lindsay G (1997) Secrets, Sex and Money: Ethical Dilemmas of Psychologists and Psychotherapists. Poster of research results displayed at British Psychological Society Division of Counselling Psychology Annual Conference, 30 May–1 June, Stratford-upon-Avon.

Clarkson P, Lindsay G (in press) Ethical Dilemmas of UKCP Psychotherapists. The Psychotherapist (UKCP Publications).

Clarkson P, Winter D (in press) User's Voice.

Consumer Reports (1995, November) Mental Health: Does Therapy Help? pp. 734–9.

Corsini R (ed.) (1984) Current Psychotherapies. Itasca, IL: FE Peacock.

De Mare P, Piper R, Thompson S (1991) Koinonia – From Hate through Dialogue to Culture in the Large Group. London: Karnac Books.

Denzin NK, Lincoln YS (eds) (1994) Handbook of Qualitative Research. Thousand Oaks, CA: Sage.

Dryden W (ed.) (1984) Individual Therapy in Britain. Milton Keynes: Open University Press.

Elkin I (1995) The NIMH treatment of depression collaborative research program: major results and clinical implications. Changes 13(3): 178–85.

Farrell BA (1979) Work in small groups: some philosophical considerations. In Babington Smith B, Farrell BA (eds) Training In Small Groups: A Study of Five Groups. Oxford: Pergamon, pp. 103–15.

Fiedler FE (1950) A comparison of therapeutic relationships in psychoanalytic, nondirective and Adlerian therapy. Journal of Consulting Psychology 14: 436–45.

Foucault M (1980) Power/Knowledge: Selected Interviews and Other Writings 1972–1977. New York: Pantheon.

Foucault M (1988) Politics, Philosophy, Culture: Interviews and Other Writings 1977–1984 (Lawrence D. Kritzman, ed.). London: Routledge.

Frank JD (1979) The present status of outcome studies. Journal of Consulting and Clinical Psychology 47: 310–16.

Frank JD, Frank JB (1993) Persuasion and Healing – A Comparative Study of Psychotherapy. Baltimore: The Johns Hopkins University Press.

Gee H (1995) Supervision: Relating and defining (the essence of supervision). Talk delivered at Spring Conference and Special General Meeting of Group for the Advancement of Therapy Supervision (now the British Association for Psychoanalytic and Psychodynamic Supervision), 20 May 1995, London.

Gergen M (1994) Free will and psychotherapy: complaints of the draughtsmen's daughters. Journal of Theoretical and Philosophical Psychology 14(1): 13–24.

Gleick J (1988) Chaos: Making a New Science. London: Heinemann.

Gleick J (1992) Genius: Richard Feynman and Modern Physics. London: Abacus.

Grosskurth P (1986) Melanie Klein. London: Maresfield Library.

Hahn H (1997) Meeting of Choreo Committee, 21 June 1997.

Harré R, Gillett G (1994) The Discursive Mind. Thousand Oaks CA: Sage.

Hauke C (1996) Book review of The Therapeutic Relationship by Petrūska Clarkson, British Journal of Psychotherapy 12(3): 405–7.

Heine RW (1953) A comparison of patients' reports on psychotherapeutic experience with psychoanalytic, nondirective and Adlerian therapists. American Journal of Psychotherapy 7: 16–23.

Heisenberg W (1959) Physics and Philosophy. New York: Harper & Row.

Helman CG (1994) Culture, Health and Illness: an Introduction for Health Professionals. 3rd edn. Oxford: Butterworth-Heinemann.

Hinshelwood RD (1990) Editorial. British Journal of Psychotherapy 7(2): 119–20.

Hynan MT (1981) On the advantages of assuming that the techniques of psychotherapy are ineffective. Psychotherapy: Theory, Research and Practice 18: 11–13.

Jung CG (1928) Analytical psychology and education. In Contributions to Analytical Psychology. Trans. Baynes HG and Baynes FC. London: Trench Trubner, pp. 313–82.

Koestler A (1989) The Act of Creation. London: Arkana. First published 1964.

Lambert MJ (1992) Psychotherapy outcome research: implications for integrative and eclectic therapists. In Norcross JC, Goldfried MR (eds) Handbook of Psychotherapy Integration. New York: Basic Books, pp. 94–129.

Lepper G (1996) Between science and hermeneutics: Towards a contemporary empirical approach to the study of interpretation in analytical psychotherapy. British Journal of Psychotherapy 13(2): 219–31.

Liddell HG, Scott R (1996) Greek-English Lexicon (abridged). Oxford: Oxford University Press.

Lipsey MW, Wilson DB (1993) The efficacy of psychological, educational and behavioral treatment. American Psychologist 48(12): 1181–209.

Luborsky L, Crits-Christoph R, Alexander L, Margolis M, Cohen M (1983) Two helping alliance methods of predicting outcomes of psychotherapy. Journal of Nervous and Mental Disease 171: 480–91.

Lyotard J-F (1989) The Postmodern Condition: A Report on Knowledge. Manchester: Manchester University Press.

Malcolm J (1981) Psychoanalysis: The Impossible Profession. New York: Knopf.

Marcel G (1950) The Mystery of Being. Trans. Fraser GS. London: Horvill Press.

Marshall I, Zohar D, Peat D (1997) Who's Afraid of Schrödinger's Cat? New York: William Morrow.

Moodley R (1998) Cultural return to the subject: traditional healing in counselling and therapy. Changes 16(1): 45–56.

Morrow-Bradley C, Elliott R (1986) The utilization of psychotherapy research by psychotherapists. American Psychologist 41(2): 188–97.

Norcross JC (ed.) (1986) Handbook of Eclectic Psychotherapy. New York: Brunner/Mazel.

Norcross JC (1997) Light and Shadow of the Integrative Process in Psychotherapy. Post-conference seminar: Psychotherapy in Perspective, 29 June 1997, at the Seventh Annual Congress of the European Association for Psychotherapy, Rome.

Norcross JC, Goldfried MR (1992) Handbook of Psychotherapy Integration. New York: Basic Books.

O'Malley SS, Suh CS, Strupp HH (1983) The Vanderbilt psychotherapy process scale: a report on the scale development and a process outcome study. Journal of Consulting and Clinical Psychology 51: 581–6.

Parry G, Richardson A (1996) NHS Psychotherapeutic Services in England. Department of Health.

Plaut F (1996) Why people still want analysis. Harvest 42(1): 7–26.

Polkinghorne DE (1992) Postmodern epistemology of practice. In Kvale S (ed.) Psychology and Postmodernism. London: Sage, pp. 146–65.

Roth A, Fonagy P (1996) What Works for Whom? A Critical Review of Psychotherapy Research. New York: The Guilford Press.

Russell R (1995) What works in psychotherapy when it does work? Changes 13(3): 213–18.

Ryle G (1960) Dilemmas: The Tarner Lectures. Cambridge: Cambridge University Press.

Schlipp PA (ed.) (1949) Albert Einstein, Philosopher-Scientist. Evanston IL: Northwestern University Press.

Seligman MEP (1995) The effectiveness of psychotherapy. American Psychologist 50(12): 965–74.

Shapiro DA (1996) Foreword. In Roth A, Fonagy P (eds) What Works for Whom? A Critical Review of Psychotherapy Research. New York: The Guilford Press, pp. viii–x.

Shotter J (1992) 'Getting in touch': the meta-methodology of a postmodern science of mental life. In Kvale S (ed.) Psychology and Postmodernism. London: Sage, pp. 58–73.

Silverman D (1997) Discourses of Counselling – HIV Counselling and Social Interaction. London: Sage.

Smail D (1987) Taking Care: An Alternative to Therapy. London: JM Dent.

Smith E (1997) Knowing what we're doing. The Therapist 8: 6.

Smith ML, Glass GV (1977) Meta-analysis of psychotherapy outcome studies. American Psychologist 32: 752–60.

Stewart I (1996) Signing off. Tate Magazine (Winter): 80.

Storr A (1979) The Art of Psychotherapy. London: Heinemann.

Strupp HH (1979) Specific versus non-specific factors in psychotherapy. Archives of General Psychiatry 36: 1125–36.

Tillich P (1973) The Boundaries of Our Being. London: Collins.

Watkins CE (ed.) (1997) Handbook of Psychotherapy Supervision. New York: Wiley.

Winter DA (1997) Everybody has still won but what about the booby prizes? Inaugural address as Chair of the Psychotherapy Section, British Psychological Society, University of Westminster, London.

Wittgenstein L (1922) Tractatus Logico-Philosophicus. Trans. Ogden CK. London: Routledge & Kegan Paul.

Youngson HA, Alderman N (1994) Fear of incontinence and its effects on a community-based rehabilitation programme after severe brain injury – successful remediation of escape behaviour using behaviour modification. Brain Injury 8(1): 23–36.

Chapter 2
Working with
Countertransference

PETRŪSKA CLARKSON AND JOHN NUTTALL

The transference–countertransference relationship is only one of five modalities of relationship that research (Clarkson, 1995) has identified as potentially present in the therapeutic encounter. This chapter defines and gives the background to one aspect of this – countertransference – and traces the development of the concept from Freud's first use of the term in 1910 to the contemporary view that it is a useful tool of psychotherapy.

The first part explains its connection with the Kleinian concept of projective identification and discusses its elaboration by the object relation school. There is general acceptance nowadays that countertransference contains a great deal of information about the client's psychological world. It is therefore important to understand this process and the authors have identified three main dimensions to countertransference. These are its **vector** (or direction and force), its **variance** (the quality it represents) and its **valence** (its effect on the client).

The second part of the chapter illustrates, through the use of example and metaphor, how these three dimensions are defined and can be recognized. Common themes and paradigms of countertransference are identified and discussed along with some ways in which experience has shown how these might be contained and worked with constructively. Finally a clinical vignette is presented in which some of the dimensions of countertransference are identified and used to understand the client's psychic world and foster therapeutic change.

This chapter is intended for those in our profession who would like some background to, and explanation of, countertransference and how it might be recognized and dealt with in clinical practice, supervision and teaching. Of course, not all psychotherapists and counsellors recognize the notions of transference and countertransference as significant or necessary for effective therapeutic work. Jung (1998) wrote that anyone who thinks he must demand a transference is forgetting that this is only

15

one of the therapeutic factors (p. 8). The other relational modes are the **working alliance**, the **reparative**, the **person to person**, and the **transpersonal** relationships.

This chapter does not deal with those feelings, fantasies and thoughts that the client has about the therapist; that is the client's transference and countertransference. It concentrates only on those feelings, fantasies and thoughts that are evoked and invoked in the therapist by virtue of the interpersonal and therapeutic nature of the client–therapist relationship.

This is also not an attempt to cover the subject in the depth it deserves as this has been done elsewhere (Casement, 1985; Clarkson, 1995; Racker, 1982; Sandler, 1988). The intention here is to give some background to the concept and, by the use of metaphor and clinical vignette, illustrate some of the key issues around countertransference that might impinge on the therapeutic encounter. In illuminating these we have highlighted three dimensions to countertransference around which we have structured this chapter. These are its vector, its variance and its valence. Exploring it in this way, we hope, has made the chapter as clear and as immediately useful as possible about the issues of working with the concept of countertransference in practice, supervision and teaching.

Background and definition

Although the first modern thinker to be credited with a clear formulation of 'the unconscious' was Leibniz, it was Freud who began the systematic investigation into its structure and function (Stevens, 1991, p. 11). In his practice he began to notice an unconscious process in which a whole series of psychological experiences are revived, not as belonging to the past but as applying to the physician at the moment (Freud, 1905). He called this unconscious process 'transference'.

By 1910 in his paper 'The future prospects of psychoanalysis' he wrote, 'we have become aware of the "countertransference" which arises in him (the physician) as a result of the patient's influence on his unconscious feelings, and we are almost inclined to insist that he shall recognise the countertransference in himself and overcome it' (pp. 144–5). Freud's view was that all such feelings towards the patient were representative of the analyst's own pathology – that they are the therapist's own transferences on to the patient. He felt that all kinds of countertransference interfered with the physician's ability to understand his client. Freud did not regard it, as it is regarded today, as an empathic response to the patient's unconscious issues and a useful and informative process in therapy.

The view that countertransference was a useful tool of therapy was developed extensively following Klein's conception of 'projective identification'. This is a process by which, in phantasy, the individual projects their unwanted parts (say feelings of anger or fear) into its bad internal objects to ward off attack and omnipotently control them. Klein posited this as a very early defensive phantasy used by the infant who associates the process with its bodily function of evacuation; and anybody who has observed a baby in a temper tantrum will understand why. In her seminal paper 'Notes on some schizoid mechanisms' she gives flavour to the mixture of physical and emotional feelings that make up this process:

> Together with these harmful excrements, expelled in hatred, split off parts of the ego are also projected onto the mother, or, as I would rather call it, into the mother. These excrements and bad parts of the self are not meant only to injure but also to control and take possession of the object. This leads to a particular form of identification which establishes the prototype of an aggressive object relations . . . I suggest for these processes the term 'projective identification'.
>
> (Klein, 1946, p. 8)

However Klein emphasized that it is 'not only the bad parts of the self which are expelled and projected, but also the good parts of the self' and this is important in the normal development of good object relations. Only when such projections are excessive, with over-idealization of the object, does the ego become depleted and vulnerable.

'Projective identification is intimately involved in the phenomenon of countertransference' (Grotstein, 1997, p. 200) and this concept of being able to place 'into' the other, parts of the self that need to be disowned (bad parts) or preserved (good parts) was developed as a way of understanding countertransference by Paula Heimann in 1950. She wrote: 'the analyst's unconscious understands that of his patient. This rapport on the deep level comes to the surface in the form of feelings which the analyst notices in response to his patient; in his "countertransference".'

In 1962 Bion (1993) suggested that projective identification played a normal role in the communication between mother and baby, but if there is a lack of 'maternal reverie' and the infant's projections cannot be contained, then projective identification is carried out with increasing force and frequency and continues to be used as an ego defence in adulthood. Projections of this texture are picked up by the receptive therapist in their countertransference, and it might represent one of the ways in which the patient communicates what they need from therapy (Maroda, 1994, p. 31).

Such countertransferences are a good indicator of the type of developmental deficit experienced by the client, and can bring into focus the requirements of the reparative or developmentally needed relationship. Thus the therapist has to 'sustain the feelings which are stirred up in him, as opposed to discharging them (as does the patient), in order to subordinate them to the analytic task in which he functions as the patient's mirror reflection' (Heimann, 1950).

The result of this analysis of the therapist's feelings, fantasies and thoughts towards the client is that two broad categories or vectors of countertransference can be identified. The first kind, which Freud identified, has been called **proactive countertransference** and is primarily concerned with the therapist's own past experience, current preoccupation or future hopes and fears. The second kind is called **reactive countertransference** and are those countertransferences identified by Heimann (1950) and enumerated by Little (1951), and concern the therapist's reactions or responses to the client's past experience, current preoccupation or future hopes, fears and fantasies (Lewin, 1963; Clarkson, 1995, p. 90).

Heimann's and Little's formulations, based on Klein's concept of projective identification, constituted a major contribution to, and extension of, psychoanalytic theory and practice. From there onward countertransference was viewed as a potential valuable source of information about the client's transference that can form the basis for effective therapeutic understanding, interpretation and intervention.

However, in the same way that we can say transference is a kind of 'distortion' of the here-and-now reality of the therapeutic relationship experienced by the client, countertransference can be said to be a kind of distortion of the here-and-now reality experienced by the therapist. Whether or not this distortion is used for good or ill will depend on the awareness, insight, integrity and skill of the therapist. Later, we shall be discussing ways in which the valence of countertransference might manifest itself as facilitative or destructive in the therapeutic relationship.

It is important to note that countertransference, like transference, 'is everywhere and unavoidable' (Clarkson, 1995, p. 75) and generally unproblematic. 'The countertransference that is likely to cause trouble is the unconscious one on the analyst's side, whether it be an infantile negative or positive one or both in alternation' (Sharp, 1947). It becomes a problem when such feelings are (a) out of awareness, (b) chronic or repetitive, (c) detrimental to the therapeutic work, or (d) persistently distressing to the therapist. 'We deceive ourselves if we think we have no countertransference. It is its nature that matters' (Clarkson, 1995).

The nature of countertransference and the Object Relations school

Klein extended psychoanalytic theory to give interpersonal relations and instinctual drives equal consideration in determining human development (Segal, 1995) but it was left to her followers to elaborate her formulations to the point where 'it is now accepted that patients can behave in ways that get the analyst to feel the feelings that the patient, for one reason or another, cannot contain within himself or cannot express in any other way except by getting the analyst to have the experience too' (Bott Spillius, 1995, p. 6). For the object relations psychologist these projected feelings are invariably those associated with 'bad' early internalized object relations that have not been fully resolved.

Fairbairn (1952) offered one of the best descriptions of the internal world of object relations that the infant builds as a result of its attempt to master a frustrating or 'bad' external reality that might be the earliest relationship with the mother or caregiver. He posited that such internalized relationships form 'endopsychic structures' that are comprised of split-off parts of the ego in dynamic relationship with the split exciting and rejecting parts of the object. They continue their existence as semi-autonomous parts of the self, whose *raison d'être* is to continue living out these 'bad' experiences so that they can be refuted or confirmed.

> Their existence . . . leads to the seeking of relationships that will be consonant with the specific neurotic paradigm of early experience; to the distortion of current relationships so that they can be experienced in accordance with such paradigms; and to the patterning of activity in the world so as to be expressive of such a relationship and as a result, to restrict the freer, more situationally appropriate expression of the self and experience of the world.
>
> (Rubens, 1994, p. 162)

This is typically the kind of experience the counsellor will become aware of in the countertransferential relationship of the therapeutic setting. It leads to a distortion in the therapeutic relationship that has more to do with re-enacting earlier relationships than just, as Freud posited, the displacement or transfer of instinctual impulses from an earlier Oedipal object to the therapist (Sandler et al., 1979, p. 41).

Anna Freud in her book *The Ego and the Mechanisms of Defence* (1936) acknowledged the more relational paradigm when she wrote about the 'transference of defence' where clients transfer not only their instinctual wishes but also their earlier ego defences or archaic mode of ego functioning on to the psychotherapist. There is a sense here of how the client is wont to displace on to the physician not only the multifarious feelings towards their objects but aspects of the relational paradigm as well. This is a basic relational process, and experienced therapists will be aware of their own tendency to do the same on to the client. By 1952 Klein was writing of the 'transference situation' in which 'it is essential to think in terms of total situations transferred from the past into the present, as well as of emotions, defences and object relations' (Klein, 1952, p. 209).

The object relations position on countertransference was probably best summarized by Racker in 1968 (see Racker, 1982). He identified how, through projective identification, the client might displace parts of either the ego or the internalized object on to the therapist and evoke in the therapist the feelings that correspond with these different parts of the self. Thus there is a varying quality or **variance** in the way the counsellor might identify with the client. The therapist's feelings might correspond with the object part of the client and be complementary to the client's feelings; or they might correspond with the client's ego part and be concordant with the client's feelings. Thus when in complementary identification with the client the therapist is induced to experience the client in the same way the original object was presumed to have felt. But when in concordant identification the therapist feels similar to the way the client felt in dealing with the original object.

These developments in the concept of countertransference represented a stark contrast to the original definitions introduced by Freud, and it might have saved considerable controversy if they had been renamed or defined differently. Grinberg (1962) attempted to do this by calling reactive countertransference **projective counter-identification** to differentiate it from Freud's original formulation. And it is interesting to note here the contribution of Harry Stack Sullivan (a North American psychoanalyst) who in his lectures of the 1940s developed a theory of interpersonal psychology that was not so much based on structural models of the mind as observable and subjectively experienced interpersonal processes. He saw transference in its broadest sense as a distortion in the client's parataxic mode of experiencing, a process that is 'a variant of the human tendency towards misconception or incorrect interpersonal attribution' (Barton Evans, 1996, pp. 187–93). The corresponding feeling induced in the therapist he called 'reciprocal emotion'. As a 'participant observer' the therapist can use these feelings to understand the client's 'security operations', the meaning of which need to be brought into awareness in the therapeutic relationship. Any further speculation about unconscious processes, he felt, would be fruitless as they are essentially unknowable (Sullivan, 1954).

Different dimensions of countertransference – the three Vs

There is then a matrix of different dimensions of countertransferences made up of its vector – proactive and/or reactive; and its variation – complementary and/or concordant. Because such a detailed breakdown of these psychological processes is unusual in many approaches, we would like to illustrate and discuss how these different aspects of countertransference might be experienced in the everyday therapeutic encounter.

However there is a third dimension to this matrix, that of the valence or the potential for countertransference to be facilitative or destructive. All countertransferences can be used for the benefit or detriment of the client. They are generally beneficial when contained by the therapist and consciously used to illuminate the client's instinctual or object relations world. They are generally detrimental when they invoke inappropriate interventions or are acted out by the therapist, thereby helping to confirm the client's distorted view of reality. In the following sections we have attempted to illustrate, by the use of example and metaphor, the three dimensions of countertransference discussed.

Proactive countertransference

The notion of proactive countertransference refers to those feelings, fantasies and bodily experiences that affect the therapeutic process primarily as a result of the practitioner's own unresolved past or current issues. In colloquial terms, the source of the distortion in the therapeutic relationship has to do with the therapist's own baggage. For example, if therapists are afraid of authority figures – perhaps because of an abusive authoritarian father – they may feel too afraid of a successful high-powered client to be truly effective, or find they get inappropriately angry with an obstinate father figure. If therapists are motivated primarily by an unconscious desire to save a depressed mother, they are probably not as effective as a therapist who is less influenced by such unresolved past issues. This might be the case with a counsellor whose mother was, say, bereaved shortly after giving birth – just when the baby needed her emotional attention the most. The counsellor might re-experience archaic feelings of failure, frustration, anger or sadness if the depressed client does not become happy. Clients might even pick up, unconsciously, the counsellor's hidden agenda and belligerently resist help or, worse, in complementary identification with the counsellor, comply by a flight into health at the cost of not dealing with their own issues.

Here it might be useful to illustrate a specific type of proactive counter-transference that sometimes emerges in the supervision and training of supervisors and therapists: that of how our own early experience of helping might unconsciously affect and influence our therapeutic practice now, and not always for the good. Although Freud considered it damaging, unhelpful or obstructive to the therapeutic process it is, to some extent, present in all of us. It is probably the primary reason why personal psychotherapy is an essential requirement in many types of training and why analysis is sometimes considered 'interminable' – so that we can separate 'what's mine and what's theirs'. It means 'that he or she (the counsellor) must have worked on himself or herself' (Fromm, 1994, p.

193). However, we can never eradicate proactive countertransference. The best we can do is to understand and tolerate it, and recognize its potential to help or hinder the therapeutic process.

Over many years of experience in this field we have often found that what motivates people to enter this and similar professions is a sincere and persistent yearning to understand and deal with the confusion or pain stemming from their own childhood. In certain profound ways this provides the empathy, the compassion and a willingness to accompany another vulnerable human being on their journey towards fulfilment. On the other hand these same sensitivities can sometimes interfere or interrupt the process between the practitioner and the client in unhelpful ways.

Archetypally this notion of how our own injuries bring us to this kind of work constellates the image of the wounded healer. This is embodied in the mythical figure of Chiron, the centaur, about whom many stories, books and clinical speculations have developed. It is therefore important for all psychotherapists to understand and be aware of their own unconscious identification with this archetype and to work in their own therapy and supervision on recognizing its facilitative or destructive impact on the relationship with their clients. In working with the training and supervision of hundreds of wounded healers of all levels of experience I (PC) have frequently participated in the process of sorting and sifting through the therapist's feelings, fantasies and avoidances in order to help the healer deflate their over-identification with this archetype.

It is often useful for the therapist to get in touch with the healer-story of the child within them (usually pre-seven). This child is often highly intuitive, deeply loving, compassionate, intelligent, emotionally literate and desperate to restore a confused, barren or dysfunctional family to health. People with such histories often have a remarkable capacity for making others feel that they can be trusted or confided in, and for establishing the initial phase of a therapeutic relationship through dedicated care, attention and attunement to the emotional processes of the client. These are often the innate talents of the kids who, early in life, took on the mantle of the family doctor, nurse or therapist. It is only in the later stages of the therapeutic relationship that they begin to re-experience the same impotence and helplessness that they experienced in their original family situation. Such difficulties might then emerge as recurrent problems in their work (stuckness, confusion, anxiety with clients) which are, or at least should be, brought to supervision.

The danger here is that unaware therapists could, by projective identification, induce the client to fail (due to unconsciously expecting the same outcome as the child experienced) – at the same time as re-experiencing their own sense of failure and disappointment in the repetition.

Searles (1975) believed that many clients with the same sensitivities are able to tune into such feelings of distress in the therapist (client counter-transference) and might attempt to cure the therapist or, at least, correct their disruptive effect on the therapeutic relationship. 'The patient's unconscious curative powers are remarkably sensitive and strong' (Langs, 1992, p. 238) and they will endeavour, usually in the unconscious commu-nication, to advise the therapist on how to rectify the frame or reconsider their interventions if they perceive the therapist's own baggage to be a disruptive influence (Langs, 1992; Smith, 1991).

By considering the shape of their early healing ambitions therapists can become skilful in the work of understanding and forming relationships, and also become, and remain, effective and successful in the work of trans-formation. By understanding their own internal world and parataxic distor-tions the therapist is in a better position to reflect on their client's early relations with others, and can be prepared for the client's unconscious invitations to repeat or re-enact such relations or, indeed, be attuned to the client's desire and attempts to be curative and helpful to them.

Reactive countertransference

Reactive countertransference occurs when the therapist is reacting with feelings, fantasies, thoughts or bodily sensations that are induced or evoked by the client, the issues they bring and the way they bring them. For example, therapists working with bulimic clients often report that they experience some apparently inexplicable eating-disordered behav-iour themselves from time to time. Or a therapist may be left feeling depressed and despairing, or enraged, after a session with a client who reported grievous experiences of childhood abuse in an apparently light-hearted or matter-of-fact tone. It is sometimes experienced as if the client deposited their unexpressed, and probably unwanted or denied, feeling **into** the therapist. These could be examples of concordant reactive countertransference, because what the therapist is attuned to is the sadness or anger that belongs to the client's own very early ego that suffered the abuse.

Conversely, when a normally patient and loving therapist feels repeat-edly angry, bored or irritable with a client, it might be because that is the way the client's parents felt towards him. Equally the therapist may feel pity towards the client in the way that school friends or siblings pitied the weak 'runt' of the pack during childhood. Acting out or censoring appropriate therapeutic interventions because of such feelings might be doing the client a disservice. If psychotherapists become aware of these feelings and can contain and reflect on them, then they can be offered back to the client in a sensitive and intelligent way as helpful information and can become

very valuable and important helpmeets in the therapeutic process. These
are examples of complementary reactive countertransference.

Having differentiated between complementary and concordant
countertransference it is important to point out that, with some clients,
especially those with severe personality disorder, the therapist might be
subject to several different dimensions of countertransference in the same
session. These might change suddenly and without warning. 'Projections
tend to be relatively stable in patients with neurotic personality organisation, but they are unstable and rapidly alternating in patients with severe
character pathology and borderline personality organisation' (Kernberg,
1992, p. 115). Such clients are able to subliminally induce feelings in the
therapist, which alternate between aspects of the client's own dissociated
self and their object representations, and our view is that it is usual for
feelings of both to be residual at the end of the session. Indeed, a true
empathic response to the client may require it.

'It is of crucial importance that the analyst tolerates the rapidly alternating, at times completely contradictory, emotional experience that
signals the activation of complementary self and object representations of
a primitive internalised object relation' (Kernberg, 1992, p. 116). One way
of checking the variance of countertransference requires therapists to
carefully note down their feelings, mood and preoccupation before going
into the session, so that they can be conscious of any changes in these
parameters during, or especially after, the session. Also, in the same way
that the client's dreams and parapraxes provide information and guidance
about the transference, the therapist's own dreams, mistakes and manifes-
tations of the unconscious may contribute understanding about the
origins of their own countertransference.

In situations of such complexity it is also very important for the therapist
to be able to differentiate what is proactive in themselves (projected) and
what is reactive (introjected) in response to the client. Indeed the therapist
must be able to tolerate such feelings that are aroused, especially those of
hate (Winnicott, 1975) or sexual arousal (Mann, 1997). One of the most
frequently asked questions in training and supervision concerns this differentiation: 'How do I know whether it is my issues or the client's issues that
are being evoked in the therapeutic encounter?' 'Is it my pathology or
theirs that is causing the problem?' 'How do I distinguish between reactive
and proactive countertransference?' (its vector). This is clearly a very
complex problem requiring understanding and serious considerations of
manifold factors – many of them unknown or even unknowable.

Here is one technique that many supervisees find helpful: During the
session in the consulting room (unless you know to the contrary) assume
that all feelings, fantasies and thoughts are **reactive countertransferences**.

Pay attention and work carefully with them in the therapeutic relationship with your client. Then after the session, during reflection, supervision and writing up, or in planning or preparation for future sessions (unless you are sure to the contrary), firstly assume that all feelings, fantasies and thoughts are **proactive countertransferences**. Pay attention and work carefully with them in your own therapy or with a trusted supervisor.

In this way you will benefit from both perspectives and neither will get neglected, ignored or, worse, denied. One can move between them as shifting concentration from figure to ground and then back again. This exercise is, in itself, a valuable one for sharpening nuances of self awareness, and of understanding the dynamics of the therapeutic relationship; as well as a process aiding the development (or revision) of therapeutic skills and efficiency.

Another technique that other practitioners have found useful is to develop maps or schemata that anticipate the likely patterns of countertransference. Who is expected to do what to whom, and are the issues likely to be concerned with dependency, power, sex or ingratiation (Cashdan, 1988)? What kind of interpersonal games does the client play (Nuttall, 1999)? Such templates are not meant to substitute the subjective experience but, until time and space allows, to assist the therapist's own 'internal supervisor' (Casement, 1985). For example, in a situation where a therapist experiences the client as seductive, would the 'transference map' suggest that such feelings originate from the client's own need to please the transferential object, or originate from the therapist's attitude which has induced a pleasing response in the client?

To help and summarize so far, Table 2.1 shows the matrix of countertransference that emerges when vector and variance are considered together.

Table 2.1 The matrix of countertransference

Variance vector	Concordant	Complementary
Proactive	Client evokes feelings in the therapist related to the therapist's own past ego experiences and phantasies.	Client evokes feelings in the therapist related to the therapist's own archaic object representations.
Reactive	Client evokes feelings in the therapist that replicate the client's dissociated or denied ego experiences and phantasies.	Client evokes feelings in the therapist that replicate the client's archaic object representations.

The valence of countertransference – its potential for good or bad

Facilitative countertransference

Reactive countertransference is generally accepted as the true empathic response to the client's feelings, and is therefore seen as the most therapeutically facilitative. Proactive countertransference can also be facilitative. It might help the self-aware therapist, who has suffered similar experiences to the client, to be particularly understanding of, or attuned to, the client's experience. Sometimes positive and nurturing object representations are evoked in the therapist that can be healing and facilitative and might help replicate in the therapeutic relationship the good experience the therapist had with their own father or mother.

Winnicott (1975) argued that even 'hate in the countertransference', if acknowledged and tolerated by the therapist, can be beneficial as it helps clients to understand that their own hate or aggression can also be tolerated and survived. In this way the therapist is seen to be real by the client and can therefore equally trust the therapist's love.

However, such ostensibly authentic reactions from the therapist may be an indication that a more person-to-person relationship with the client is taking shape (Clarkson, 1995). Other kinds of transferences or elements that the therapist might carry across from a previous situation into the therapeutic relationship are, for example, a liking or talent for particular kinds of clients – say creative people, intuitive introverts, young people or those with psychotic conflicts. This may come from a particular understanding or sensitivity for certain types of human condition. Of course such subtle preferences may change over time as therapists evolve and progress in their own journeys. Before many years in therapy, working with abusive or violent individuals might have been anathema for therapists who suffered at the hands of cruel parents. After resolving such traumas some therapists and counsellors grow in compassion and ability to deal effectively with the very clients they did (and should have) avoided earlier in their careers.

Destructive countertransference

Countertransferences can also be destructive for the therapist, the client, both or even others involved, such as children. The therapeutic relationship can be endangered to the extent that psychotherapists are unconscious of the shadow or destructive elements in their personality. Examples range from therapists in the midst of their own marital traumas subtly encouraging clients to divorce regardless of circumstances, to the subtle feelings of envy the therapist may feel towards a client who is more successful.

This negative potential in the countertransference is probably the main reason why personal therapy is considered to be important in those approaches where the transferential relationship is paramount. It might also be the root of many incidents of ethical misconduct. In our experience few of these are actually committed intentionally. More often they are due to a lapse in judgement, a suspension of normal questioning, compliance with group pressure or overwhelming personal needs that erupt into the consulting room, causing distress to all concerned. Supervision has a major part to play in imparting the knowledge, experience and skills needed to identify under what conditions, when and how and with whom the counsellor's well-trained functioning is likely to become impaired or disempowered (Clarkson, 1998a).

All therapists need to know and find out their particular vulnerabilities in this regard. It constitutes the particular 'veer' in their driving, just as motor vehicles have unique 'veers' in which the steering tends more to the right or to the left, requiring the driver to make frequent small adjustments along the way. We all have veers in our personalities for which, with vigilance, self-awareness, and the processes of supervision and therapy, we have to make regular adjustments when relating to others. Such tendencies probably embrace all human qualities but might show subtly, say, in the way in which we intervene too quickly or too late, in having too much or too little self-doubt, in our resistance to training or supervisory inputs; in becoming too engrossed in content or in process; becoming overly sensitive or insensitive to cultural context; using reason at the expense of feeling or vice versa and so on. Such veers, developed from early experience, reside in all of us and it was Fairbairn who stressed 'that a total state of health is only a theoretical possibility' (Greenberg and Mitchell, 1983, p. 161).

To feel or sense one's destructive countertransference being activated in or before a session requires immediate and effective preventive action. Internal alarm systems need to be put in place and regularly checked for optimum functioning, and when the alarm signal goes off it should always be taken seriously – just like the domestic smoke alarm. Counsellors can develop their own metaphorical alarm system depending on their most effective primary sense system – touch, hearing, sight or even smell. One supervisee reported that whenever she felt 'her buttons being pressed' she used the visual and auditory metaphor of a fire alarm button being hit. She felt this signalled the need for a disciplined escape from the involuntary blazing in her body associated with the feelings and fantasies that had more to do with her own childhood trauma than with her client's issues.

Knowing and recognizing the kinds of countertransference that can be facilitative or destructive to one's work is a fundamental quality of a proficient therapist and is a key test of the therapist's sense of responsibility. It is always worth reminding ourselves that 'patients come to us because they believe that we have sufficient knowledge, skill and self-awareness to enable us to guide them through their own self-discovery' (Maroda, 1994, p. 31).

A clinical vignette

The following section describes a case where, as counsellor and supervisor, we were able to experience and use the various dimensions of countertransference to deepen our understanding of the client's anxieties and needs. Richard (a pseudonym) was a young gay man who had been diagnosed HIV positive a year earlier. He was acutely depressed and distressed at his diagnosis, which led him to want to explore the difficulties of his childhood, his current relationship, and his feelings of low self-esteem. Throughout his childhood he and his siblings had suffered physical abuse from his parents, especially the father, who had also been violent towards the mother. His depression revolved around his feelings that he had not had a happy childhood and that, following infection, he would not have the chance of a happy future. As his virology results worsened he faced decisions about anti-viral therapy. This rekindled his anxieties and depression and evoked 'the return of the bad object' (Fairbairn, 1952, p. 59; Shelby, 1995, p. 121; Nuttall, 1998). He felt he was 'bad and weak' and deserving of his plight. Richard was in counselling for just over a year, representing about 60 sessions in all.

Richard was a well-dressed and pleasant young man. He felt 'knocked down' by HIV and wanted to 'rebuild his life and get things in order'. He had taken on the 'burden of badness' (Fairbairn, 1952, p. 65). Identifying with the 'bad' object, he blamed himself for his difficulties. He said in tears, 'I feel as though I've failed; the virus is the ultimate failure. I've always failed; at relationships, job – a sorry pathetic life really. Whenever I have things together, I do something to spoil it.' He mitigated this badness by being 'a perfectly presented package', polite, well mannered and charming, which constituted his moral defence of the superego (Fairbairn, 1952, p. 65), and was the way he presented in therapy. Challenge to this defence, such as feeling belittled at work, the HIV infection, a simple rebuke by a friend, resulted in aggressive behaviour that destroyed all the goodness, and left him feeling depressed and unable to cope with life, as if he might as well already be dead.

This internal world was reflected in his transference, and he saw the counsellor 'as an authority figure' and 'someone I shouldn't upset or anger'. Yet 'being here for this hour is the safest place to be', and he said he wanted the counsellor to be his mentor. In the transference he experienced the counsellor as both the exciting and rejecting father figure; someone he needed, yet someone he also feared would reject him. By about session 25 this transference abated and was replaced by a much stronger one based on aspects of his mother. This had less idealizing qualities and was full of anger and hate for his mother who had failed to 'protect us from dad'; feelings that seemed difficult and dangerous for him to express. She had often been 'grotesquely angry' herself and would report her children's bad behaviour to the father.

The counsellor's countertransference vacillated correspondingly, ranging from the erotic, to the irritable, to the needed mentor. The erotic feelings might have represented the counsellor's reactive concordant identification with Richard's own sexual feelings for his father, whilst the irritation represented his reactive complementary identification with the rejecting father. The strong desire to be his mentor was also the counsellor in complementary identification with the client's phantasy of the ideal father he needed to heal the wounds of the past (Mann, 1997). However, in supervision, this was identified as proactive countertransference as it represented the counsellor's own desire to give him the helpful father of his own childhood.

When the bad mother transference was in ascendancy the counsellor felt hated, and desperately frustrated at not being able to take away the client's pain and dread. There were times when, in trying to avoid acting out this countertransference, the counsellor felt as though he were walking on eggshells. In supervision we sensed that this might have been how Richard experienced his family life; terrified to show any kind of emotion, joy or sadness, for fear that it would provoke violence, leaving Richard in a cocoon of suppressed rage. This matrix of feelings is what Klein (1952, p. 55) might have referred to as the transfer of a 'total situation' from Richard's past into the present. Supervision helped the counsellor to realize that it might be destructive to act out Richard's desire for him to be the mentoring father or needed mother, as these needs might get more onerous and encourage a more 'malignant regression' (Balint, 1989, pp. 144-8).

Recognizing how the countertransference could be facilitative gave the counsellor an insight into the client's internal world and brought him to understand how important constancy in the therapeutic relationship was for this client. This facilitated a 'benign regression' (Balint, 1989) in which the counsellor was experienced as someone who could contain and tolerate the client's pain without reacting aggressively or endearingly. The corollary of this, however, was that the counsellor was left with a residual concordant countertransference of a 'sad little boy'; an identification, again, that he recognized as having some proactive origins in himself. However this countertransference was, nevertheless, probably indicative of the dominant feeling that Richard himself was unable to tolerate. This was an understanding that proved useful to reflect back to Richard and eventually helped him to a position in which he felt safe to release the sadness and rage associated with his childhood and his existential givens.

'If we were omniscient analysts, the only countertransference we should experience would be that belonging to those intuitive periods when all is going well' (Money-Kyrle, 1996, p. 31). Of course none of us is all knowing, about ourselves, about the client or about the workings of the mind. We may use a number of working models or orientations but, as research has shown, 'there is no significant evidence that theoretical approach is relevant to the successful outcome of psychotherapy . . . it is the therapeutic relationship that potentiates the beneficial effects of psychotherapy' (Clarkson, 1998b). One of the five modalities of this relationship is the way in which two individuals, in this case the client and the therapist, subliminally communicate their feelings to one another and the meaning that can be derived from such communication. Although Freud (1915, p. 194) wrote 'it is a very remarkable thing that the Ucs of one human being can react upon that of another, without passing through the Cs', he viewed any such reaction in the therapist as something to be overcome, expunged or at least ignored. It was only after the insight intro-duced by the Kleinian and object relations schools in Britain, and maybe the interpersonalists in the US, that psychotherapists began to understand how the form of affective communication in adulthood is residual of the preverbal infant–caregiver relationship or reverie. The intimate nature of the therapeutic encounter is evocative of such early object relations and so any disturbance in the infant–caregiver reverie is replayed in the transfer-ential–countertransferential relationship. If this disturbance or distortion can be discerned and understood by the therapist it can be used as 'an instrument of research into the patient's unconscious' (Heimann, 1950) and form the foundation for interpretation or for the reparative or devel-opmentally needed relationship.

However, it is important for us all, as therapists, to recognize the distor-tions that we also bring to the therapeutic encounter and the dangers of these being tuned into by the client. It is therefore imperative for all in our profession to be aware of the many facets of countertransference, what vector or direction it has, what variance or quality it conveys, and what valence or potential effect it might have on the client. Is it proactive, reactive, concordant, complementary, destructive or facilitative? Irrespective of the theoretical history and background to the concept these are all aspects of the therapeutic relationship to which the therapist should be subjectively and phenomenologically attuned. It is hoped that this chapter has provided some illustration and practical guidance to aid this attunement, but our views need to be contextualized within the vast sea of literature on the subject.

As Jung (1928) warned, 'Learn your theories as best you can, but put them aside when you touch the miracle of the living soul'. He wrote that the soul 'is a function of relationship' (Jung, 1998, p. 105) so it seems that he, too, felt that theory was subordinate to the therapeutic relationship itself. Working with countertransference, in whatever theoretical guise, recognizing it, understanding it, and using it to the benefit of the client, is one of the fundamentals of the optimum therapeutic relationship.

References

Barton Evans F (1996) Harry Stack Sullivan: Interpersonal Theory in Psychotherapy. London: Routledge.

Bion WR (1993) A theory of thinking. In Bion WR (1993) Second Thoughts. London: Karnac.

Bott Spillius E (1995) Clinical experience of projective identification. In Clinical Lectures on Klein and Bion. London: Routledge.

Casement P (1985) On Learning from the Patient. London: Routledge.

Cashdan S (1988) Object Relations Therapy: Using the Relationship. New York: WW Norton.

Clarkson P (1995) The Therapeutic Relationship. London: Whurr.

Clarkson P (ed.) (1998a) Supervision (Psychoanalytic and Jungian Approaches). London: Whurr.

Clarkson P (1998b) Beyond schoolism. Changes 16(1): 1–11.

Fairbairn WRD (1952) Psychoanalytic Studies of the Personality. London: Tavistock.

Freud A (1936) The Ego and the Mechanisms of Defence. London: Hogarth.

Freud S (1905) Fragments of an Analysis of a Case of Hysteria, Standard Edition 7. London: Hogarth.

Freud S (1910) The Future Prospects of Psychoanalysis, Standard Edition 11. London: Hogarth.

Freud S (1915) The Unconscious, Standard edition 4. London: Hogarth.

Fromm E (1994) The Art of Listening. London: Constable.

Greenberg JR, Mitchell SA (1983) Object Relations in Psychoanalytic Theory. London: Karnac.

Grinberg L (1962) On specific aspects of countertransference due to the patient's projective identification. International Journal of Psycho-Analysis 43: 436–40.

Grotstein JS (1997) Splitting and Projective Identification. London: Jason Aronson.

Heimann P (1950) On countertransference. International Journal of Psycho-Analysis, 31: 81–4.

Jung CG (1928) Analytical Psychology and Education. In Baynes CF (ed.) Contributions to Analytical Psychology. London: Trench Truber & Co.

Jung CG (1998) The Psychology of the Transference. London: Routledge.

Kernberg O (1992) Aggression in Personality Disorders and Perversions. London and New Haven: Yale University Press.

Klein M (1946) Notes on some schizoid mechanisms. In Klein M (1997) Envy and Gratitude. London: Vintage.

Klein M (1952) The origins of transference. In Mitchell J (ed.) (1991) Selected Melanie Klein. London: Penguin.

Langs R (1992) A Clinical Workbook for Psychotherapists. London: Karnac.

Lewin K (1963) Field Theory in Social Sciences: Selected Theoretical Papers. London: Tavistock.

Little M (1951) Countertransference and the patient's response to it. International Journal of Psycho-Analysis 32: 32–40.

Mann D (1997) Psychotherapy: An Erotic Relationship. London: Routledge.

Maroda K (1994) The Power of Countertransference. London: Jason Aronson.

Money-Kyrle R (1996) Normal countertransference and some of its deviations. In Money-Kyrle R, Melanie Klein Today, vol. 2. London: Routledge.

Nuttall J (1998) Fairbairnian object relations: the challenge to the moral defence in gay men with HIV. Psychodynamic Counselling 4(4): 445–61.

Nuttall J (1999) Games – a behavioural manifestation of projective identification? Psychodynamic Counselling 5(3): 339–55.

Racker H (1982) Transference and Countertransference. London: Maresfield Reprints.

Rubens RL (1994) Fairbairn's structural theory. In Rubens RL, Fairbairn and the Origins of Object Relations. London: Free Association Books.

Sandler J (1988) Projection, Identification, Projective Identification. London: Karnac Books.

Sandler J, Dare C, Holder A (1979) The Patient and the Analyst. London: Maresfield Library.

Searles H (1975) The patient as therapist to his analyst. In Giovacchini P (ed.) Tactics and Techniques in Psychoanalytic Therapy, vol. 2: Countertransference. New York: Jason Aronson.

Segel J (1995) Melanie Klein. London: Sage.

Sharp EF (1947) The psychoanalyst. International Journal of Psycho-Analysis 28: 210–13.

Shelby DH (1995) People with HIV and Those Who Care for Them. New York: Howarth.

Smith D (1991) Hidden Conversations. London: Routledge.

Stevens A (1991) On Jung. London: Penguin Books.

Sullivan HS (1954) The Psychiatric Interview. New York: WW Norton.

Winnicott DW (1975) Hate in the countertransference. In Winnicott DW, Through Paediatrics to Psycho-analysis. London: Tavistock, pp. 194–203.

Chapter 3
The Therapeutic Relationship in the Existential Psychotherapies – 5 Relational Dimensions

PETRŪSKA CLARKSON

'The best thing for being sad', Merlin advised the fatherless young Arthur, 'is to learn something. That is the only thing that never fails. You may grow old and trembling . . . you may miss your only love, you may see the world around you devastated by evil lunatics, or know your honour trampled in the sewers of baser minds. There is only one thing for it then – to learn. Learn why the world wags and what wags it. That is the only thing which the mind can never exhaust, never alienate, never be tortured by, never fear or distrust, and never dream of regretting. Learning is the thing . . .'

(White, 1987)

At this moment (1994) there seems to me to be five approaches to psychotherapy that primarily occupy themselves with existential themes. Different exponents may identify themselves differently and (as is common) may not agree with this classification. Some will certainly not thank me for placing them within the same rubric as others. However, for the purposes of this discussion, I want to focus on similarities and the work of inclusion, rather than the differentiation and unpicking of differences between these approaches. What follows here is based on an unpublished paper presented to the Oxford Psychotherapy Association in 1994 and an adaptation for practitioners with an existential/phenomenological interest of the paper 'A multiplicity of therapeutic relationships', published in the *British Journal of Psychotherapy* in 1989.

Five approaches

We may begin with **existential psychotherapy**, which draws its primary genealogy from Husserl (1931), Heidegger (1949), Jaspers (1913/1962)

33

and others such as Sartre (1948), Binswanger (1968), and Boss (1979), Yalom (1989), Van Deurzen-Smith (1988) and Spinelli (1989). Arguably Frankl's logotherapy should be included here. Then we come to **phenomenological/client-centred psychotherapy**; this is the approach that is predicated on the work of Rogers (1951) with his colleagues, Laing and Esterson (1964) and the European phenomenologists such as Marcel (1952), Minkowski (1970) and Merleau-Ponty (1962). This leads us on to **gestalt psychotherapy**, the brainchild of the European gestalt psychologists, but popularized by Fritz and Laura Perls and their colleagues in the US and which subsequently filtered back into Europe and the rest of the world. **Archetypal and cultural psychology** are developments from Jungian and cultural theory as exemplified in the work of Hillman (1990), Estes (1992), Moore (1992) and other post-Jungian derivatives such as Cobb (1992) and Loewe (in Clarkson, 1997), which brings us, lastly, to forms of **integrating or integrative or pluralistic psychotherapy**, which is based on my five-dimensional model of the therapeutic relationship since it specifically **includes** the acknowledgement and use of the existential or the real dimension among the other modalities of relationship in the therapeutic encounter.

Common existential themes between these disparate approaches

- A rejection of the predominant role of the Freudian or Kleinian 'unconscious' in psychic life or a relegation of this notion and its associated construct of 'transference' to an equal or even rather minimal role along with other explanatory principles or a redefinition of the term itself.
- A privileging of choice, responsibility, agency, authorship, an inescapable freedom and choicefulness in human action, thought, fantasy and life – 'man is condemned to be free' (Sartre, 1948, p. 34) paradoxically at the same time as...
- An emphasis on awareness, contact, engagement, mutual co-creation and a dialogic relation not only with other people, but also with other things (as they converse with us) and other forces of a spiritual, ecological, mythical or cultural nature.
- A preoccupation with the perennial existential themes of human life such as guilt, anxiety, death, the body, time, alone-ness, the 'other', the arbitrary nature – or in Heidegger's (1949) words the 'thrown-ness' – of our existence.
- A suspicion or rejection of cultural standardization or mental hygiene norms imposed from outside the individual and purveyed in

unacknowledged counselling or psychotherapy values that suggest, model or encourage utopian, salvationist or medical model types of solutions to the dilemma of being human.
- An acknowledgement and honouring of the importance of values and valuing in all human action and inaction, explicitly in the helping process and as part of the changing, growing or evolution of every person, whether temporarily in the role of bystander, helper or seeker, or permanently.
- Intentionality, teleology and synchronicity are viewed as at least equally eligible with genetic causality as temporal constructs and therefore humans are conceived to be influenced and influencing the future as much as, if not more than, being influenced by the past.

Implications for psychotherapy

- Increased respect for the individuality and autonomy of the client – rejection of infantilization and dependency-creating structure and content.
- Avoidance of pathologizing individual concerns in isolation from issues that are collective and culturally based such as race, class, gender, body image, sexual choices.
- An unabashed return to beauty, value, commitment, care (Kierkegaard's *Sorgen*) in life, relationships and a resumption of the quest for meaning, story, poetry and myth, thoughtfulness about others, a philosophy of life (see Clarkson, 1998).
- A humble differentiation between what can and cannot be changed. What is the true nature of the phenomenon, the person's temperament, the kind of world in which we live, as opposed to a guilt-inducing obsessive-compulsive search for perfection.
- A willingness to share wisdom, to safeguard it, to prize learning and to be wrong.
- An acceptance that life is the great co-therapist and that symptoms may be teachers and keys to dimensions of life not glimpsed in the consulting room.
- A trust in the organismic process, the actualizing tendency or the **Physis** (for example, Heraclitus, Heidegger) of each life, the unfolding of our evolution and a knowledge that this trust will frequently have to be regained after being lost in despair, the void and the 'dark night of the soul'.
- The relinquishing of product orientation to human problems and ideals in favour of a process orientation where the **how** becomes more important than the **why** or the **how much**?

- A contextualization of therapy where the events, relationships, social justice commitments and contemporary local or international issues outside the consulting room are considered more important and even potentially more 'therapeutic' than those inside it.
- A return to the body, the senses, the breath, movement, touch and being moved, as well as to relationship in groups, membership of organizations and the human family at large; a call to the abundance of life.
- The co-existence of paradox, contradiction and circularity, the chaos of complexity (Clarkson, 1992), multiple levels of reality, pluralistic perspectives, an essential constructivism and a postmodernist broadening, without the abandonment of the fundamental human ethical project (Bauman, 1993).

A multiplicity of relationships in existential psychotherapy

A human being becomes a self only by relating itself to another.
(Kierkegaard, 1980, pp. 13-14)

The relationship in existential psychotherapy

Kierkegaard (1846) held that one of the root problems of our time was that detachment had replaced commitment in human relationships:

A father no longer curses his son in anger, using all his parental authority, nor does a son defy his father, a conflict which might end in the inwardness of forgiveness; on the contrary, their relationship is irreproachable, for it is really in process of ceasing to exist, since they are no longer related to one another within the relationship; in fact it has become a problem in which the two partners observe each other as in a game, instead of having any relation to each other, and they note down each other's remarks instead of showing a firm devotion. (pp. 44–5)

The phenomenological assertion that 'Dasein is essentially Being-with' has an existential-ontological meaning. It does not seek to establish ontically that factically I am not present-at-hand alone, and that others of my kind occur . . . Being-with is an existential characteristic or Dasein even when factically no Other is present-at-hand or perceived. The Other can be missing only *in* and *for* a Being with.
(Husserl, 1936, pp. 156–7)

The existentialist May (1969) focuses on the existential nature of the psychotherapeutic relationship. In existential and phenomenological approaches to psychotherapy one can distinguish perhaps two opposite poles of articulation about human relationships. Sartre (1946) often exemplifies the position of 'hell is other people' considering isolation as fundamental to the human experience and social life as intrinsically alienating the individual from his authentic self. Also on the basis of Sartre's autobiographical works, Atwood (1989, p. 208) comments that 'one gains the overpowering impression from these descriptions that Sartre's personal sense of nothingness was rooted in severe empathic voids in his relationships with early caregivers. One also sees how closely his later descriptions of the various struggles of being-for-itself mirror his lifelong efforts to avoid enslavement by others and establish a sense of his own autonomous identity.'

Marcel (1952, p. 77), on the other hand, would be an exemplar of a very different kind of commitment to relationship as *a priori* fundamental to human existence and development:

> The more I am present to another the more I am present to myself, the greater my density, my realization, my plenitude of being; and in the mutuality of love, belonging to one another, is an exchange of being, beyond the judgement of knowledge of a third party, which gives a concrete meaning to the notion of absolute taken strictly, and discloses a limit not of frustration but of achievement.

Five Relational Dimensions

I have identified an integrative psychotherapeutic framework containing five possible modalities of client–psychotherapist relationship (Clarkson, 1990; Clarkson, 1995) as being present in any effective psychotherapy. These are: the working alliance; the transferential/countertransferential relationship; the reparative/developmentally needed relationship; the person-to-person relationship; and the transpersonal relationship.

It has also been used explicitly or implicitly in many other contexts for the training and supervision of counsellors and psychotherapists. This framework provides an integrative principle that focuses on similarities and differences between different approaches to psychotherapy and differentiates the relationships that each approach tends to favour. A consistent and coherent integrative approach to psychotherapy has been developed using this framework. It is one means of intellectually and experientially engaging with the systemic complexity of the relationship matrix in all psychotherapies or approaches to psychological counselling. It also provides a conceptual principle for integration between different approaches to psychotherapy, notwithstanding the apparently irreconcilable schisms between schools or theories.

On the other hand, from a postmodern perspective, there is no necessity to 'integrate' these therapeutic relationships, because they are probably all already potentially present in the practice of any developing, maturing psychotherapist of any one or any multiple model narrative perspective. This section explores these therapeutic relationships within an **existential psychotherapeutic idiom**.

The working alliance

In order for 'help' to be of any use, a **working alliance** needs first to be established. This involves co-operation between patient and therapist that underpins all effective helping. 'The therapeutic alliance is the powerful joining of forces which energizes and supports the long, difficult, and frequently painful work of life-changing psychotherapy' (Bugental, 1987, p. 49). I suppose Sartre might have called it the 'joint project'.

Although as an existential psychotherapist, Yalom (1989, p. 30) emphasizes the importance of working with feelings and fantasies about death, he insists on a solid working alliance as in the following example:

> Also, Thelma, I can't work well with a suicide threat hanging overhead. I need a solemn promise from you that for the next six months you will do nothing physically self-destructive. If you feel on the verge, call me. Phone me at any time and I'll be there for you. But if you make any attempt no matter how slight – then our contract is broken, and I will not continue to work with you. Often I put this down on paper and ask for a signature, but I respect your claim always to honor your resolutions.

The biased relationship

This mode of psychotherapeutic relationship is the one most extensively written about, for it is extremely well developed, articulated and effectively used within the theoretically rich psychoanalytic tradition as well as other approaches (Racker, 1982; Heiman, 1950; Cashdan, 1988; Langs, 1976; Clarkson, 1992c). It is most frequently referred to as the transferential/countertransferential aspect of the therapeutic relationship. It is important to remember that Freud did not intend psychoanalysis to be a **cure** but rather a search for understanding, and he frowned upon psychoanalysts who wished to change patients rather than analyse them.

In this regard it is essential to notice that many existential psychotherapists since Jaspers (1913/1965), for example May and Yalom, use the notion of transference as distortion of the patients' typical needs in different ways. Jaspers (1913/1963, p. 28) writes that the psychotherapist has to be a philospher whether he is aware of it or not, examining himself and his own psychology constantly. In this light:

> This transference is unavoidable in psychotherapy and it can be a dangerous reef on which to break if we do not recognize it and deal with it. Many doctors bask in the superior position that has been foisted on them by their patients.

On the other hand, the desire of many other doctors to dismiss all these transferences, submissions and dependencies, these one-sided erotic relationships
in order to create the one desired relationship of understanding communication founders on the elementary needs of the patients who simply want
someone they can dearly love and who will save them.

Other existential psychotherapists also describe transference as the distor-
tions that are experienced in the relationship by the therapist and/or client
as **bias** (van Deurzen-Smith, 1997, pp. 219–24). She differentiates beween
therapist bias and client bias, each of which can be affected by biases from
attitudes, orientation, state of mind and reaction to each other. For Boss
(1957, p. 123):

> Transference is not a mere deception based on faulty linking of affects and
> instincts to the 'wrong' object as Freud thought. Transference is always a
> genuine relationship between the analysand and the analyst. In each being-
> together, the partners disclose themselves to each other as human beings; that
> is to say, each as basically the same kind of being as the other. Not secondary
> 'object cathexes', not 'transfer of libido' from a 'primarily narcissistic ego' to the
> 'love-object', no transfer of an affect from a former love object to a present-day
> partner, are necessary for such disclosure, because it is of the primary nature of
> Dasein to disclose being, including human being.

The reparative/developmentally needed relationship

The reparative/developmentally needed relationship is another relationship mode that can occasionally be differentiated from the others. This is
the intentional provision by the psychotherapist of a corrective/reparative
or replenishing parental relationship (or action) where the original
parenting was deficient, abusive or overprotective. The lens through
which the therapist refracts the relationship may be **developmental** in the
classical and well-known Freudian, Eriksonian or Piagetian sense, or in the
sense of the unfolding of a whole – all the potentialities of which are
already present from the beginning. (This perspective is more like that of
Sterne, Clarkson and Bohm of the Implicate Order.)

Merleau-Ponty's critique of Piaget's child psychology is that it 'misrep-
resented as inferior, primitive or at best derivative, any consciousness
other than that of a white male adult natural scientist... in other words:
Piaget. This negates the structural integrity of child consciousness as it
would that of women, the mentally ill, the working classes, ethnic minori-
ties or any non-Western culture' (Morley, 1998; Merleau-Ponty, 1964).

> I am not myself a succession of 'psychic' acts, nor for that matter a nuclear *I* who
> brings them together into a synthetic unity, but one single experience insepa-
> rable from itself, one single living cohesion, one single temporality which is

engaged, from birth, in making itself progressively explicit, and in confirming
that cohesion in each successive present.

                                                                   (Merleau-Ponty, 1962, p. 407)

As a result of Freud's disapproval of Ferenzci there are many psychotherapists who would deny that they provide such a 'corrective emotional
experience'. However it is patently obvious that even if all 'gratification' is
eschewed, according to the existentialist Boss (1979, p. 277):

> very few adults indeed ever experience from another adult the kind of
> enduring, unshakeable, benevolent, and tactful devotion that a patient
> regularly receives from an analyst, whatever his school of thought. For many
> people who have become neurotic through loneliness, such being-together is
> in itself a very effective therapeutic tool.

In a similar way the steady respectful, congruent empathy of Bugenthal
and other existentially oriented client-centred therapists such as Rogers or
Gendlin shows upon investigation to be providing something very similar,
providing that which has been deficient in the person's life as a child. Just
the fact of being there regularly, on time, with the client's interests in the
foreground is something very few people seem to have been able to have
taken for granted in their early years. Most human beings thus seem to
experience this kind of 'selfless' attention or availability from their therapist as reparative, corrective or healing.

Boss (1979, p. 262) indeed makes it very clear that his patient's
relationship to him was 'very much like the genuine, healthy love of a
small daughter for parents worthy of this name'. It was this unshakeable
daughter–father relationship with her physician that let the patient see
how very difficult her relationship to her actual parents had been and how
she gradually matured in her analysis with Boss. He describes how his
initial feelings of resistance and revulsion towards her behaviour (bias or
countertransference?) turned into a lively interest and enduring benevo-
lence characterizing that of a healthy 'father–daughter relationship' (p.
263) where he could also educate her into revising her attitudes and
feelings about sex and happiness and suggest explicitly that 'she would
find freedom, fulfilment, and happiness if she were to face steadfastly
everything that presented itself to her with responsible concerned care of
the unfolding of its being' (p. 264).

Boss provides us with an excellent case study demonstrating all five
relationship modes. Although he insists on seeing transference as 'decep-
tion', he sensitively deals with the patient's passionately erotic love
towards him whom she wanted to accede to her sexual demands. His
explanation in terms of the working relationships – that it would compro-

mise his freedom as an analyst in the therapeutic process which was absolutely necessary for the therapy to succeed – succeeds in avoiding 'the humiliating rejection of the sort she had experienced so much during childhood'. The reparative intent of this intervention is to 'confirm her womanhood' and 'take her very seriously as a woman' – exactly the opposite of her previous traumatic experiences. Either a humiliating personal or 'transference interpretation' type of rejection or an ill-considered return of her erotic attentions could have been a retraumatization.

This section in Boss (pp. 257–72) shows how exquisitely the reparative relationship dovetails with the potential for acting out or reliving the events which shape the preconceived assumptions or transference expectations (whether conscious or not) in the patient's life. Boss sees the role of the therapist as opening 'a new place for her existence to dwell in the world' and freeing her from limitation and the impairment of her potentialities to be free and autonomous through her human relationship with him and his vision of the process of genuine healing 'involves the way the patient is existentially related to the world at the time, his whole existence' (p. 275).

The phenomenological psychologist Moustakas (1966, pp. 4–5) writes about the reparative developmental dimension of the therapeutic relationship as follows:

> The therapist who lives in the existential sense maintains his own uniqueness, meets the requirements as they emerge, faces life openly with a willingness to recognize his own limitations and his own uncertain, groping nature in a life that has never existed before, with a child who is entirely new, no matter how much his behaviour may appear like that of other children. Such a therapist remains with himself, utilizes his own being as the central resource . . . He remains with the child and enables him to come to terms with his own rejection, immorality, or hatred, not by utilizing a dialectical maneuver or a professional technique, but by bringing to the child the full resources of a real self, interested and committed to the child's well being.

In the same way that the experienced clinician discovers the reparative or corrective therapeutic value of empathic attunement or resonance in ways similar to Jaspers (and Rogers and then Kohut), in a similar way we notice that what Marcel would call the simple 'fidelity' of being there regularly, at a particular time with the client's interests in the foreground, provides reparation for the wounds of being neglected, slighted, pushed into the background and disrespected.

In view of the regressive nature of this kind of work and the likely length of time involved, the professional and ethical responsibilities of the psychotherapists are also concomitantly greater and perhaps so awesome that many psychotherapists try to avoid it. The work of Grof (1985), Reich

(1945), Lake (1966) and other controversial figures outside mainstream psychotherapies, as well as some from the very centre, belong in this category. It is certainly true that this depth of long-standing psychotherapeutic relationship as the primary psychotherapeutic relationship modality is more frequently reported between psychotherapists and their more severely damaged patients.

The dialogic relationship

> In the experience of dialogue, there is constituted between the other person and myself a common ground; my thought and his are interwoven into a single fabric, my words and those of my interlocutor are called forth by the state of the discussion and they are inserted into a shared operation of which neither of us is the creator. We have here a dual being, where the other is for me no longer a mere bit of behaviour in my transcendental field, not I in his; we are collaborators for each other in consummate reciprocity (Merleau-Ponty, 1962, p. 354).

Particularly (but not exclusively) within the existential tradition, there is an appreciation of the **person-to-person relationship** or **real relationship**. This psychotherapeutic relationship modality shows most continuity with the healing relationships of ordinary life. Buber (1970) called this the I–Thou, or I–You relationship to differentiate it from the I–It relationship. The I–You relationship is referred to elsewhere in psychotherapeutic literature as the real relationship or the core relationship (Barr, 1987). Van Deurzen-Smith writes that 'The existential counselling relationship strives to monitor its inevitable public dimension as closely as possible. It also aims at being open to the intimacy of an I–You recognition of subjectivity in the client. It further aims at enabling clients to build an I–You relationship with themselves' (1988, p. 108).

It is very likely that those ordinary relationships that human beings have experienced as particularly healing over the ages have been characterized by the qualities of the I–You relationship (Buber, 1970). This has been retrieved and valued for its transformative potential in the psychotherapeutic arena if used skilfully and ethically (Rogers, 1961; Laing, 1965; Polster and Polster, 1973). There has always been, and there is again, recognition within psychoanalytic practice that the real relationship between analyst and analysand – following Freud's own example – is a deeply significant, unavoidable and potentially profound healing force also within the psychoanalytic paradigm (Malcolm, 1981; Klauber, 1986; Archambeau, 1979).

With Freud's discovery of the importance of the transference relationship came deep clinical suspicion of the real relationship – the psychotherapeutic relationship most similar to ordinary human relationships.

Object relations theorists have offered psychotherapy profoundly useful concepts and theoretical understandings, but the I–You psychotherapeutic relationship is the **opposite** of an object relationship. For Buber, the other is a person, not an object or part object.

> Whoever says You does not have something for his object. For wherever there is something there is also another something; every It borders on other Its; It is only by virtue of bordering on others. But where You is said, there is no something. You has no borders. Whoever says You does not have something; he has nothing. But he stands in relation.
>
> (Buber, 1970, p. 55)

Emotional involvement in the relationship between psychotherapist and patient is that between **person and person** in the existential dilemma where both stand in a kind of mutuality to each other. Indeed, as Friedman (1985) points out, it is a kind of mutuality because the psychotherapist is also **in** role. However, in the immediacy of the existential encounter, the mutuality is almost complete and the Self of the psychotherapist becomes the instrument through which the healing evolves.

> I find myself engaged along with others in a world that makes demands on me: I respond to others and undertake responsibilities to and for them. (This is so different from the old Gestalt prayer.)

So far from my being myself the ground of my certainty in knowing and the motive of my constancy in willing, it is the existence of another that gives me my primary notion of existence and it is in so far as I believe in the existence of others and act on that belief that I affirm my own existence.

> Life is achieved by resolving the tension in responsive feeling and creative activity, in which having is not eliminated but is assimilated to being, in which one and another become I and thou; in which science is integrated with metaphysics; in which autonomy (managing my own affairs) is transcended in liberty, which is participation; in which my body and the world with which it is consubstantial and which enlarges and multiplies its powers is the place in which I bear witness to Being; in which I work out my fidelity and my hope and keep myself open, fluid and ready to spend.
>
> (Marcel, 1952, p. 66)

Such presence of the psychotherapist as a real self, a dialogic partner, needs, of course, extreme care and, in its worst abusive form, has been an excuse for inauthentic acting out of the psychotherapist's own need for display, hostility or seductiveness. Genuine well-judged use of the I–You relationship is probably one of the most difficult forms of psychotherapeutic relating. Doubtless this was the very good reason behind the early analysts regarding it with extreme suspicion. Also, of course, it is in the name of I–You relationship that many personal relationships have been destructive. It probably requires the most skill, the most self-knowledge and the greatest care because its potential for careless or destructive use is so great. Its influence is unavoidable.

'There can be no psychoanalysis without an existential bond between the analyst and the analysand', writes Boss (1963). 'This means that to imagine there can be analysis without countertransference, without involvement and response on the part of the analyst, is an illusion. The analyst can deny but cannot avoid having an emotional relationship with the analysand: even the objectifying attitude of indifference is a mode of emotional relating' (Friedman, 1985, pp. 79-80).

The I–You relationship is characterized by the **here-and-now existential encounter** between the two people. It involves mutual participation in the process and the recognition that each is changed by the other. Its field is not object relations, but subject relations. The real person of the psychotherapist can never be totally excluded from an interactional matrix of therapy. Existential psychotherapy (Boss, 1963; Binswanger, 1968; May, 1969) specifically includes the I–You genuine encounter as a major psychotherapeutic modality, but analysts are also addressing the issue.

What Freud calls 'transference' Boss (1979) describes as 'always a genuine relationship between the analysand and the analyst'. Despite the difference in their positions the partners disclose themselves to each other as human beings. It seems that Freud and Boss are describing psychotherapeutic relationship modalities which are intrinsically different in intent, in execution and in effect; not merely a semantic blurring.

Jaspers already wrote in 1913 that: 'Empathic understanding . . . always leads directly into the psychic connection itself. Rational understanding is merely an aid to psychology, empathic understanding brings us to psychology itself.' Jaspers adds, 'We can have no psychological understanding without empathy into the **CONTENT** (symbols, forms, images, ideas) and without seeing the **EXPRESSION** and sharing the **EXPERIENCED PHENOMENA**'. Jaspers, then, appears by this emphasis to be ranking empathy on a par with 'understanding' as a major therapeutic technique – a manoeuvre followed years later (without acknowledgement) by Kohut.

This person-to-person relationship can also be found in child therapy, as Moustakas (1966), the editor of the excellent and rare book *Existential Child Psychotherapy*, writes (p. 7):

> In the encounter between therapist and child, each person enters into a meaningful tie, where mental power and compassion mingle . . . the life of the therapeutic encounter is a two-way process. It is a person-to-person meeting in

which child and therapist collaborate in their search to unravel the hidden meanings; to clarify the distortions and confusion; to disclose real feelings and thoughts in a closed and fragmented self; to create a climate of learning, where conflicts, challenge, and emerging insight and awareness integrate with sensitivity and compassion in restoring a child to mature and healthy self-hood. New potentialities are actualized in the solitary inner dialogue and in the exquisite fullness of communal life.

In all cases the person-to-person relationship will be honoured by truthfulness or authenticity – not at the expense of the client but in the spirit of mutuality. According to Buber the genuine psychotherapist can only accomplish the true task of regenerating the stunted growth of a personal centre by entering as 'a partner into a person-to-person relationship, but never through the observation and investigation of an object' (1970, p. 179). Significantly though, this does not mean injudicious honesty.

Buber also acknowledges the limited nature of the psychotherapeutic person-to-person relationship. 'Every I–You relationship in a situation defined by the attempt of one partner to act on the other one so as to accomplish some goal depends on a mutuality that is condemned never to become complete' (p. 179). The real relationship is one of a set in clinical practice.

The transpersonal relationship

Contact is the means by which we feed ourselves, by which we understand, orient, and meet our needs, but *cast in the light of I–Thou, contact also stands at the ontic center of the psychological and spiritual development unique to our human existence.*

(Jacobs, 1989, p. 34)

The transpersonal relationship refers to the spiritual or inexplicable dimensions of relationship in psychotherapy. This category of relationship thus ranges from (a) a simple miscellaneous basket into which we place all those aspects of relationship that do not fit into any other category; (b) those images of relationship which are concerned with notions of chaos and complexity as well as quantum physics where modernist norms of causality and duality become redundant and (c) those aspects of mystical or transcendent relationships that correspond to the esoteric, mystical or archetypal universes of discourse. See also Clarkson (1995) and Chapter 10 of this book.

Within the Jungian tradition (Jung, 1940) there has always been an acknowledgement of the ontological domains which presently transcend the limits of our understanding ('There are more things on heaven and earth, Horatio, than are dreamt of in your philosophy' – Shakespeare *Hamlet* Act I, Scene V). However defined, some implicit or explicit recognition of the possibility, if not the existence, of a **transpersonal relationship** between healer and healed as it unfolds within the psychotherapeutic *vas* (container) is gradually beginning to gain more acceptance (Clarkson, 1990a). Merleau-Ponty and van Deurzen-Smith, for example, both use the notion of 'soul'. Van Deurzen-Smith writes that in addition to the physical, social and personal dimension there is also a spiritual dimension: 'On this dimension we connnect through what we may think of as our soul to the absolute world of ideas and their concrete significance in our everyday existence' (1997, p. 101). Merleau-Ponty (1983, p. 210) writes that

> the notions of soul and body must be relativized: there is the body as mass of chemical components in interaction, the body as dialectic of living being and its biological milieu, and the body as dialectic of social subject and his group; even all our habits are an impalpable body for the ego of each moment. Each of these degrees is soul with respect to the preceding one, body with respect to the following one.

This dimension in the psychotherapeutic relationship cannot be proved and can hardly be described. Buber (1970, p. 174) concludes: 'Nothing remains to me in the end but an appeal to the testimony of your own mysteries . . .'

A letting go of skills is implied, and of knowledge, of experience, of preconceptions, even of the desire to heal, to be present. It is essentially allowing 'passivity' and receptiveness for which preparation is always inadequate. But paradoxically you have to be full in order to be empty. It cannot be made to happen, it can only be encouraged in the same way that the inspirational muse of creativity cannot be forced, but needs to have the ground prepared or seized in the serendipitous moment of readiness. What can be prepared are the conditions conducive to the spontaneous or spiritual act.

The atmosphere is more suspension of ego-consciousness – a trance-like meditation. The quality is conveyed by the being-with of highly evolved psychotherapists such as Gendlin (1967) working with patients in acute psychosis.

There are many atheists who could be categorized as existentialists or phenomenologists. However, simply because there is an absence of specific reference to the transpersonal in one of its many disguises in a particular author's work, does not mean that awe and mystery are not inhabitants in those spheres. Some authors such as Heidegger (1959) work explicitly with the notion of **Physis** or **élan vital.**

Merleau-Ponty (1983) writes:

> But quantum physics has doubtless taught us to introduce 'acausal' givens into our image of the physical world, behind which there is no reason in principle for affirming a causality of the classical type; . . . In order to maintain definitively the originality of vital categories, it would be necessary to make every organism

a whole which produces its parts, to find in it the simple act from which the partial phenomena derive their being, to return therefore to the notion of vital élan. (pp. 158–9)

The relation of the vital élan to that which it produces is not conceivable, it is magical. Since the physico-chemical actions of which the organism is the seat cannot be abstracted from those of the milieu, how can the act which creates an organismic individual be circumscribed in this continuous whole and where should the zone of influence of the vital élan be limited? . . . In reality, the two arguments consider the organism as a real product of an external nature, when in fact it is a unity of signification, a phenomenon in the Kantian sense . . . The totality is not an *appearance;* it is a *phenomenon.* If it is impossible to affirm in principle a discontinuity of physical correlations throughout this phenomenon, the affirmation of a real continuity is not any more permissible. Vital acts *have* a meaning, they are not defined, even in science, as a sum of processes external to each other, but as the spatial and temporal unfolding of certain ideal unities. 'Every organism', said Uexkull, 'is a melody which sings itself'. This is not to say that it knows this melody and attempts to realize it; it is only to say that it is a whole that is significant for a consciousness which knows it, not a thing which rests in-itself (en soi). (pp. 158–9)

Of course one of the first and most profound of existentialists, Kierkegaard, had a depth of genuine relationship with a Christian God of poignant and powerful conviction. Marcel (1966) too is a Christian – a Catholic this time – who presents us with his highly personal reflections of his existence. He claimed that in his philosophical work he was open to Christian and non-Christian but a deep and mysterious sense of the sacredness of life permeates all his writing:

Whatever the metaphors used, there is a persistent sense of Being as enfolding my own being and the other beings who are present to me and to whom I am present, like a mother liquid in which it is my true destiny to remain in solution and my perpetual tendency to crystallize out . . . But salvation has no meaning unless things have really gone wrong; faith in the integrity of the universe, on which hope is grounded, only means something in a world which is rent by real and serious breaks.

Then there is also Tillich (*The Courage to Be*) whose truly existentialist struggles with faith, life and despair represent not an easy and simple solution to the exigencies of existence and the anguish of being human, but a more complete engagement.

Heidegger (1959), who also died as a Catholic, thought that

the early Greek understanding of being as physis is not one outlook among others. Rather it is definitive of who we are as participants in Western History . . . As a result, any new beginning [turn] will involve recapturing the insights flowing from those initial 'wellsprings' of understanding that set our civilization on its course, the new beginning is 'realizable only in a dialogue [*Auseinandersetzung*] with the first' (p. 17).

The later Heidegger unequivocally admitted a nonmetaphysical relationship to God in which he did not conceive God as the 'primal cause' but the truly 'divine God' before whom one can dance or bend one's knee (Heidegger, 1969).

> The default of god and the divinities is absence. But absence is not nothing, rather it is precisely the presence, which must first be appropriated of the hidden fullness and wealth of what has been and what, thus gathered, is presencing, of the divine in the world of the Greeks, in prophetic Judaism, in the preaching of Jesus.
>
> (Heidegger, 1971, p. 184)

Summary

This chapter has briefly overviewed five kinds of psychotherapeutic relationship as they are engaged with by existential writers and practitioners.

It is perhaps time that psychotherapists of whatever persuasion acknowledged explicitly that these five forms of relationship are intentionally or unintentionally present in most approaches to psychotherapy or psychoanalysis. Which are used, and how explicitly and purposefully, may be one of the major ways in which some approaches resemble each other more and differ most from others.

It may need to be recognized in psychotherapy training that experience and supervision are required to distinguish between the different forms of psychotherapeutic relationship and in assessing and evaluating the usefulness of each at different stages of psychotherapy. Equally, different modes may be indicated for individuals with characteristic ways of relating so that there is not a slipshod vacillation due to error or collusive countertransference.

Confusion and lack of clarity abound when types of psychotherapeutic relationship are confused with each other or if one is used as if substituting for the other. It is possible that all of these forms of relating are needed some of the time, or for some patients, and that psychotherapists with flexibility and range can become skilful in the appropriate choices. As Boss (1957, p. 259) would have it:

> In the course of our test subject's therapy, the human relationship of physician and patient was the phenomenon that forced itself into the foreground, demanding treatment. It was clear even at the start that success would depend

primarily on the physician's ability to allow this being-together to ripen in a way that would be fruitful to the patient. The first precondition for such a development is the physician's constant awareness of the way he himself relates to the patient, no matter how this relationship may change.

The far-ranging implications of this perspective for psychotherapy research, assessment and treatment need to be developed further. Integration of a multiplicity of psychotherapeutic relationship modalities does not mean eclectic or unconscious use. Indeed if relationship is the declared field, the responsibility is awesome. Freedom does not mean that we forgo discipline. Courage in actively embracing the fullest range of potentials of the self, theory and the soul needs to be accompanied by the severest form of testing, and forged anew with each client from moment to moment as part of the unfolding of **Being** (physis).

References

Bauman Z (1993) Postmodern Ethics. Oxford: Blackwell.

Binswanger L (1968) Being-in-the-World. New York: Harper Torchbooks.

Boss M (1957) The Analysis of Dreams, London: Rider.

Boss M (1979) Existential Foundations of Medicine and Psychology. New York: Jason Aronson.

Clarkson P (1988) Gestalt Counselling in Action. London: Sage.

Clarkson P (1993) New perspectives in psychotherapy. In Clarkson P, On Psychotherapy, Vol. I. London: Whurr.

Clarkson P (1995) The transpersonal relationship. In Clarkson P, The Therapeutic Relationship. London: Whurr, pp. 181–221.

Clarkson P (1996) The Bystander – An End to Innocence in Human Relationships. London: Whurr.

Clarkson P (ed.) (1998) On the Sublime. London: Whurr.

Clarkson P (in press) Values in Counselling and Psychotherapy.

Cobb N (1992) Archetypal Imagination. Hudson NY: Lindisfarne.

Detrick DW, Detrick SP (eds) (1989) Self Psychology – Comparisons and Contrasts. London: The Analytic Press.

Estes CP (1992) Women Who Run with the Wolves: Contacting the Power of the Wild Woman. London: Rider.

Gergen KJ (1992) Toward a postmodern psychology. In Kvale S (ed.) Psychology and Pos modernism. London: Sage.

Heidegger M (1949) Existence and Being. Chicago IL: Henry Regnery.

Heidegger M (1959) An Introduction to Metaphysics. Trans. Mannheim R. New Haven CT: Yale University Press.

Heidegger M (1969) Identity and Difference. Trans. Stambaugh J. New York: Harper & Row.

Heidegger M (1971) Poetry, Language, Thought. Translated by Albert Hofstandter. New York: Harper & Row.

Hillman J (1990) The Essential James Hillman: A Blue Fire. London: Routledge.

Husserl E (1931) Ideas: General Introduction to Pure Phenomenology. New York: Macmillan.

Husserl E (1936/1970) The Crisis of European Sciences and Transcendental Phenomenology. Evanston IL: Northwestern University Press.

Jaspers K (1962) General Psychopathology. Manchester: Manchester University Press. First printed 1913.

Kierkegaard S (1846/1962) The Present Age. Trans. Dru A. New York: Harper & Row.

Kierkegaard S (1985) Philosophical Fragments. Trans. Hong HH and Hong EH. Princeton NJ: Princeton University Press.

Kohut H (1977) The Restoration of the Self. New York: International Universities Press.

Laing RD, Esterson A (1964) Sanity, Madness and the Family: Families of Schizophrenics. London: Tavistock Publications.

Levant RF, Schlien JM (1984) Client Centered Therapy and the Person Centered Approach: New Directions in Theory, Research and Practice. New York: Praeger.

Marcel G (1951) Introduction to a Metaphysic of Hope. Trans. Craufurd E. New York: Harper and Brothers.

Marcel G (1952) The Metaphysical Journal. Trans. Wall B. London: Rockliff. First published 1927.

Merleau-Ponty M (1962) Phenomenology of Perception. Trans. Smith C. London: Routledge & Kegan Paul.

Merleau-Ponty M (1964) Structure et conflicts de la conscience enfantine. Bullétin de Psychologie 18: 171–202.

Merleau-Ponty M (1983) The Structure of Behavior. Duquesnes University Press: Pittsburgh.

Minkowski E (1970) Lived Time. Trans. Metzel N. Evanston IL: Northwestern University Press. First published 1933.

Moore T (1992) Care of the Soul: How to Add Depth and Meaning to Your Everyday Life. London: Piatkus.

Morley M (1998) Ontogenesis and Epigenesis: A Dialogue between Merleau-Ponty and Erik Erikson. In Hass L (ed.) Merleau-Ponty: Across the Continental–Analytic Divide. New Jersey: Humanities Press International.

Moustakas C (ed.) (1966) Existential Child Therapy – The Child's Discovery of Himself. New York: Basic Books.

Perls FS, Hefferline R, Goodman P (1951) Gestalt Therapy Verbatim. Moab UT: Real People Press.

Rogers C (1951) Client Centered Therapy. London: Constable.

Sartre JP (1948) Existentialism and Humanism. Trans. Mairet P. London: Methuen. First published 1946.

Spinelli E (1989) The Interpreted World: An Introduction to Phenomenological Psychology. London: Sage.

van Deurzen-Smith E (1988) Existential Counselling in Practice. London: Sage.

van Deurzen-Smith E (1997) Everyday Mysteries: Existential Dimensions of Psychotherapy. London: Routledge.

White TH (1987) The Once and Future King. New York: Fontana.

Yalom I (1989) Love's Executioner. Harmondsworth: Penguin.

Chapter 4
Psychotherapy, Memories of Abuse and Intersubjectivity – an Epistemological Study with Clinical Applications

PETRŪSKA CLARKSON

> What can be said at all can be said clearly; and whereof one cannot speak thereof one must be silent . . . Here I am conscious that I have fallen far short of the possible. Simply because my powers are insufficient to cope with the task – May others come and do it better.
>
> (Wittgenstein, 1922, pp. 27 and 29)

Introduction

This chapter explores the themes of memories of abuse by presenting 12 fictionalized case vignettes drawn from actual experiences in the light of the theories of intersubjectivity and entanglement as well as a philosophical exploration of epistemological domains in order to facilitate clarity and precision in speech, literature and clinical practice about these issues. It seeks to raise some other fundamental questions about our professional assumptions and practices in dealing with so-called 'recovered memories', the nature of psychological truth as well as the epistemologies and appropriate responsibilities of psychoanalysts and psychotherapists.

> An emerging clarity about the trauma-based nature of many severe mental states was thrown into confusion by the realisation in the early 1990s that some memories of childhood abuse might be 'false memories'. However, the debate about memory often generates simplistic and unproductive arguments in an area which is inherently complex and confusing and pervaded by ambiguity.
>
> (Mollon, 1996, p. 193)

51

This chapter is an attempt to clarify the conceptual ground, honour the complexity and reduce some of the confusion in our talk, our writing and our practice about these matters.

Useful guidelines for practitioners are available from most professional organizations. These generally advise care and caution in making interventions that can suggest to patients that, for example, sexual abuse occurred in the absence of genuine evidence.

Other writers have reviewed the issue of memory in detail, generally concluding that false memories of negative events can be created not only by therapists, but by peer or social pressure and any number of other factors. Memories can also be created and be significantly influenced by post-event information. It is also a fact that the brain itself cannot distinguish between real experiences and vividly imagined experiences. (See Brown et al., 1999 for a comprehensive review.)

The fictionalized vignettes that follow here are meant to raise some of the questions that we as psychotherapists face through engagement with actual case material drawn from real but composite experiences. They can later be combined with further discussion to deepen and nuance the professional discussion, supervision and training on these themes.

Case vignettes

Case vignette 1: the abuse of compassion

A 40-year-old woman (let's say Melanie) suffers from long-standing and intractable bowel pain. Melanie was a particularly loving child, very kind towards animals and others who suffered. In analysis it emerges that her parents used to beat her beloved little sister Janet in front of her – on occasions when Melanie had been naughty. They knew that beating Janet for Melanie's misdemeanours meant Melanie suffered the more from the injustice of her sister's beatings. In this way the parents believed they could cause the maximum pain to Melanie in order to discipline her. Melanie says that she was the lucky one and her sister has 'real reasons to be ill'. Melanie absolutely **knows** that she was never herself physically abused in her childhood, yet her body screamed with pain until she eventually died from cancer of the bowel.

Was Melanie physically abused?

Case vignette 2: the vindictive wife

A man and his ex-wife come for couples therapy because the estranged wife believes that he sexually abused their daughter from when she was four years old. The man has lost his (very respectable) job, been hounded out of their community of friends and colleagues and has faced his daughter's repeated accusations in family therapy sessions where she has vividly described to him what she remembered in therapy (when she was 24), how he had anally raped her as a young child. The man denies this accusation. The wife is convinced, with the bitterness of absolute conviction that he is lying. There is a substantial divorce settlement at stake. The therapist – with decades of clinical experience – feels sure that it is the wife who is lying.

How can the therapist ever be certain? (What is the epistemological status of such certainty?)

Case vignette 3: looking for evidence

In psychotherapy a patient starts reliving vivid intrusive scenes of sexual and ritual abuse as a very young child. There are scenes of having to kill her own favourite cat with her father's gun (otherwise father would have killed her). She also recalls vividly that a baby was killed and buried in the garden of her childhood home in one of these ceremonies. She is wondering whether what she remembers is 'real' or not. She is too scared to ask the police to dig up the garden in case it is not true and too convinced about her own memories to feel that she would ever be anything but a victim in life unless she 'found out the truth'. She reports that her father is still, at the moment, in your town conducting these rituals with other young girls.

What would you do?

Case vignette 4: identification with the victim

The son was brought up South Africa surrounded by wealth and servants. He was adored by his parents and received all privileges of money, status, education and loving parents in an accepting and supportive local community. Yet the therapist, who has a great deal of experience with adults who suffered abuse as children, senses that this man has been physically abused. His body reacts nervously in social situations as if he unconsciously expects to be hurt by others; he suffers from suspiciousness, hyperarousal as well as severe nightmares of being beaten up and horsewhipped until he defecates from fear and is eventually kicked to death.

When he relives the event in a regressive episode he screams and winces as if he himself is being attacked. Yet there is no indication in any way of how these embodied psychological scars could have been left – until he mentions one day in passing that his father was very cruel to his horses and farm labourers and once even kicked a black house servant (his nanny) down the stairs of the house.

Does the body lie?

Case vignette 5: evidence in an ethics complaint

A patient reports that a previous therapist had physically abused her. The new psychotherapist, having been convinced by Alice Miller's work, 'stakes his reputation on the fact that his patient is telling the truth'. After some years of disciplinary procedures and severe distress to all concerned, the patient withdraws the accusation.

Psychotherapists are not trained to evaluate 'evidence', so is this therapist behaving unethically by exceeding the limits of his competence?

Case vignette 6: institutional abuse or not?

A patient is sexually abused by a married psychotherapist who tells her that he is in love with her. When she becomes a psychotherapist (under his supervision) he refers other women patients to her who complain to her that he is also sexually abusing them. She takes care to, in her words, 'maintain her professional boundaries'.

Eventually the professional is found guilty by admission **for the second time** of sexually abusing his patients. (He had been suspended once before by his professional association for a similar complaint with other women patients.) When he undertakes (to the disciplinary board) not to practise clinically again (again!), the professional association declines to discipline him. He therefore remains on the register as an honoured professional colleague lecturing to students at universities in this country and abroad. The woman considers suicide. She feels that the professional collusion with her abuser is far more damaging to her than his original abuse of her – he was weak and bad, but surely they could have been firmer than that? Isn't the point of professional registers that they will remove people when they are found guilty of severe and serious misconduct?

In what sense could it be true that genuine victims of cruelty, abuse and injustice experience the indifference of bystanders who do not get involved in a constructive way as more damaging than the actions of the perpetrators?

Case vignette 7: the headmaster and his schoolboy lover

An adolescent boy and a headmaster start a sexual relationship. The boy feels loved and honoured, the headmaster is gentle and encouraging of all his abilities. When their relationship is discovered, the headmaster is brought to court and the boy has to give witness against him. The boy is very bewildered and terrified that he is being forced by his parents to betray 'his best friend'. In psychotherapy he reports that the court case caused him more psychological damage from guilt as well as physical and emotional distress than the 'love affair' ever did. He never felt wrong or bad or abused about the sexual relationship – indeed it was the only period of his life when he felt loved and accepted as a person. As far as he is concerned there was absolutely nothing wrong with it. It was common practice in ancient Greece and is still common practice in many parts of the world. The court case made him feel shamed, dirty and humiliated and guilty because, through their relationship, his lover had been professionally ruined and sent to prison. Even years later he says that he has never recovered from the aftermath of it – all his attempts at sexual relationships with men or women end in failure and humiliation.

What do you really feel about this?

Case vignette 8: video porn

A hardened and experienced senior police officer in the course of his duties has to watch the pornographic home videos made by a couple such as Fred West and his wife. (The Wests had sexually and physically abused and murdered girls and young women.) He is haunted and troubled for years, physically nauseated and troubled by intrusive memories – just as if he had himself been forced to participate in the actual acts.

Is there scientifically proven evidence that watching video material (or film) can create trauma?

Case vignette 9: who can help me find the truth?

A young man, gradually in the course of therapy, begins to believe that he had been orally raped by his father when he was an infant. He cannot be certain of whether this actually happened. The therapist responds neutrally, but the young man becomes more and more distressed that he cannot actually know whether his father had done this or not. The patient wishes to terminate analysis and go to a recovered memory specialist who works with hypnosis in order to establish the 'truth'.

What do you think the therapist should do?

Case vignette 10: the therapist as witness?

A 50-year-old mother of three children knows that her father and mother had sexually abused her as a child. She wishes to bring a court case against them even though they are now quite old and frail. The patient wishes to have the analyst give evidence that they actually sexually abused her throughout her childhood. The analyst is convinced by her congruence and attachment behaviour over many years in analysis that these events in fact did happen. (Third party witnesses have since died.)

Should the analyst give evidence in court?

Case vignette 11: Holocaust heritage

During psychotherapy a young man vividly recalls and re-experiences being tortured in a Nazi concentration camp where he was born. He did not in fact grow up there, as his mother was removed to another camp shortly after his birth and he was taken away to grow up with a family in neutral Switzerland. Yet he seems to be reliving the traumas of the camp as if they actually happened to his body, not his mother's. Years later he found his mother again and she could corroborate that what he experienced and relived – as if it were his own experiences – were indeed actual events that had happened to her in the camps.

How do you explain this theoretically?

Case vignette 12: the eleventh foetus and the dead twins

The client presented with a phobia of dying. Every time she tried to sleep, she had panic attacks. She was constantly anxious, very paranoid and severely impaired in forming loving relationships. Extensive exploration finally led to the fact that her mother had spontaneously aborted 10 foetuses before this one, the patient, managed to survive. An interpretation of the precariousness of her intra-uterine existence began the process of dissolving the existential transference and a gradual integration of her personality. Another client of the same therapist was a twin sharing the womb for some months with her dead twin.

Is there any positivistic scientific evidence that the clinician can draw on in these cases?

Epistemological domains in psychotherapeutic discourses

Discussion of these vignettes usually surfaces a multitude of real and imagined problems – every one of them serving to illuminate the ways in which we work – and also the ways in which we think. Easy answers there are not – only increasing complexity. In addition it is also possible that a thorough engagement with these questions may even lead us to use them as a kind of litmus test for that perennial question – what is psychotherapy?

All these vignettes are to do with knowing, not knowing, wanting to know and the responsibility for what we know. In that sense it places under question some foundational assumptions about the nature of knowledge in psychotherapy – the epistemology of psychology. It is possible that the whole trauma/memory debate could benefit from the kind of therapy that Wittgenstein recommended: an attempt to separate out (delimit) our thinking and speaking from the 'opaque and blurred' thoughts that too often attend our work.

In order to progress this conceptual work, it is necessary to review some of the principles of how we know, what is knowledge and different kinds of knowledge as reflected in different languages, universes of domains of discourse. By 'domain' I mean:

> domain of reality, constituted in three interlocking dimensions, the criteria for accepting explanations, different operational coherences structuring such explanations, and the actions seen as legitimate. Together, these define a cognitive domain – a domain of possible viable existence. Each is equally rational and equally consistent, and to the extent that we can choose between them the choice depends only on our preference.
>
> (Mingers, 1995)

Philosophy is the discipline of thinking about thinking. 'The object of philosophy is the logical clarification of thoughts. Philosophy is not a theory, but an activity. The theory of knowledge is the philosophy of psychology' (Wittgenstein, 1922, p. 77). The basis and *sine qua non* for all disciplined thinking is the avoidance of logical fallacies (for example Copi, 1961), category errors (for example Ryle, 1960) and spurious conclusions (for example Aristotle). According to Wolman (1965): 'The business of scientific inquiry is not to ascribe rationality to men but to study in a rational way the irrational ways of mankind.' (p. 11)

For our purposes here we can distinguish at least four different categories or universes of discourse in the debates about memory and trauma:

The 'facts'

- The positivistic scientific language where empirical propositions can be proved (by consensual 'contemporary scientific' standards of that culture) to be true or untrue, likely or unlikely to be the case by precisely defined limits of probability (for example, 0.05 or 0.01 degrees). The proposition 'that abused children identify with the aggressor' is not an empirically true or false statement, for the concept of 'identification with the aggressor' is not a behavioural pattern but a theoretical construct. It is however a scientifically proven fact that eye-witness evidence can be unreliable and the scientific procedures used to establish this have been proved to be replicable, valid and reliable. Of course, 'The "scientific" paradigm, which in the field of depth psychology as well as in other social sciences has dominated models of practice, theory and presentation of though, is not necessarily the only, and possibly not the best way, to do analysis (of every kind). By this I do not mean, however, that we can give up a rigorous analytic attitude' (Lepper, 1996). What is considered positivistically proven 'facts' of the kind of rigorously analytic attitude which is consensually accepted is nonetheless still qualified by the culture which so defines and accepts it. For example:

> The Western conception of the person as a bounded, unique, more or less integrated motivational and cognitive universe, a dynamic centre of aware-ness, emotion, judgement and action, organized into a distinctive whole and set contrastively against other such wholes and against a social and natural background is, however incorrigible it may seem to us, a rather peculiar idea within the context of the world's cultures.
>
> (Geertz, 1973, p. 229)

- Then there is the language (or universe of discourse) containing theoret-ical propositions which are profoundly different from empirical proposi-tions. Such propositions are **theoretical**, precisely because they cannot be proved. The same goes for 'hypotheses' or 'explanations'. If they were to be proved, they would not be theories, but facts. For example 'the body records the traces of all trauma which actually happened to it' is a theoretical narrative, not a fact proven beyond dispute in our scientific community. However, there are criteria for judging whether a particular theory is better or worse – for example, dimensions such as coherence, lack of internal contradictions, elegance, utility, economy of explanation (for example Occam's razor), 'fit' with surrounding theories and already proven scientific facts (cf. Wolman, 1965).
- Then there is the **normative** universe of discourse concerned with praxeological 'clinicopsychological propositions dealing with what ought to be done to help the patients. For example, [what is good practice? Not asking coercive or interrogatory questions of the patient, being empathic and not suggesting abuse. None of these would be an empirical or theoretical proposition. Each one] is a device, a norm, a rule to obey or disobey' (Wolman, 1965, p. 10).
- Meltzer asked: 'When we talk about psychic reality, which language should we use? Psychic reality is the world that is real for the patient, yet how is his subjective world real for another person?' (Meltzer, 1981, p. 178 quoted in Hinshelwood, 1989, p. 425). Indeed Mackay (1981) suggested that Klein's metapsychology is a phenomenological one that privileges the individual's own subjective perceptions and experiences and denies other realities (Hinshelwood, p. 427).

The language of **phenomenology** is the description of subjectively experi-enced realities of the analyst and the analysand. This descriptive method (or universe of discourse) attempts to describe subjective experiences without assumptions, impositions of value or 'objectively provable truths'. It is concerned with experience as such, '*die ding an sich*'; e.g. the experience of horror as such. Phenomenological description concerns itself with the pre-verbal worlds of emotion and physiological experiences. Is it the state that Bion described as 'without memory or desire'? As soon as we start interpreting, we are imposing theoretical narratives upon the pure description. Of course, when and how we interpret or otherwise intervene is usually co-existent with our values (or normative preferences).

Category errors between different domains

So the first communication and philosophical problem is when discussants, writers and practitioners confuse these universes of discourse, do not distinguish between them, conflate them or overemphasize one at the expense of the other. Whilst some therapists may be inclined to give too much weight to the influence of exogenous trauma, others may err in the opposite direction of discounting experiences of trauma and abuse and ascribing pathology to essentially endogenous conflict (Mollon, 1996, p. 201).

For example Brierley (1942, p. 110) pointed out that: 'We must distinguish between the patients' language (describing their phantasies) and scientific language – between living experience and our theoretical inferences.' Although he succeeds in separating out the universe of discourse from 'living experience', unfortunately it seems as if Brierley himself here is mistakenly equating 'scientific language' with 'our theoretical inferences'. These discursive domains are not the same and cannot be judged by the same criteria or 'truth values'.

The approach used here is both **ontological** in that it is concerned with existence (or being) as well as **epistemological** in that it is concerned with knowledge (what and how we can know and the methodologies we use in distinguishing varieties of truth values between different domains).

> The objects that the observer brings forth in his or her operations of distinction arise endowed with the properties that realise the operational coherences of the domain of praxis of living in which they are constituted. [This path entails] the recognition that is the criterion of acceptability that the observer applies . . . that determines the reformulations of the praxis of living that constitute explanations in it . . . each configuration of operations of distinctions that the observer performs specifies a domain of reality.
>
> (Maturana, 1988, p. 30)

A form of **category confusion** indicating a wrong identification of domains, for example, is when a statement that expresses a group norm is taken to be rational definition or fact. Something like 'because we think it is good therapy to believe our clients, what they say must be true' (I'm aware that these examples are simplified – but not much!)

Imprecise language supports many domain confusions such as taking the metaphorical phrase 'the body doesn't lie' literally or concretely. If what is meant is to pay attention to the language of the body in therapy as having its own kind of visceral truth – it is good clinical advice. When it is taken to mean that the traces of our experiences are accurately laid down in our physiology to correspond with the actual events of observable reality – it is nonsense. Bodies do lie – they respond physically, vicariously attuned with the emotions of others, as anyone who has been to a rock concert or the funeral of a public figure could testify. Under hypnosis bodies show blisters when they have not been burnt. Bodies register physical trauma when only a word or a look has passed. In some parts of the world, people die from no known physical cause when they are 'hexed' by their communities.

According to Hinshelwood (1989), for example, Kleinians use the terms 'introjection' and 'projection' to refer to the subjective experiences of their patients, yet the terms were originally developed to refer to psychological features and processes objectively described in a scientific manner – Freudian 'metapsychology' (Hinshelwood, 1989, p. 425). (He is emphasizing that Freud used a scientific manner to describe his theories; he is not saying that Freudian metapsychology is a science.) Introjection is thus, for example, **not** an 'objective scientific term'; it is a technical name given to an hypothesized psychological process.

Conflict between epistemological domains exists when one or more levels of language are in opposition – and, in fact, they usually are. There is a world of difference between a client saying 'daddy was just messing around' and 'daddy raped me'. Another indication from a psychotherapist would be a phrase like: 'Because my physiological countertransference indicates that the client is telling the truth, I will testify that the event actually happened.' That is taking 'knowledge' from my own body – which is a kind of physiological/emotional knowledge and equating that with the kind of knowledge (or truth) that judges and police officers are trained to evaluate. It is a **different** kind of truth and the domains (the court, the consulting room, the imagination, the dream) where these truth values can be enacted are different.

It is argued that rigorous definition of terms and conscientious specification of domains of discourse would be of inestimable help to clinical and supervisory practice, the courts, our profession and particularly for our patients who already suffer from enough confusions of feeling and thinking, moral values and fact, fantasy and phantasy, observation and trance induction, truth and lies.

At the metaphorical heart of much of the confusion and conflicts in the field of memory, psychotherapy and abuse lies the unresolved mind–body problematique. If a dual world is posited in which 'a ghost in a machine' pulls the levers of the body (to use Ryle's famous phrase) it becomes logically impossible to make valid 'scientific' statements about the psyche. Psychotherapists often write or speak as if we can observe someone objectively and as if we can also sample their subjective experience through our own psycho-physiological and symbolic experiences through empathic identification with their subjectivity. There is a major problem with the notion of objectivity and a minor one with the notion of subjectivity.

The minor problem is the assumption that we can ever know another person's world subjectively through empathy. In this regard it is salutary to read Abrams (1993). What kind of knowledge is based on empathic attunement and how could we ever know if their experience of red or being burnt with cigarettes is the same as mine – or what I imagine theirs to be? We also usually assume that the 'attunement is one-way' – but intensive counter-transference studies (Searles, 1975; Casement, 1985; Langs, 1976) have other narratives which are highly persuasive and have clearly been used to conduct effective therapy in many cases. Few exponents of the current panacea of empathic attunement take into account the possibility that that very attunement can be **iatrogenic**. If attunement is good and non-attunement is bad, then it follows that bad attunement could be disastrous.

Some theorist-clinicians for example consider that a story of being raped as a child told to the therapist encodes the patient's experience of being psychologically raped by (for example) over-intrusive interpretations or breaks in the analytic frame. (See Smith, 1991, for example.) This may be 'true knowledge' at the symbolic narrative level of discourse – verifiable by the verbal or physiological response to the interpretation. But what if they are intentionally deceiving themselves (Mollon, 1999), you are being hypnotized (for example projective identification) or they are manifesting what is commonly called 'multiple personality disorders' or dissociation as a result of abusive trauma? (See Wolman and Ullman, 1986.)

> In these states of dissociative pathology, where the unity of consciousness (always illusory) is sharply breached, we are faced with another puzzling question. Who is remembering? Who has forgotten? Is it a matter of memory at all? One state of consciousness seems to know something (or fantasise something) which another part does not know. Perhaps it is better to think of this as a kind of epistemological pathology.
>
> (Mollon, 1996, p. 198)

And might the pathology lie in our professionals and the expressions of our professional thinking itself?

The major epistemological problem with the notion of objectivity (the idea that randomized control studies can provide evidence of effectiveness) is that there are a very large number of scientific studies that question the possibility of there ever being a neutral or objective observer. Experimenter effects have, for example, even been observed in rats learning mazes. They have also been observed in the famous Elkington studies.

Furthermore, the arch-scientists, the physicists, have already (albeit reluctantly) come to the inescapable conclusion that the observer is **always** part of the field. 'Objective observation' as is commonly understood is scientifically impossible. (Of course constructionists and constructivists have always had their philosophical doubts about it too.) If this is a fact in the consensually accepted domain (and it appears that it is) classical notions of self and other, objective and subjective, individual and group, inside and outside, the very nature of psychological knowledge and what we as psychotherapists think we do with it, need to come under very serious review.

Quantum entanglement (Isham, 1995), for example, indicates that, scientifically, self and other are inseparable – at some levels we exist in interrelationship, affecting each other, forever. 'Ordinarily, we regard separate objects as independent of one another. They live on their own terms, and anything tying them together has to be forged by some tangible mechanism. Not so in the quantum world. If a particle interacts with some object – another particle, perhaps – then the two can be inextricably linked, or entangled . . . In a sense, they simply cease to be independent things, and one can only describe them in relation to each other' (p. 27).

'In 1935 Einstein recognised that if two particles were entangled, doing something to one could immediately affect the other, even at a great distance. As a result, Einstein doubted that entanglement could be real. But since then, experiments have provided strong evidence that this "non-local" linking of distinct parts of the world really happens' (New Scientist, 6 March 1999, p. 26). Might this explain how clients sometimes arrive at the next session quite improved after the therapist had some good supervision or a particularly fruitful turning point in their personal therapy? One of the fashionable currents that can be used in that direction is the notion of intersubjectivity.

Intersubjectivity

In recent years the term **intersubjectivity** has come to be promiscuously used to cover a multitude of meanings – all characterized by the fact that they refer to the **relationship** between people. In that loose sense all books about the therapeutic relationship are books about intersubjectivity. This point may be so obvious as to escape comment.

Trevarthen (1979) applied the term to developmental psychology to indicate the way in which the infant is always in relation as well as its awareness of other beings in his world. Stern (1985) explains that affect attunement is a qualitative state that goes beyond the basic definition of intersubjectivity as he understands it. However it is not the original sense of the word and is used by developmental theorists in his wake out of its epistemological context to indicate a specific quality of relating sometimes found between caretaker and infant and extrapolated to the relationship between analyst and analysand. So then we have the implication that intersubjectivity 'is a good thing' – a praxeological notion.

Careless use of the term intersubjectivity could land us back in a similar mess to where we came from – unless we define the meaning of the concept as we are using it and specify the domains in which we are using it to constitute our different kinds of therapeutic knowledge about the practice of psychotherapy.

'There has been a certain incompatibility in some contemporary writings that attempt to combine a theory of intersubjectivity with a brand of psychoanalytic thought, presuming a sharp demarcation between inner world and external reality' (Diamond, 1996, p. 303). Wittgenstein in his Cambridge lectures of 1930 said:

> The simile of 'inside' or 'outside' the mind is pernicious. It is derived from 'in the head' when we think of ourselves as looking out from our heads and of thinking of something going on 'in our head'. But then we forget the picture and go on using language derived from it . . . We can only use such language if we consciously remember that picture when we use it.
>
> (Lee, 1980, p. 43)

Intersubjectivity is of course **in the first place** a philosophical term first used by Husserl and then by Merleau-Ponty. In the philosophical branch of phenomenology it has a rather precise meaning as a condition of human existence of primary interrelatedness. It connotes a philosophically necessary view of the world in contrast to (and completely different from) that posited by Kantian style idealism on the one hand and positivistic scientisms on the other. Intersubjectivity is ontologically different from object relations which, although based on the primacy of the individual's desire to be in relationship with others, does not emphasize the *a priori* and omnipresent nature of the interworld that we all occupy. As Diamond (1996, p. 308) puts it:

> A notion of intersubjectivity which derives from a phenomenological perspective challenges any a priori distinction between individual and social world. There is not division, only primary relation . . . Intersubjectivity implies different ontological premises, a different model of human existence, which is fundamentally incompatible with a psychological theory which begins with the individual. It cannot be a matter of supplementing an individual-based approach with an intersubjective approach. Intersubjectivity involves an entire reworking of founding principles.

'Classical analysis construes the core of mental life as a discrete entity that can be relative interpretively captured as such. In contrast, the intersubjectivists construe core psychic processes are inseparable from a relational matrix' (Dunn, 1995, p. 723) 'Interpersonal interactions and enmeshments of interacting subjectivities are conceptually closer to the way such mental experiences and images are structuralized in the mind' (Dunn, 1995, p. 728).

Heimann's broadening of the classical Freudian countertransference formulation also stressed 'that it is a relationship between two persons . . . the degree of the feelings experienced and the use made of them, these factors being interdependent' (1950, p. 82).

> But attention to countertransference, no matter how totalistic, does not require an intersubjective perspective in the strict sense of the term. The most sensitive account of the analyst's subjectivity may still be considered solely a reaction to (rather than necessarily an active constructing force of) both the patient's transference and the analytic material as a whole. A totalistic formulation of countertransference may be used as a positivistic vehicle to determine what is *in the patient's mind* that made the analyst respond in this or that particular way.
>
> (Dunn, 1995, p. 727)

Ogden (1994) postulated that that the analytic couple must attempt to understand the experience of their individual subjective realities interacting with the intersubjective realities that they create together and that this reciprocal tension is the motor of the psychoanalytic process. Unfortunately who is influencing whom most is still not clarified by this formulation. Even an empirical cognitive scientist such as Gudjonsson (1997) in his study of members of the British False Memory Society conclude:

> While many of the respondents in the present survey blamed the therapists for the recovered memories, this may not give a complete picture of the problem in all cases. In some cases the patient may have gone to the therapist with the belief of having suffered abuse already in her or his mind, but without having any memory of abuse. The real question in these circumstances is who is

shaping the responses of whom? A patient may be well able to shape the interpretations and comments given by the therapist in an attempt to find an explanation for his or her distress and psychological problems. Therefore, placing
the responsibility for the recovered memory phenomenon exclusively on therapists may be unfair.

(Gudjonsson, 1997)

Of course we know from scientific studies of the importance of client
motivation to effective outcomes from psychotherapy that it is unfair to
place the responsibility for recovery exclusively on the therapist! Indeed
having watched patients improve with unethical, untrained and abusive
therapists and patients deteriorate with ethical, well-trained and empathic
therapists, I am phenomenologically convinced that this is 'true'.

However, intersubjectivity in the quantum sense means that there are
not dual worlds but that we all interpenetrate each other. From
complexity theory we also learn that out of such relational fields new
properties emerge not attributable to one or the other, but from the interrelated whole. 'Not **how** the world is, is the mystical, but **that** it is'
(Wittgenstein, 1922, p. 187).

Some guidelines for clinicians

Consider that the search for certainty in an uncertain world might often be
dysfunctional in itself – whether this is initiated by the client who, for a
'fact' for example, 'wants to know the truth' or by a clinician who believes
that adult pathology is caused by childhood trauma.

Such a desire for certainty is, however, physiologically and emotionally
understandable as phenomenological yearnings and desires. There is
substantial reason to believe that a beneficial **relationship** can alleviate
some of the distress in human beings and perhaps facilitate a more
resilient response to the vicissitudes of existence – without certainty
necessarily ever being achieved.

Cultural theorists have described our contemporary culture as postmodern and our task as coming to terms with the co-existence of multiple
narratives, some of which may contradict each other. The contemporary
situation in psychotherapy and psychoanalysis mirrors this situation.

There is no real scientific evidence that any one of the 450 or more
theoretical approaches make much difference to the outcome of
psychotherapy – no matter how measured. Perhaps therefore our choices
of the narrative that accompanies our practice are just subjective preferences, permeated with notions of value and ideologically based norms.
(See Chapter 1 of this book.)

This is not to say that our subjectivities, our clinical intuitions, our
countertransferences and physiological resonances with our clients do not

convey valid and important information – only to stress that the discursive and experiential domain for these is the consulting room, not outside where other truth values may be required.

Consider remaining within the remit of psychotherapy – the healing of the soul – not the evaluation of evidence in any sense. Consider remaining with your patients in a world where their subjective truth is completely validated; whether or not it corresponds with what actually happened or not – and that your belief in them is required for their phenomenological experiencing, not for the facts of their history.

Consider that if, after thorough discussion with you, it is still important that your client pursues the 'facts', another psychologist or forensic specialist works with them specifically on that issue – and that you continue to attend to their emotional life as the events unfold – or not. In this way you can keep your working relationship with them clear and focused on accompanying them on their life's journey whatever the 'facts' may be.

Do not offer or agree to give objective expert evidence in any way – unless you are compelled by the court. In such a case, all you can say is that this is what you were told by your patient – any attempt to make a statement of truth about what you heard about third parties in a session is outside of the competence of most psychotherapists and unlikely to fall within the remit of psychotherapy as a profession anyway.

Even if the implications of intersubjectivity in the entanglement sense make it impossible for us at a theoretical (or even scientific) level to separate out who is doing what to whom and why, as professionals we are still responsible for thinking and questioning about our therapeutic relationships. In the end, for the sake of doing something intentionally, 'there are types of relating within the intersubjective field that are important to identify and distinguish' (Diamond, 1996, p. 322). And that *is* the task of psychotherapy.

Addendum: discussion points and questions from the case vignettes

1. The abuse of compassion

Was Melanie physically abused? In what sense could one say that she might be even more injured in her body than her sister? Would the scientifically proven evidence that plants physiologically register the injuries made to their neighbours have relevance in understanding Melanie's subjective experience? From the clinical perspective, does it matter that the blows did not actually 'in observable reality' fall upon her? Would the psychotherapy be any different if she had been directly abused? If so, how? Which psychological theories are most useful to conceptualize this situation? Do you think it possible that her therapist's personal unresolved countertransference reactions could have led to the undermining of the analysis and the eventual death of the patient?

2. The vindictive wife

How can the therapist ever be certain? What information would constitute valid evidence? Since, in the opinion of the therapist, an innocent man is being falsely accused and punished, what is the therapist's ethical responsibility? Is it possible that the man never actually abused his daughter but fantasized about doing so? Is it possible that such a fantasy 'in his head' could cause damaging **physical** trauma to his daughter? Have you ever seen adults in regression relive the times when a murderously enraged parent looked at them 'with killing eyes' and they felt they died? Have you ever seen a black child come home from being called 'dirty nigger' by racist bullies and heard someone say: 'sticks and stones may break your bones, but words will never hurt you'? In what sense may this not be true? If you're a woman – have you ever felt physically undressed and raped by the gaze of a man (or men?) – so much so that you felt you had to go home and wash? If you're a man, ask your female friends this question.

3. Looking for evidence

What is the therapist's role? Is it at all possible to have no opinions or no feelings about what the patient needs to do? What are some of those opinions or feelings? Is it possible **not** to communicate these to your patient – in some overt or covert way? Supposing your client dreams that you go to help her and the bones of the baby are found? Would that affect your psychotherapy differently than if she dreamt that you refused to help her and the bones of the baby were not found? If she reports that her father is still, at the moment, in your town conducting these rituals with other young girls, what would you do?

4. The lying body

Does the body lie? Yes, bodies can behave as if they were actually burnt by producing blisters, for example, under hypnosis. Some bodies react with palpitations, fear and sometimes even screaming with terror in some frightening films. Films are not 'real'. Is the body of the South African patient lying? In what sense of the word? Is it possible that if he is cured from his current difficulties psychopathic and cruel behaviours towards weaker creatures may occur? Which theory would be helpful in anticipating and dealing with such an event? In what sense does growing up in a country such as apartheid South Africa traumatize everyone – whether or not they were directly involved?

5. Evidence in an ethics complaint

What happened there? A clinician's subjective feelings (or countertransference) does not constitute evidence in any objective sense. What would constitute evidence in an ethics case? In court? Are psychotherapists trained to evaluate evidence? How is evidence evaluated in court? Trained judges or a jury of 'twelve good men and true' listen to witnesses on all sides – including the cross-examination of their testimonies under oath. The accused is even then presumed innocent until proven guilty – and that proof needs to be beyond any **reasonable** doubt. Might it be unethical (as in outside the limits of one's competence) to claim to 'know' the truth based on the therapist's own evaluation of the 'evidence' provided by a patient in psychotherapy? What kind of personal pathology can lead a therapist or colleague to claim 'knowledge' of an event that they did not witness in such a way? Might it be a naive and ill-considered belief that it was good practice always to demonstrate publicly that the therapist believes that the client is telling the therapist the actual objective truth?

6. Institutional abuse or not?

Who has committed the most damaging abuse? In the client's experience, the refusal of the professional organization to deal justly with her assailant was the most profound abuse. At least she said: 'he was one sick man, but they should have known better. Now I feel that the whole profession has abused me.' Many abused children report, for example, that the greatest betrayal was not that one parent abused them, but that the other one did not protect them. In studies of crimes committed in front of witnesses who did not intervene (such as three youths dragging a girl to be raped from a crowded shopping mall in Birmingham) the victims also report that the greatest violence they experienced was the indifference of others, not the actual assault by the perpetrator. What is your responsibility in this case?

7. The headmaster and his schoolboy lover

What do you feel about this? What are your values about under-age sexual relationships between teachers and children? Do you believe that these opinions can be genuinely hidden from the unconscious of your patients? What do you think the therapist should do?

8. Video porn

Is there scientifically proven evidence that watching video material (or film) can create trauma? What is the status of that research? How would you approach psychotherapy with this man? With others who are affected by gruesome pictures of massacres on TV? With children who watch violent movies?

9. Who can help me find the truth?

What do you think the therapist should do? Do you know of any literature that could be provided to help this patient decide? Would it make any real difference to his mental health (or his psychotherapy) if he could establish whether the abuse actually happened or not? Could this be established beyond doubt by hypnotic techniques? Are you familiar with the hypnotic techniques used to implant new memories? (See Erickson's February man, 1979.) Hypnosis can indeed uncover additional information (Watkins, 1989). However, false memories are often increased. For instance, 90% of new memories recalled under hypnosis subsequently proved to be incorrect (Dywan and Bowers, 1983) and the Laurence and Perry (1983) study showed that people who have been so hypnotized are remarkably confident that their false memories are literally true.

10. The therapist as witness?

Should the analyst give evidence in court? What can the therapist say as 'being the truth, the whole truth and nothing but the truth'? What is the effect on the patient if he refuses? The clinician can of course be subpoenaed – compelled by the court to give his evidence. What does that do to the transference and countertransference?

11. Holocaust heritage

How is this to be explained? It is a comparatively common phenomenon anecdotally reported in clinical practice that children can experientially reproduce their parents' behaviour and feelings including sometimes the historical facts of their parents lives, without having had previous factual knowledge of the events or experiences concerned. How would one 'prove' this? If it were to be proved true, how would it affect one's psychotherapy? Which theorists can be particularly useful in understanding and dealing with such phenomena?

12. The eleventh foetus and the dead twin

There is some scientific evidence that intrauterine experiences can dramatically affect later development. However anecdotal clinical evidence presents with many cases where people have been traumatized by intrauterine experiences – in some of which we could never establish the 'actual' truth. (See Rossi and Cheeck, 1988, on 'ideomotor questioning revealing an apparently valid traumatic experience prior to birth' – pp. 432–7.)

References

Abrams D (1993) Self-attention and the ego-centric assumption of shared perspective. Journal of Experimental Social Psychology 29: 287-303.

Bagshaw R (1996) Cross and Wilkins Outline of the Law of Evidence. 7th edn. London: Butterworth.

Bion W (1970) Attention and Interpretation. London: Karnac.

Brierley M (1942) 'Internal objects and theory'. International Journal of Psycho-Analysis 23: 107–20.

Brown D, Sheflin A, Hammond C (1999) Memory, Trauma Treatment, and the Law. New York: WW Norton.

Casement P (1985) On Learning from the Patient. London: Tavistock.

Copi IM (1961) Introduction to Logic. 2nd edn. New York: Macmillan.

Diamond N (1996) Can we speak of internal and external reality? Group Analysis 29: 303–17.

Dunn J (1995) Intersubjectivity in psychoanalysis: a critical review. International Journal of Psycho-Analysis 76: 723–38.

Dywan J, Bowers KS (1983) The use of hypnosis to enhance recall. Science 222: 184–5.

Erickson MH, Rossi EL (1979) The February man: facilitating new identity in hypnotherapy. In Rossi EL (ed.) Innovative Hypnotherapy: The Collective Papers of Milton H Erickson on Hypnosis. Vol. IV. New York: Irvington Publishers, pp. 525–42.

Geertz C (1973) The Interpretation of Cultures. New York: Basic Books.

Gudjonsson GH (1997) Accusations by adults of childhood sexual abuse. Applied Cognitive Psychology 11: 3–18.

Haley J (ed.) (1967) Advanced Techniques of Hypnosis and Therapy. Selected Papers of Milton H Erickson. New York and London: Grune & Stratton.

Heimann P (1950) On counter-transference. International Journal of Psycho-Analysis 31: 81–4.

Hinshelwood RD (1989) A Dictionary of Kleinian Thought. London: Free Association Books.

Husserl E. (1931/1960) Cartesian Meditations. Trans. Cairns D. Nijhoff.

Isham CJ (1995) Lectures on Quantum Theory – Mathematical and Structural Foundations. London: Imperial College Press.

Langs R (1976) The Bipersonal Field. New York: Jason Aronson.

Laurence J, Perry C (1983) Hypnotically created memory among highly hypnozable subjects. Science 222: 523–4.

Lee D (ed.) (1980) Wittgenstein's Lectures Cambridge 1930–1932. Oxford: Basil Blackwell.

Lepper G (1996) Between science and hermeneutics: towards a contemporary empirical approach to the study of interpretation in analytical psychotherapy. British Journal of Psychotherapy 13(2): 219–31.

Mackay N (1981) Melanie Klein's metapsychology: phenomenological and mechanistic perspectives. International Journal of Psycho-Analysis 62: 187-98.

Maturana H (1988) Reality: the search for objectivity or the quest for a compelling argument. Irish Journal of Psychology 9: 25–82.

Meltzer D (1981) The Kleinian expansion of Freud's metapsychology. International Journal of Psycho-Analysis 62: 177–85.

Merleau-Ponty M (1962) The Phenomenology of Perception. Trans. Colin Smith. London: Routledge & Kegan Paul.

Mingers J (1995) Self-Producing Systems. Implications and Applications of Autopoiesis. New York and London: Plenum Press.

Mollon P (1999) 'Memories are made of . . . what?'. In Greenberg S (ed.) Mindfield: The Therapy Issue. London: Camden Press, pp. 89–94.

Ogden T (1994) The analytic third: working with intersubjective clinical facts. International Journal of Psycho-Analysis 75: 3–19.

Rossi EL, Cheek DB (1988) Mind-Body Therapy – Ideodynamic Healing in Hypnosis. New York: Norton & Company.

Ryle G (1960) Dilemmas: The Tarner Lectures. Cambridge: Cambridge University Press.

Searles HF (1975) The patient as therapist to his analyst. In Giovacchini PL (ed.) Tactics and Techniques in Psychoanalytic Therapy, vol. 2. New York: Aronson, pp. 94–151.

Smith D (1991) Hidden Conversations: An Introduction to Communicative Psychoanalysis. London: Routledge.

Stern D (1985) The Interpersonal World of the Infant. New York: Basic Books.

Watkins JG (1989) Hypnotic hypermnesia and forensic hypnosis: a cross-examination. American Journal of Clinical Hypnosis 32: 71–83.

Watson L (1983) Supernature. London: Coronet Books.

Wittgenstein L (1922) Tractatus Logico Philosophicus. Trans. Pears DF, McGuinness BF. Reprinted London: Routledge, 1961.

Wolman BB (ed.) (1965) Handbook of Clinical Psychology. New York: McGraw-Hill.

Wolman BB, Ullman M (eds) (1986) Handbook of States of Consciousness. New York: Van Nostrand Reinhold Company.

Chapter 5
Heraclitus

Petrūska Clarkson

> It belongs to all men to know themselves and to think well.
>
> (Heraclitus, Fragment XXVI)

Introduction

Heraclitus is the spirit who influenced me most in my development as a psychologist psychotherapist. The extant 'Fragments of Heraclitus' in *The Art and Thought of Heraclitus* are available in a good translation with the Greek original texts by Kahn (1993). Heraclitus wrote them in Ephesus, on the coast of Asia Minor (north of Miletus) around 504–501 before the Common Era and deposited the book as a dedication in the great temple of Artemis. He was a poet with an interest in perfume.

Why Heraclitus? As a philosopher he addressed himself to the nature of the **psyche**. According to Friedman (1964), Heraclitus was the forerunner of existentialism. He was also the first psychologist who said: I go in search of myself (Fragment XXVII) and concluded that you will not find out the limits of the soul by going, even if you travel every way, so deep is its report (Fragment XXXV).

My searching into the Heraclitean fragments shows this to be true of the fragments themselves – they are inexhaustible, no matter how long and how deep his work has been studied over the last 2,500 years. Their process and their content embody each other, each is a part **and** the whole. Although a multiplicity of languages co-exist in which experience can be described, his claims that direct experience is of a different level of discourse than what is 'heard' from others also makes him the first phenomenologist in the Occidental tradition.

> The world order speaks to men as a kind of language they must learn to comprehend. Just as the meaning of what is said is actually 'given' in the sounds

which the foreigner hears, but cannot understand, so the direct experience of the nature *[physis]* of things will be like the babbling of an unknown tongue for the soul that does not know how to listen. This is apparently the first time in extant literature that the word psyche 'soul' is used for the power of rational thought.

(Kahn, 1981, p. 107)

Thinking and acting well (phronein)

For Heraclitus self-knowledge leads to the knowledge of what is 'shared by all' – a universal principle of wholeness. There is no part of the whole that does not remain in relationship with every other part that is also a whole. The fragments are concerned with how people live their lives and die – how to make sense of our experience. In the Heraclitean epistemology questions of cognition are inseparable from questions of action and intention, questions of life and death (Kahn, 1981, p. 100).

At the same time as deserving of the epithet Heraclitus, the Obscure, he is also very clear in his thinking. The Oxford philosopher Gilbert Ryle (1966) again had to clarify for modern (and postmodern) philosophers a kind of thinking error – category confusion – when one class of domain or kind of discourse is assigned a truth value that is logically inappropriate to that domain. Let's take an example of Heraclitus at work spelling this out:

Most men do not think *[phroneousi]* things in the way they encounter them, nor do they recognize what they experience, but believe their own opinions. (Fragment IV)

Phronesis is translated by the word **thinking**, with the meaning of intelligence, understanding; and **phroneousi** as **think** in the sense of understand, think straight, act with intelligence. Heraclitus here in fragment IV is distinguishing three universes of discourse: (a) the way in which humans **encounter** things; (b) the way in which they **recognize** (*ginoskousi,* know, be acquainted with) what they experience and (c) the way in which they **believe their own opinions**.

There is thus (a) a domain of direct encounter that I might provisionally call the **physiological** level; (b) there is a domain of recognizing experience – which I consider to be the **phenomenological** level of pure description and (c) there is also another epistemological level of **having opinions** – which could be called a normative level. Heraclitus is critical of people who listen to authorities without using their own direct experience, 'listening like children to their parents' (Fragment XIII), and those who believe the poets of the people and take the mob as their teacher (Fragment LIX).

Yet in other places he clearly holds opinions himself about what is good or **ethical** for humankind. For example: the people must fight for the law as for their city wall (Fragment LXV) and justice will catch up with those who invent lies and those who swear to them (Fragment LXXXVII) and one must quench violence quicker than a blazing fire (Fragment CIV). He has firm values: Thinking well is the greatest excellence and wisdom: to act and speak what is true, perceiving things according to their nature (*physis*) (Fragment XXVI).

It is therefore not **having opinions** that Heraclitus criticizes, but **believing opinions** – even one's own. **Opinions (beliefs) are in a different universe of discourse than that which is true at an 'objective' level of consensual reality at a particular time in a particular culture**.

Throughout the extant fragments Heraclitus can be seen to differentiate different domains of discourse such as direct experience, passions, rational thought, beliefs, opinions, and the different **kinds of truth** that co-exist at individual, collective, human, inanimate and cosmic levels. Take *sophronein* as a vantage point for looking epistemologically at the state of thinking in psychoanalysis – one of the primary psychological ways in which the Caucasian peoples over the last hundred years or so have attempted to 'know themselves and to think well'.

> Psychoanalytic theory is replete with dichotomies, intrapsychic/interpersonal, drive/relational, fixation/regression, deficit/conflict, even the hoariest of all, nature/nurture. One is always tempted to say, Why not see and use both perspectives? But these are not different perspectives on the same reality: They are different realities, entirely different pervasive sets about what reality is. They are opposing philosophies of life. Therapists who talk about character and character disorders see patients, psychotherapeutic devices, and outcomes differently from therapists who talk about personality. Just because we are using the same words, we are not using them in the same way. We talk to each other, we must begin with the assumption of difference. I believe that our particular Tower of Babel is built on the paradoxical illusion that we are all speaking the same tongue . . . Any reader, not totally committed to one **ideology** or another, cannot fail to be impressed – and one might hope, dismayed – by the total conviction with which prominent analysts proclaim diametrically opposed clinical strategies for what they diagnose as the very same characterological category.
>
> (Levenson, 1991, p. 244, author emphasis)

As Heraclitus says, much learning does not teach understanding (in Fragment XVII). So, as we babble at each other in our different psycho-languages (from our different 'schools') not realizing that we are talking about the same experience (or about different experiences in the same language), we, as healers, could do with some healing understanding ourselves. 'The business of scientific inquiry is not to ascribe rationality to men but to study in a rational way the irrational ways of mankind' (Wolman, 1965, p. 11).

According to Wittgenstein (1922) philosophy itself is a medicine (physic). Philosophy *is* the discipline of thinking about thinking. The object of philosophy is the logical clarification of thoughts. Philosophy is not a theory, but an activity. The theory of knowledge is the **philosophy of psychology** (p.77, emphasis added).

Confronted with the speed of change, the growing complexity of the world and with the new (?) challenges of history, the 1998 UNESCO International Symposium – Towards Integrative Process and Integrated Knowledge – recognized how the nature of reality itself, with its inherent complexity and multiform character, but at the same time with its deep unity, requires transcending the boundaries of single disciplines. It was also observed that the probable reason for these global issues to necessitate a transdisciplinary approach is that they tend to reveal, more than others, the underlying complexity of reality (p. 8).

So how can we gain clear understanding of ourselves and this our complex multilingual world? Definitely not by just listening to monolingual authorities (theoretical learning):

> The way to attain an integrated concept and practice of knowledge, and consequently to address many crucial issues of our age through a transdisciplinary approach, does not lie in applying ready-made, 'mechanical' procedures based on automatic, stereotyped formulas and standardized recipes.
>
> (UNESCO report, 1998, p. 7)

Heraclitus would be pleased. The philosopher for all ages says that we need to search and search again. **Research means to search again**. Into many things. People who love wisdom must be good inquirers into many things indeed. (Fragment IX) Why? Because **physis loves to hide** (Fragment X).

Since Plato fractured the original mind/body unity, physis has sometimes been mistranslated (as the Romans did) with the limited word 'nature'. According to Heidegger (1959/1987) the later concepts of 'nature' must be set aside: **physis** means the emerging and the arising, the spontaneous unfolding that lingers. In this power, rest and motion are opened out of original unity (Heidegger, 1987/59). When Heidegger uses the word Being, he means **physis** in the original ancient Greek sense. Furthermore, the Greeks did not learn what **physis** is through natural phenomena, but the other way around; it was through a fundamental poetic experience of being that they discovered what they had to call **physis**. Heidegger thinks that physis as logos is the poesis of **physis** – the ultimate source of thought as well as of language and poetry. The human **logos**, as it shows itself in language and poetry, is merely a response to the **logos** of **physis**.

There are three further themes that, although they overlap and are in relationship with each other as constantly changing wholes, between them embrace perhaps the most important emphases for me as a psychologist psychotherapist. These are:

- everything is in relationship to everything else;
- everything changes; and
- everything is a whole.

Everything is in relationship to everything else

So, the first theme is process, or dynamic interrelatedness. Colloquially, **everything is in relationship to everything else** – even our relationship with the first **physicians**.

Heidegger thought that 'the early Greek understanding of **being as physis** is not one outlook among others. Rather, it is definitive of who we are as participants in Western History. As a result, any new beginning [turn] will involve recapturing the insights flowing from those initial wellsprings of understanding that set our civilisation on its course, the new beginning is realizable only in a dialogue (*Auseinandersetzung*) with the first' (Heidegger, 1959).

The warrior-philosopher Jan Smuts was the founder of the forerunner to the United Nations – and the last South African Prime Minister before 'apartheid'. He bequeathed the word **holism** to philosophy and wrote that wholes are not closed isolated systems externally: they have their field in which they intermingle and influence each other. The holistic universe is a profoundly reticulated system of interactions and interconnections (Smuts, 1926, p. 333).

> Epistemologically, the things we see (people, objects etc.) exist only in relation-ship and, when analysed microscopically, they too are best viewed as relation-ships . . . Relationships become the primary source of our knowledge of the world. . . . in fact things ultimately are relationships.
>
> (Cottone, 1988, p. 360)

As shown in Chapter 1, there is no significant objective evidence that theoretical approach is relevant to the successful outcome of Eurocentric psychotherapies – no matter how measured. There is substantial evidence that it is in fact the **psychotherapeutic relationship** rather than theory, diagnosis or technique that potentiates the beneficial effects of psychotherapy (see Clarkson, 1998b, for a review).

This finding is consistent with experience and research reporting that (as long as the explanation or narrative is culturally congruent) experiences of mental and emotional healing have **always** existed in human societies. Furthermore such healing practices are **right now** helping many people in distress across the world through what is sometimes referred to as indigenous medicine. According to Frank and Frank's 1993 masterly survey, (a) the therapeutic relationship, (b) a culturally congruent narrative, (c) a dedicated space, and (d) a prescription for some action constitute the four necessary ingredients for all healing practices throughout the world and throughout all of history.

In addition to the multitude of studies which have testified to the overriding importance of the therapeutic relationship, it has been found that there are **different kinds** of relationship required for different kinds of patients, and this factor is more important than diagnosis in predicting effectiveness of psychotherapy.

Evidence also exists that there are experiences of psychotherapy by which people feel harmed – abuses of relationship. With the exception of sexual abuse, one of the most salient facts here is that the harmfulness seems to have to do with the extent to which psychotherapists entrench into a theoretical position when challenged or questioned by their clients (see Winter, 1997 for a review).

As the Oxford philosopher of psychology Farrell pointed out in 1979, participants, 'trainees' or clients are usually considered to be 'cured' or 'trained' or 'analysed' or 'qualified' by one single criterion – they have adopted the WOT ('way of talking') of the leaders, governing bodies, examination boards and others of perceived status or power. An empirical study by Silverman (1997) from London University also found repeatedly that 'rather than being a deviant case, such adoption by clients of the professionals' rhetoric is common . . . each centre [of counselling] offers an incitement to speak structured according to its own practical theories' (p. 209).

So perhaps our Eurocentric theories are our culturally congruent narratives – our WOTS. In this way each different psycho-language can be spoken well or made into gibberish, but each unique language (game) also has its rules of grammar, as well as the potential for poetry. There are in existence 'pure' languages that are no longer spoken. Most languages in use are also in a process of constant change. There are also integrative languages such as Esperanto, Yiddish and Fangalo. In any case, the narratives of psychotherapy theory are located in a different universe of discourse from that of facts or even research. Theory cannot properly substitute for these other universes of discourse, nor be conflated with them. That would not be 'thinking well'.

As Norcross (1999) puts it, let's confront the unpleasant reality and say it out loud: in the dogma-eat-dogma environment of **schoolism,** clinicians traditionally operated from within their own particular theoretical frameworks, often to the point of being oblivious to alternative conceptualizations and potentially superior interventions.

The dynamic interrelatedness of all of human life is now a well-established scientific fact. Like quantum physics, the chaos and complexity sciences highlight the importance of relationships (for example, Lewin, 1992). The observer (researcher, clinician) is always part of the field – always affecting and being affected in that relationship. Our current physicists have shown us that everything and potentially everybody is in relationship in a kind of dance. It is impossible **not** to have a relationship with another person **and** we will continue to affect each other's states, even should we never see them ever again (Isham, 1995 and personal communication 1999). Pictures showing entanglement demonstrate how we physically interpenetrate each other. Everything is in this sense connected with everything else and any separation is therefore theoretical or descriptive rather than actual.

Examples of '**tele**' from psychodrama (Greenberg, 1974/1975) or synchronicity in Jungian thought (1972/1955) abound in psychotherapy and supervision and give credence to the notion that there are meaningfully interconnecting patterns in all of human existence (see Clarkson, 1998a). Repeatedly, many of us experience that, whenever we stop to pay attention to a particular conjunction between events and people, some significance – often profound – is laid bare.

So it seems that the Heraclitean notion that everything is in relationship to everyone and everything else forever is in a sense philosophically, experientially, scientifically and psychotherapeutically accurate.

Everything changes

Heraclitus was *par excellence* the philosopher of change. The second theme, which I see as a continuous flow around the cycle of awareness from 500 BC to my work today, shows how

> He regarded the universe as a ceaselessly changing conflict of opposites, all things being in a state of flux, coming into being and passing away, and held that fire, the type of this constant change, is their origin. From the passing impressions of experience the mind derives a false idea of the permanence of the external world, which is really in a harmonious process of constant change.
>
> (Hawkins and Allen, 1991, p. 663)

So, Heraclitus postulated that change is the only thing in the whole world of which we can be certain. The nature of this change, according to him, is usually cyclic. One cannot step twice into the same river, nor can one grasp any mortal substance in a stable condition, but it scatters and again gathers; it forms and dissolves, and approaches and departs (Fragment LI).

Structure is slow process and process is fast structure. The unifying force of all life phenomena, which is suggested by Heraclitus, is **physis**. The river water symbolizes the one **physis**, or life force. It is similar to Bergson's 'élan vital' but is conceived of as 'all-embracing – everything'.

The coincidence of opposite values in one action allows it to be a symbol of the one **physis**. It was conceived of as the healing factor in illness, the energetic motive for evolution, and the driving force of creativity in the individual and collective psyche – and the universe.

This sense that **everything is changing all the time**, as a result of relationship, is the very heartbeat of the Heraclitean message. The ordering, the same for all, no god nor man has made, but it ever was and will be: fire everliving, kindled in measures and in measures going out (Fragment XXXVII). Guerrière's translation stresses the **auto-poiesis** (self-making) of physis even more: kindling itself in measures and quenching itself in measures (Heraclitus in Guerrière, 1980, p. 97).

Heraclitus suggests, therefore, that the nature of change is intrinsically rhythmic – kindling and quenching. 'The beginning and the end are shared in the circumference of a circle' (Fragment XCIX). Any psychotherapist (any human being too) is familiar with the rhythms of breathing in and breathing out, of eating and excreting, of arousal and orgasm, the seasons, the generations, civilizations. This is the intrinsic and inevitable cyclic nature of human existence.

> The god: day and night, winter and summer, war and peace, satiety and hunger. It alters, as when mingled with perfumes, it gets named according to the pleasure of each one. (Fragment CXXIII)

One of the many corollaries of appreciating the cyclic nature of phenomena is the importance of the void – the abyss space – when **physis** is in hiding. However, it is from the void that the new emerges; it was in the deepest darkness that Moses found God, and it is when we most truly let ourselves go into the emptiness (of despair or illness) that fullness (and healing) can begin to arise. 'Creativity happens at far from equilibrium conditions' (Briggs and Peat, 1989).

The recent scientific thrill of discovering evidence that our known world emerged with a Big Bang from the void (for example, Davies, 1992) echoes human experience of a sudden insight, a figure/ground shift, a turnaround (or **metanoia**) that obliterates one phenomenological world and brings another into being. Like death, it is inescapable and yet human beings so often try to avoid it. It is my conviction that if we only had time to teach the human race one thing before we self-destruct, it would not be the linear skills of making 'training standards', but rather the cyclic skills of navigating the endless changes in our bodies, our lives and in our worlds.

> With its very coming-to-life every living thing already begins to die, and conversely, dying is but a kind of living, because only a living being has the ability to die. Indeed, dying *can* be the highest 'act' of living. PHYSIS is the self-productive putting-away of itself, and therefore it possesses the unique quality of delivering over itself that which *through it* is first transformed from something orderable (e.g. water, light, air) into something appropriate for it alone (for example, into nutriment and so into sap and bone).
>
> (Heidegger, 1998, p. 227)

Everything is a whole

> Graspings: wholes and not wholes, convergent, divergent, consonant, dissonant, from all things one and from one thing all.
>
> (Fragment CXXIV)

A meditation on the meaning and implications of this Heraclitean fragment tends to invite us into feeling how profoundly Heraclitus understood and wanted to communicate the intrinsic oneness of all phenomena.

It also gives a new and contemporary articulation to the original Heraclitean ideas. For example, Briggs and Peat (1989) state: 'The whole shape of things depends upon the most minute part. The part *is* the whole in this respect, for through the action of any part, the whole in the form of chaos or transformative change may manifest' (p. 75). However, we need to understand that this wholeness includes its **opposite**. 'The name of the bow is life; its work is death' (Fragment LXXXIX).

Thus cosmic unity includes the notion of **enantiodromia**, a term subsequently used both by Jung (1969b) and by Perls (1969). This refers to the nature of the unity of apparent polarities. Opposites may have contrary qualities, yet they can turn into each other at their apotheosis. 'The same . . . living and dead, and the waking and the sleeping, and young and old. For these transposed are those, and those transposed again are these' (Fragment XCIV).

In a letter (1952) Jung wrote:

> The language I speak must be ambiguous, must have two meanings in order to be fair to the dual aspect of the psyche's nature. I strive quite consciously and deliberately for ambiguity of expression, because it is superior to singleness of meaning and reflects the nature of life. My whole temperament inclines me to be very unequivocal indeed. That is not difficult, but it would be at the cost of

truth. I purposely allow all the overtones and undertones to chime in, because they are there anyway while at the same time giving a fuller picture of reality. Clarity makes sense only in establishing facts, but not in interpreting them. (This letter appears only in the original Swiss edition of *Memories, Dreams, Reflections,* p. 375.)

See also *Mysterium Coniuncionis,* par. 715: 'Unequivocal statements can be made only in regard to immanent objects; transcendental ones can be expressed only by paradox.' Moreover 'Nicholas of Cusa, in his *De Docta ignorantia,* regarded antinomial thought as the highest form of reasoning.'

The more fully I configure my anger, the more likely that it can turn into love or understanding – and of course vice versa. In chaos theory a similar phenomenon has become known as the 'flipover' effect (Gleick, 1989, p. 29) – the sudden figure/ground shift from one polarity to another. It appears to apply to both process and content. Rarely can one polarity remain the same for long without calling its diametrical pole into being. It is not better for human beings to get all they want. It is disease that makes health sweet and good, hunger satiety, weariness rest (Fragment LXVII).

> Although Physis is wont to hide itself, it manifests itself in multiple ways . . .The form in which Physis does manifest itself through phenomena is their one-ness. That is to say, it suggests a certain one-ness in multiple things, a certain 'coincidentia oppositorum' (co-incidence of opposites).
>
> (Guerrière, 1980, p. 103)

Heraclitus is sympathetic to the fate of the exceptional individual and he expresses his contempt for the Ephesians: since they drove out their best man, Hermodorus, saying, 'Let no one be the best among us; if he is, let him be so elsewhere and among others' (Fragment LXIV). Yet he realizes that the individual and the collective are in irretrievable relationship and conflict is necessary. 'The counter-thrust brings together, and from tones at variance comes perfect attunement, and all things come to pass through conflict' (Fragment LXXV).

From this perspective, whether defended or concealed, whatever part or particularity is present, the whole is enfolded in that fragment in the same way as a fractal of anything enfolds the whole and a moment of time enfolds all of eternity.

The **fractal** – a concept from chaos theory – is an immensely fruitful metaphor to draw upon within psychotherapy today. The word 'fractal' was coined by Mandelbrot (1974) to describe this phenomenon of a repeating pattern – the whole repeated in every fragment, and thus spiralling off each other towards creative evolution.

The final net result is that this is a whole-making universe, that it is the fundamental character of this universe to be active in the production of wholes, of ever more complete and advanced wholes, and that the Evolution of the universe, inorganic and organic, is nothing but the record of this whole-making activity in its progressive development.

(Smuts, 1987, p. 326)

But Smuts speaks only of the progressive development. Heraclitus' **physis** is both creative and destructive (destructuring). So is the **auto-poeisis** of modern complexity theory. Mingers (1995, p. 1) makes the very explicit connection. He postulates that Heidegger practically invented the word auto-poeisis as in the following quote: 'Physis also, the arising of something from out of itself, is a bringing forth, poeisis. Physis is indeed poeisis in the highest sense.' Wholes are made indeed, and they also fragment as planets (perhaps even our own) eventually explode in fiery conflagration.

There is one common flow, one common breathing, all things are in sympathy. The whole organism and each one of its parts are working in conjunction for the same purpose . . . the great principle extends to the extremest part, and from the extremest part it returns to the great principle, to the one nature, being and not-being.

(Jung, 1969c, p. 490, quoting Hippocrates in Precope's translation)

Of course, even (or particularly) in Heraclitus, holism, change and dynamic interrelationship (even between opposites) are also fractals of **one whole**. By extrapolating these three themes, I am merely focusing on some different facets of a unity which is intrinsically indivisible, although it is forever changing, and although its parts are forever interrelated, even as they oppose or contradict each other. Using Lyotard's (1997, p. 271) words – except for the last one:

There are stories: the generations, the locality, the seasons, wisdom and madness. The story makes beginning and end rhyme, scars over the interruptions. Everyone . . . finds their place and their name here, and the episodes annexed. Their births and deaths are also inscribed in the circle of things and souls with them. You are dependent on God, on nature. All you do is serve the will, unknown and well known, of physis, place yourself in the service of its urge, of the *physein* which urges living matter to grow, decrease and grow again. This service is called [psychotherapy].

The poetic summary

Physis (or **phusis**) is an ancient Greek word very rich in meaning. It is used to refer to life energy as it manifests in nature, in growth and healing as well as in all dimensions of creativity. **Physician** or **physic** (as in medicine) and **physics** (as in quantum and chaos understandings of the world) are both derived from it. Here it is used as a concept to concentrate some of the most significant qualities and aspirations of my work – in honour of everlasting change, unlearning as well as learning, living as well as dying well, bodysoul, the cycle as potent paradigm for human evolutionary processes, the individual and society, relationship and archetype, the importance of nature as teacher and inspiration, the drive towards complexity, quality and wholeness, the co-existence of contradictions. Whether in individuals, children, couples, groups, organizations or artistic work, the central and organizing theme is simply to have life and to have it more abundantly.

The competency based summary

The praxis of systemic integrative relational psychotherapy (or any 'pure' form of psychotherapy from Kleinian analysis to bio-energetics) is based on intentional **being** – physis – which is understood as a relational co-creation of healing, growth and emergent creativity – auto-poiesis (for example, Clarkson, 1996a) and a philosophically informed choice of known or invented interventions between **seven epistemological and ontological levels** of complexity (physiological, emotional, nominative, normative, rational, theoretical and transpersonal) (for example, Clarkson, 1975, and Clarkson, 1992a) manifested through the **five relationship modalities** (the working alliance, the transference/ countertransference relationship, the developmentally needed or reparative relationship, the dialogic relationship and the transpersonal relationship).

These five relational modes are present in any relationship from supervision to parent–child relationships, to casual sexual encounters (Clarkson, 1990, 1995b and 1996b) guided by the Invariant Action Sequence (danger, confusion, conflict, deficit, development) (see for example Clarkson, 1998c) in terms of the understanding and appropriate use of **systems principles** as articulated by Von Bertalanffy, Maturana and Varela and current quantum physics and complexity understandings of the world (Clarkson and Lapworth, 1992 and Clarkson, 1998d).

Characteristics:
transdisciplinarity and valuing singular theories (for example, Clarkson, 1992b);
culturally pluralistic (for example, Clarkson and Nippoda, 1997);
beyond schoolism (for example, Clarkson 1998b);

integrating practice and research (for example, Clarkson, 1998e)
with ethics (for example, Clarkson, 1995a, 1996c & 2000),
culture (for example, Clarkson, 1997),
and organizational context (for example, Clarkson, 1995b);
attentive to contemporary debates as well as to history and future
    aspirations (for example, 1993)

Consultation, training, supervision and practice-based PhD research can
be formal and structured or based on psychologically based principles of
learning by enquiry (*Dieratao*) as Heraclitus advised (in Clarkson, 1998e,
1998f, pp. 242–72).

Outcomes

I hope I have clarified the language question. Our common language is
English. Furthermore, contrary to Turner's (1998) expectations, veterans
and trainees find this approach to our field very valuable, as evidenced by
their success, for example, with BACP and UKCP registration, BPS
counselling psychology examinations as well as Master's and Doctoral
degrees at different universities.

Finally: Lifetime is a child at play, moving pieces in a game. Kingship
belongs to the child (Fragment XCIV).

References

Avens R (1984) The New Gnosis: Heidegger, Hillman and Angels. Dallas TX: Spring
    Publications.
Bergson H (1965) Creative Evolution. London: Macmillan.
Briggs J, Peat FD (1990) Turbulent Mirror. New York: Harper & Row. First published
    1989.
Clarkson P (1975) The seven-level model. Paper delivered at University of Pretoria,
    November.
Clarkson P (1990) A multiplicity of psychotherapeutic relationships. British Journal of
    Psychotherapy 7 (2): 148–63.
Clarkson P (1992a) Systemic integrative psychotherapy training. In Dryden W (ed.)
    Integrative and Eclectic Therapy: A Handbook. Buckingham: Open University
    Press, pp. 269–95.
Clarkson P (1992b) Transactional Analysis Psychotherapy – An Integrated Approach.
    London: Routledge.
Clarkson P (1993) New perspectives in counselling and psychotherapy, or adrift in a
    sea of change. In Clarkson P, On Psychotherapy. London: Whurr, pp. 209–32.
Clarkson P (1995a) The Therapeutic Relationship in Psychoanalysis, Counselling
    Psychology and Psychotherapy. London: Whurr.
Clarkson P (1995b) Change in Organisations. London: Whurr.

Clarkson P (1996a) The archetype of physis: the soul of nature – our nature in harvest. Journal for Jungian Studies 42(1): 70–93.

Clarkson P (1996b) Researching the 'therapeutic relationship' in psychoanalysis, counselling psychology and psychotherapy – a qualitative inquiry. Counselling Psychology Quarterly 9(2): 143–62.

Clarkson P (1996c) Values in counselling and psychotherapy. Changes 13(4): 299–306.

Clarkson P (1996d) The Bystander (An End to Innocence in Human Relationships?). London: Whurr.

Clarkson P (1996e) Counselling psychology in Britain – the next decade. Counselling Psychology Quarterly 8(3): 197–204.

Clarkson P (1996f) The eclectic and integrative paradigm: between the Scylla of confluence and the Charybdis of confusion. In Woolfe R, Dryden W (eds) Handbook of Counselling Psychology. London: Sage.

Clarkson P (ed.) (1997) The sublime in psychoanalysis and archetypal psychotherapy. In Clarkson P, On the Sublime in Psychoanalysis, Archetypal Psychology and Psychotherapy. London: Whurr. (This was a revised version of the paper, 'The Sublime in Psychoanalysis and Psychotherapy', delivered at the Tenth Jung Studies Day held at University of Kent, Canterbury, 25 November 1995.)

Clarkson P (ed.) (1998a) Supervision: Psychoanalytic and Jungian Perspectives. London: Whurr.

Clarkson P (1998b) Beyond schoolism. Changes 16(1): 1–11.

Clarkson P (1998c) Supervision in counselling, psychotherapy and health: an intervention priority sequencing model. European Journal of Psychotherapy, Counselling and Health 1(1): 3–20.

Clarkson P (1998d) The Organisational Psychology of Complexity. OACES Organisations as Complex Evolving Systems Conference, Warwick University.

Clarkson P (1998e) Counselling Psychology: Integrating Theory, Research, and Supervised Practice. London: Routledge.

Clarkson P (1998f) Learning through Inquiry (the Dierotao programme at PHYSIS). In Clarkson P (ed.) Counselling Psychology: Integrating Theory, Research and Supervised Practice. London: Routledge, pp. 242–72.

Clarkson P (2000) Ethics: Working with Ethical and Moral Dilemmas in Psychotherapy. London: Whurr.

Clarkson P, Lapworth P (1992) Systemic integrative psychotherapy. In Dryden W. (ed.) Integrative and Eclectic Therapy: A Handbook. Buckingham: Open University Press, pp. 41–83.

Clarkson P, Nippoda Y (1997) The experienced influence or effect of cultural/racism issues on the practice of counselling psychology – a qualitative study of one multicultural training organisation. Counselling Psychology Quarterly 10(4): 415–37.

Cottone RR (1988) Epistemological and ontological issues in counselling: Implications of social systems theory. Counselling Psychology Quarterly 1(4): 357–65.

Davies P (1992) Does This Give God His P45? (Interviewed by Macpherson A.) The Mail on Sunday, 26 April, p. 17.

Farrell BA (1979) Work in small groups: some philosophical considerations. In Babington Smith B, Farrell BA (eds) Training In Small Groups: A Study of Five Groups. Oxford: Pergamon, pp. 103–15.

Frank JD (1973) Persuasion and Healing. 2nd edn. Baltimore MD: Johns Hopkins University Press.

Frank JD, Frank JB (1993) Persuasion and Healing: A Comparative Study of Psychotherapy. Baltimore MD: Johns Hopkins University Press.

Friedman M (ed.) (1964) The Worlds of Existentialism. New Jersey: Humanities Press.

Gleick J (1989) Chaos: Making a New Science. London: Heinemann. First published 1988.

Greenberg IA (ed.) (1975) Psychodrama: Theory and Therapy. London: Souvenir Press. First published 1974.

Guerrière D (1980) Physis, Sophia, Psyche. In Sallis J, Maly K (eds) Heraclitean Fragments: A Companion Volume to the Heidegger/Fink Seminar on Heraclitus. Alabama: University of Alabama Press.

Hawkins JM, Allen R (eds) (1991) The Oxford Encyclopaedic English Dictionary. Oxford: Oxford University Press.

Heidegger M (1959) An Introduction to Metaphysics (R. Manheim, trans.). New Haven: Yale University Press.

Heidegger M (1998) Pathmarks (ed. McNeill W). Cambridge: Cambridge University Press.

Isham CJ (1995) Lectures on Quantum Theory – Mathematical and Structural Foundations. London: Imperial College Press.

Jung CG (1928) Analytical psychology and education. In Contributions to Analytical Psychology (trans. Baynes HG, Baynes FC). London: Trench Trubner, pp. 313–82.

Jung CG (1956) Symbols of transformation: an analysis of the prelude to a case of schizophrenia. In The Collected Works, Vol. 5 (trans. Hull RFC). London: Routledge & Kegan Paul.

Jung CG (1963) Memories, Dreams, Reflections (ed. Jaffe A). London: Routledge & Kegan Paul.

Jung CG (1964) Man and his Symbols. London: Aldus Books.

Jung CG (1969a) Synchronicity: an acausal connecting principle. In The Collected Works, Vol. 2 (trans. Hull RFC). London: Routledge & Kegan Paul.

Jung CG (1969b) On the nature of the psyche. In The Collected Works, Vol. 8 (trans. Hull RFC). London: Routledge & Kegan Paul.

Jung CG (1969c) Constitution and heredity in psychology. In The Collected Works, Vol. 8 (trans. Hull RFC). London: Routledge & Kegan Paul.

Jung CG (1970) The conjunction. In The Collected Works, Vol. 14 (trans. Hull RFC). London: Routledge & Kegan Paul.

Kahn C (1981) The Art and Thought of Heraclitus. Cambridge: Cambridge University Press.

Lee D (ed.) (1980) Wittgenstein's Lectures Cambridge 1930–1932. Oxford: Basil Blackwell.

Levenson EA (1991) The Purloined Self – Interpersonal Perspectives in Psychoanalysis (ed. Feiner AH). New York: William Allison White Institute.

Lewin R (1992) Complexity – Life at the Edge of Chaos – The Major New Theory that Unifies all Sciences. London: Macmillan.

Lyotard JF (1997) Domus and the megapolis. In Leich N (ed.) Rethinking Architecture: A Reader in Critical Theory. Routledge: London.

Mandelbrot BB (1974) The Fractal Geometry of Nature. New York: Freeman.

Mingers J (1995) Self-Producing Systems: Implications and Applications of Autopoiesis. New York: Plenum Press.

Norcross JC (1999) Foreword. In Hubble MA, Duncan BL, Miller SD (eds) The Heart and Soul of Change: What Works in Therapy, pp. xvii–xix. Washington DC: American Psychological Association.

Perls FS (1969) Gestalt Therapy Verbatim. Moab, Utah: Real People Press.

Ryle G (1966) Dilemmas: The Tarner Lectures. Cambridge: Cambridge University Press.

Silverman D (1997) Discourses of Counselling – HIV Counselling and Social Interaction. London: Sage.

Smuts JC (1987) Holism and Evolution. Cape Town: N & S Press. First published 1926.

Turner M (1998) Moving Beyond Modernist Discourses of Psychological Therapy. European Journal of Psychotherapy, Counselling and Health 1(3): 435–57.

UNESCO (1998) International Symposium of Transdisciplinarity – Towards Integrative Process and Integrated Knowledge. New York: United Nations, pp. 1–12.

Winter DA (1997) Everybody has Still Won but What About the Booby Prizes? Inaugural address as Chair of the Psychotherapy Section, British Psychological Society, University of Westminster, London.

Wittgenstein L (1922/1961) Tractatus Logico Philosophicus (trans. Pears DF, McGuinness BF). London: Routledge.

Wittgenstein L (1922) In Lee D. (ed.) (1980) Wittgenstein's Lectures Cambridge 1930–1932. Oxford: Basil Blackwell.

Wolman BB (ed.) (1965) Handbook of Clinical Psychology. New York: McGraw-Hill.

Chapter 6
As Within, so Without

Petrūska Clarkson

Introduction

The title of this chapter is a horizontal version of Hermes Trimegistus's ancient adage 'As above, so below'. It is also quoted in Klossowski de Rola (1973, p. 15) from the Emerald Table as: 'that what is below is like what is above and that what is above is like what is below, to perpetrate the miracles of one thing'. Whereas the venerable alchemist was at pains to point out vertically the way in which the celestial bodies in the sky mirror the human condition, I am at pains to point out the way in which the individual mirrors the collective. How individual psychology mirrors social psychology and vice versa. Perhaps much more than psychology. As within, so without.

Groundwork

The question is asked: 'Why do the great get so mercilessly attacked? For example, Freud?' The answer comes: 'Because of the scale of his achievement.'

'Why do people feel they have to destroy great achievers?'
'Because each one of us is inside at war with our own creativity.'

For some decades I have called this **the principle of inner–outer equivalence**. It means that what happens inside the human being is mirrored in what happens outside in society. If we consider the great expanses of history – human beings on this planet for some billions of years – we will notice that this small packet of atoms arranged for the brief period of our

88

mortal lives and given a personal name is but an eyeblink in the face of eternity. Imagine speeding up the whole process in the way that we can with film on video.

Consider then the molecular arrangement of this person called Freud coming together and dispersing again within seconds as it again becomes part of the vast fabric of the seething mass of chaos and order we call life and death. This thought experiment shows that structure is slow process, and process is fast structure. The individual is a moment in eternity. However, we also know from our own subjective experience that we can enter the timelessness of eternity in a single clock-time moment of bliss or horror.

We know from (post-)modern physics about **entanglement theory** which shows that individuals interpenetrate each other. Not only that, but it demonstrates that when two so-called individuals have met once, they are an effect of each other at least for the rest of lived time – even should they never meet again. Their changing states continue to influence each other – forever. Just like atoms in a laboratory.

We have slowly come to understand from object relations theory that 'we are our others'. Relationship psychology confirms this (Clarkson, 1995). It has also been suggested that the World Wide Web can be seen as a huge neural system connecting every part of the planet (and potentially every individual on the planet) with all the others, so that metaphorically and even quite literally we have become one organism. It has also been suggested that the whole planet is one living organism – **Gaia** (Lovelock, 1989). These are also ancient ideas. In the occidental tradition 2,500 years ago Heraclitus said: 'From all things one and from one thing all' (Kahn, 1987, p. 85, CXXIV).

Of course, the notion of 'the individual' is a comparatively recent event in European culture. Artists started signing their names to their works only a few hundred years ago. Kings and queens were of the body of the people. Their illness is the illness of their people – and vice versa. We can see vestiges of this in Shakespeare's *Coriolanus* where Menenius Agrippa, his friend says to the populace:

There was a time when all the body's members
Rebell'd against the belly; thus accus'd it:
That only like a gulf it did remain
I'th' midst o' t' body, idle and inactive,
Still cupboarding the viand, never bearing
Like labour with the rest; where th' other instruments
Did see and hear, devise, instruct, walk, feel,
And mutually, participate, did minister
Unto the appetite and affection common
Of the whole body. The belly answer'd –
First citizen:Well, sir, what answer made the belly?

Men. Sir, I shall tell you. With a kind of smile,
Which ne'er came from the lungs, but even thus –
For look you, I may make the belly smile
As well as speak – it tauntingly replied
To th' discontented members, the mutinous parts
That envied his receipt; even so most fitly
As you malign our senators for that
They are not such as you.
1Cit. Your belly's answer – What?
The kingly crowned head, the vigilant eye,
The counsellor heart, the arm our soldier,
Our steed the leg, the tongue our trumpeter,
With other muniments and petty helps
Is this our fabric, if that they –
Men, What then?
Fore me, this fellow speaks! What then? What then?
1 Cit. Should by the cormorant belly be restrained,
Who is the sink o' th' body –
Men. Well, what then?
1 Cit. The former agents, if they did complain,
What could the belly answer?
Men. I will tell you;
If you'll bestow a small – of what you have a little –
Patience awhile, you'st hear the belly's answer.
Cit 1. You're long about it.
Men. Note me this, good friend;
Your most grave belly was deliberate, Not rash like his accusers, and thus
answered.
'True it is, my incorporate friends,' quote he
'That I receive the general food at first
which you do live upon; and fit it is,
Because I am the storehouse and the shop
Of the whole body. But, if you do remember,
I send it through the rivers of your blood,
Even to the court, the heart, to th' seat o' th' brain;
And, through the cranks and offices of man,
The strongest nerves and small inferior beings
From me receive that natural competency
Whereby they live. And though that all at once
You, my good friends' – this says the belly – mark me
1Cit. Ay, Sir, well, well.
Men. Though all at once cannot
See what I deliver out to each,
Yet I can make my audit up, that all
From me do back receive the flour of all,
And leave me but the bran.

(Shakespeare, *Coriolanus*, Act I, Scene I)

In some non-European cultures the notion of 'the individual' has never taken the hold it has on the Cartesian, Newtonian trained analytic mind. To the Sioux or the Australian Aborigine the earth simply cannot be conceived of as separate from my body. Indeed the very notion that mind and body can be separate (as in our poor term 'psycho-somatic') or that self and other **can** be independent is quite foreign. The very idea of 'other' is for some manifestly absurd to many people. The contemporary Japanese language for example has no word that equates with the way in which English speakers use the notion of 'individual self'. In many communities, if a crime has been committed, any member of the community can be punished or executed for it – and there is no sense of injustice.

I was shocked into personal awareness of this phenomenon recently in doing some research on experiences of group psychotherapy in a multicultural community drawn from some 150 countries. One person said: 'I just don't understand all this fuss about confidentiality, confidentiality, confidentiality – it just doesn't make sense to me. How is it possible that anything be confidential when we are in community?' Intrigued, I checked with a colleague from Ibo-land and he said: 'Of course, in our home village, if a couple is having trouble, we say: "you've got to tell us, because if you don't, we'll find out anyway." Your difficulties are everybody's business.'

So attacks on the creative achievers in our midst might also be **everybody's business**. And, in a very profound way it mirrors the way we are at war with our own creativity. Bohm (1985) introduced the scientific term of '**holon**' to try to capture **how the part is always also the whole**. Now we know that not only sheep, but also human beings can (and are) being 'cloned' from any cell of a person – a nail, an eye-lash, a slice of flesh.

Again an image from complexity theory might be helpful. A fractal is a mathematically pictorial way of describing 'self-similarity across scale'. When tracing the **pattern** of a coastline, for example, any part of it can be seen to be self-similar to any other part of it.

For ease of discussion we can use the terms **micro, meso** and **macro** to differentiate for example three sizes of scale. Whether the whole coastline is traced, a medium part of it or a very small part of the fractal pattern arrangement remains similar to each other. Not exactly the **same**, but **similar** (Mandelbrot, 1974). Anyone who has seen the colourful fractal images cannot be unmoved by the beauty of this creatively chaotic, but **at the same time** intrinsically ordered patterns of nature – and human nature.

So, if the part is also the whole, the individual is also the collective, and the collective is also the individual 'writ large', then the macro scale mirrors the micro and both mirror meso-scale – the group, the organization, the community, the nation. Engaging with the problem of attacks on creative achieving individuals, we can then see these as macro-scale examples of the micro-scale attacks of individuals on their own creativity. Is the collective at war with its own creative individual parts? Is the individual at war with his or her own creativity?

Famous people and their others – a complex relationship

The *Shorter Oxford English Dictionary* defines the notion of fame as 'renown: the state of being famous; much spoken of' (Onions, 1973, p. 510). The psychological literature does not reveal much research on this theme. Yet for example, daily newspapers devote many column inches to describing or discussing the lives and activities of people who could be regarded as famous or infamous in some way. There are many stories or biographies, which somehow refer to the effects of 'fame' on rock artists, child film starts and other people of achievement or notoriety. There is, however, not a great deal of serious study in terms of this aspect of individual and group psychology.

I have researched this phenomenon experientially, theoretically as a psychologist psychotherapist and also as an organizational consultant. Obviously I can only speak here about general psychological principles and not individual specifics. I only intend to highlight certain factors of interest here.

Famous people are those individuals who become idealized and/or demonized by the group, the organization or the society. The others – the public and the media – seem to make idols or devils of them, usually alternately. They are put on and pulled off pedestals with unsurprising regularity. The extent to which famous people live ordinary lives on a large screen is evidenced by the way many people devour every piece of gossip they can get about people of achievement or notoriety. The fame can come about by personal achievement or by association, such as marriage, luck or accident.

Many people look up to the famous. They envy what appears to be their success, fame and good fortune. But the price of success is high and painful. Sometimes it appears that the more famous a person is, the higher the price; the greater the success, the greater the pain and distress. We can think of Elvis Presley or Jacqueline Kennedy. Of course there are advantages, pleasures and satisfactions as a result of fame, but these are well known and commonly accepted. What are not so well understood are the disadvantages and the problems of success. Psychological studies have shown that positive events – such as promotion at work, buying a new house, having a longed-for baby – are actually psychologically quite stressful for the people involved, even if they very much wanted these events (Holmes and Rahe, 1967). So, fame would also have disadvantages and these have not been thoroughly understood as yet from a psychological, sociological or therapeutic point of view.

Personal experience

Although in some ways masses of people feel they know the famous person and act as if they know the famous person, famous people themselves feel less and less understood in this process. It is possible that this process is also self-similar across the scale of 'fame', and by studying micro-examples, we might illuminate the meso- or even macro examples.

My own experience of this phenomenon on a very tiny scale was when I noticed that more and more people had started talking **about** me instead of *to* me. Someone who met me for the first time would express their surprise that I was a warm and funny person because they had 'heard' that I was a cold cerebral intellectual. I found this very disorientating. A colleague whom I had advised, at their request, not to publish a research study because of failed ethical standards, made disparaging remarks about my research to a student. I even heard a rumour that I did not write my own books – apparently my secretary did. Some secretary!

Then I was to do a paper at a psychology conference. Due to unforeseen and unfortunate consequences, I was unable to deliver the paper personally. I checked in the literature and found several examples where a colleague would deliver the paper on behalf of another colleague when they could not personally be at the event. A colleague, concerned that my contribution would be absent, kindly offered to read my paper at the conference. I gladly accepted. Subsequently I heard that another colleague had said that this was unethical behaviour on my part.

My puzzlement turned to anguish at the unfairness of such an insinuation and the slur on my reputation. My helpful colleague suggested that perhaps this attack was made out of envy because so many delegates usually want to come to my workshops at conferences. It was still very hard for me to come to terms with this. Why hadn't they asked me personally about it? Perhaps the character assassin just didn't **know** that this was internationally accepted practice. What had I done to deserve such an unjustified attack? I knew (from blind peer-reviews for example) that my work on the topic was valued and respected – why this? Should I stop writing? What had I done wrong?

Phenomenological research into the psychology of fame

So, I decided to conduct some formal research on the theme of fame to gain some insight into that which was happening to me. A review of the literature was singularly unhelpful. There were no statistical quantitative studies I could find. There were also no studies of the subjective experiences of other people making this life phase transition in which I found myself.

Wanting to assure myself that my research would be of appropriate academic standard, I placed myself under the supervision of the most accomplished and respected qualitative research psychologist I knew. I thought that perhaps if I asked other much more 'famous' psychoanalysts, psychologists and psychotherapists how they **qualitatively** experienced this phenomenon, I could learn from them – understand it more, find out what my fault was and learn to deal with it with less confusion and pain.

I approached colleagues in my profession who could be described as famous ('being spoken about') because of their achievements. I hoped that as mental health professionals, they would be more self aware and able to articulate their experiences in psychological terms. I interviewed them confidentially and taped their responses to some very simple questions:

* What do you understand by the concept of fame?
* What are some of the positive effects, which you have experienced as a result of this phenomenon?
* What are some of the negative effects, if any?
* How do you feel it has impacted on your practice as a psychotherapist?
* How do feel it has impacted on you as a professional *vis à vis* your colleagues?
* How has it affected you as a person?
* Is there anything else you would like to add, perhaps in terms of coping strategies?

(The full report has been published as 'The psychology of fame' in Clarkson, 1998.)

All denied that they were really 'famous'. This is an interesting echo of a paper on the sociology of science by Woolgar (1985) where he found that participants were reluctant to treat their own activities as instances of a particularly idealized phenomenon. He reported that when he tried to get access to study scientists at work, each laboratory team would without exception say that if he was interested in real science this really was not the best place to study it. What they were doing did not actually fit what scientific work really should be. These scientists all said that work being done at some other laboratory by some other scientists would be more suited for exploration.

Surprisingly (to me) the results applied independently of gender, independently of the kind of personalities they were and independently of the scale of their achievements. Every one's experience was similar to every other one in some major ways. For the sake of this chapter, I will focus on some outstanding and perhaps helpful findings.

All ordinary communications had become endowed with exaggerated positive/idealized and/or negative/derogatory properties and associations. In a way there is an experienced **distortion** of the 'volume and importance' of one's communications. This was usually experienced as a sense of loss of control, becoming 'the *object'* of others' fantasies, others' expectations about which you may know very much or be able to do very much – except go away, retire, stop producing. Becoming better known is experienced in its opposite, subjectively becoming less well known. '*The name blinds people to fair judgement.' 'The name becomes too big [and] they can't see beyond it – they don't see anything but the name.'*

Every single respondent in this research reported specifically that they had experienced negative reactions from colleagues that they felt were envy. Envy is defined as 'a destructive attack on the good object, not on the bad object' (Hinshelwood, 1989, p. 167). It was sometimes equated with jealousy or rivalry with the home base professional group's reactions usually being the most extremely negative.

Examples of what respondents have experienced as envious attacks from colleagues ranged from malicious pathologizing gossip, outright lies, versions of being 'sent to Coventry' (colleagues not speaking to you), anonymous letters attempting to prejudice appointment or honours boards, disparaging one's abilities (for example, if so-and-so is successful in one activity, then they cannot be a good analyst, a good supervisor, and so forth), the apparent malicious causation of misunderstandings with editors and publishers on joint projects with other colleagues.

A common aspect was the fact that those of the home group (to which one would most naturally look for recognition) often ignored their colleague's achievements – they simply did not mention it. Archetypal patterns reported in the Bible were quoted: '*A prophet is not without honour except in his own land.'* Another person said that after a particularly successful achievement the reaction of colleagues was '*as if I had farted and it was better not to draw attention to it'*.

Every one of the respondents had experienced some form of depersonalization, loss of humanity, identity, absence of empathy from others, lack of fit between private and public self, being seen as being invulnerable and without feelings. Everyone had been hurt by such experiences. *'In a way you've lost your membership card of the human race.'* *'There is this film called The Invasion of the Body Snatchers . . . Yes, it's a film in which some alien thing takes over the body so it kind of looks like you, talks like you, but isn't you.'* *'You sense that the other person has got a complete travesty of the person you really are.'*

While the perception of invulnerability grows externally there is often an increase in anxiety and vulnerability due to insidious negative comments, spurious attempts, ethics complaints, the sowing of suspicion, inexplicable complications with editors, trainees and colleagues. For example *'I don't think I am being paranoid, but there is a sense in which I am being watched, with people almost hoping that I will put a foot wrong.'* *'I was at a party when someone warned me about me. They didn't know who I was, but they were telling me to be careful of this person who was me and of course I encouraged them to talk and then someone identified me and then there was an interesting moment . . . I did not recognize the person [they were talking about].'*

There seemed to be a curve which translates as encouragement in the beginning and then a diminishing return as if only a certain level of achievement can be tolerated by the collective before the productive individual must be brought down off the pedestal upon which (usually against their will) they had been hoisted. A different measurement is used than for 'other people' who may not have achieved so much in these particular ways.

There is a certain lack of compassion and a definite lack of a wish to understand or empathize. *'You are made to feel different and separated from others and subject to different rules.'* Several respondents reported loneliness, isolation from colleagues and professional communities and difficulties in maintaining previous peer relationships even in spite of the best intentions and attempts. *'You lose people's empathy – you are seen as invulnerable, not needing love and support.'* *'Finally, I think you have to acknowledge a sense of powerlessness – that there's simply not a lot you can do about it.'*

So, here we have men and women of widely differing personalities and different approaches, skilled in the arts and crafts of personal transformation, all experiencing a similar phenomenon, and acknowledging that there is *'simply not a lot you can do about it.'*

Although in some ways many people feel they know 'the famous person' and act as if they know the famous person, 'famous' people feel less and less understood in this process – less and less accepted as fellow human beings. All the people I studied experienced that, in a way, they were no longer members of the ordinary human race, no longer ordinary mortals with ordinary feelings and ordinary flaws.

People treated them in exaggeratedly positive or negative ways, almost as if they had become cardboard cut-outs on which people projected their best and worst fantasies. Anything they said or did seemed to become distorted in some way: either it was taken wrongly or made much more important than they meant it. People take an exaggerated interest in all their activities, no matter how trivial. There is usually a sense of loss of control.

So, when people like Prince Charles, Tony Blair or Liz Hurley are accused of trying to 'manipulate' the media, their inner experience is likely to be the opposite – a feeling of no matter what they do they can't win and they cannot get the bulk of people to accept them as the human beings they actually are. They become 'the stars' of other people's imaginations and expectations, and the sinks of their disappointment and feelings of disillusionment – but real contact with the human being behind 'the name' is lost.

I have come to term this dynamic process '**third party transference**' because (a) it can be seen to be 'a process of actualisation of unconscious wishes' (Laplanche and Pontalis, 1988, p. 455); (b) it is in line with the fact that 'Freud looked upon transference – theoretically at any rate – as just a particular instance of displacement of affect from one idea to another' (Laplanche and Pontalis, 1988, p. 457) and (c) it is a distortion of a potentially real or even healing relationship.

What makes this particular form of third party transference so particularly pernicious is the fact that the person on to whom this often extreme affect is displaced is not in a position, like the analyst, to use it therapeutically. In the absence of such opportunity the affect can sometimes assume psychotic proportions and is not infrequently **acted out**, for example in the idealization or demonization of public figures. This is often exemplified in the phenomenon of 'stalking'. (However there is also psychological 'stalking'.)

Symbolically or actually they are cannibalized. People tear pieces of clothing or hair from rock stars, claim an intimacy that does not exist with famous film actors, and reduce a princess to a frightened weeping photograph outside her therapist's consulting room.

In my opinion, most people who are famous have tried to make a contribution and want to leave the world a better place in some way. In this respect we have admiration for them. But too often the admiration we have for our heroes then turns into denigration. There was a certain hysteria in building up the woman founder of lastminute.com, and hardly disguised glee (*schadenfreude*) when her company failed to make the expected stockmarket killing for which the collective had bayed.

The crowning of a sports hero is all too soon followed by the desperate search for the 'feet of clay' – whether they wear sarongs or thongs, whether they beat their wives or are 'tied to the apron strings'. Historical or national heroes all too often have a brief time of glory before the collective starts attacking them for the very qualities that were found so admirable at a previous time.

Yet these are instances of behaviour statistically rather normally spread throughout any population. Apparently many people in the collective find it hard to admire those whom they envy without trying to bring them down in some way. In the classic study comparing and contrasting envy and jealousy – *Othello* – Shakespeare put into the envious Iago's mouth the words:

And by how much she [Desdemona] strives to do him good,
She shall undo her credit with the Moor.
So will I turn her virtue into pitch;
And out of her own goodness make the net
That shall enmesh them all.

(Shakespeare, *Othello*, Act II, Scene III)

It is the good object that the one who envies is going to attack – for its **goodness**. 'So will I turn her virtue into pitch.' The gifts themselves become the blemishes for which the envied person is attacked. No wonder they often go 'mad', as Van Gogh and Laing are reported to have done – it is as mad-making as living in a schizophrenogenic family.

The scales by which the behaviour of the famous are judged seem to be different from the way we judge 'ordinary mortals'. A superhuman standard of perfection is expected and the common human flaws, which we all have, are unforgiven. Madonna is called a control freak, Marilyn too compliant; Thatcher is vilified for her decisive ways, Major for his indecisive ways. It doesn't seem to matter what quality of a person is focussed upon – **the process is the same**.

Many famous people experience, along with the admiration for their achievements and the envy of their good fortune, an absence of ordinary human compassion (*ubuntu*) from the very people from whom they would hope to get some understanding. Empathy or 'fellow-feeling' (humankind-ness) disappears the more the gulf widens between the 'ordinary' members of the collective and those of extraordinary achievement or good fortune.

Attempts by 'the famous' to make public statements to explain themselves, to get the public to judge for themselves and see their ordinary humanity – in spite of their gifts – seem almost bound to fail as the Richard Gere *Times* advertisement and the Prince Charles and Ginger Spice interviews have proved. Whatever they say (or omit to say) is often construed against them, if it is not actually used negatively in a distorted, idealizing way. This can feel equally disorientating – as when people say 'I know exactly how you feel' when really they do not.

From the moment when the work is taken over and recognized by the public, or even merely offered to the public, it ceases to be the possession of the artist, not only economically but also spiritually. Just as the artist created it for his own needs, the public accepts it to alleviate its own wants, and whatever they may make of it, it never remains what it was originally. It ceases to be the personal achievement of the individual and becomes a symbol for others and **their** spiritual demands. This 'misunderstanding' which the artist feels is inevitable and the price at which fame is bought (Rank, 1932, p. 371).

Murder

Bion thought that exceptional individuals are placed on committees out of envy in order to destroy their creativity. He considered it 'a fact that every genius, mystic or messiah is both [creative and nihilistic], as the nature of his contributions is bound to destroy certain forms and conventions, the culture or coherence of some group or of some sub-group within a group' (in Grinberg, Sor and Tabak de Bianchedi, 1975, p. 21).

Klein (1957) wrote that 'the former idealised person is often felt as a persecutor [which shows the origin of idealization as a counterpart to persecution], and into him is projected the subject's envious and critical attitude. It is of great importance that similar processes operate in the internal world which in this way comes to contain particularly dangerous objects.'(p. 193) . . . 'creativeness becomes the deepest cause for envy' (p. 202) . . . 'a particular cause of envy is the relative absence of it in others' (p. 203).

The exceptional individual rarely feels his gifts as her or his own. Goethe felt compelled to describe his whole creation as a collective work that only happened to bear his name. Artists I have interviewed also say that their work comes 'courtesy of the management [God]'. Yet, the outrage of the collective at this 'contribution' is sometimes quite disproportionate. The breakdown of empathy and the psychotic proportions of the envious attack on the famous person reach their apotheosis in murder.

Why kill Gandhi who stood for peace? Why just shoot presidents? Why crucify Christ? Why did the mob scrape the flesh of the fourth-century philosopher and mathematician Hypatia from her body with broken pieces of pottery in the streets of Alexandria (Dzielska, 1995)? Orpheus was torn limb from limb.

Examples proliferate in our newspaper headlines. Why did John Lennon's fan Mark Chapman first ask for his autograph and then go back to shoot John with five hollow-point bullets until his blood vessels ruptured and his bones splintered? Judging from the micro-scale examples in my study, there might even have been a moment of horrible incomprehension when he thought: 'Why me?' 'What did I ever do to Mark Chapman, but make music and give him the autograph that he had asked for?'

'In fact, shortly before he died, John had dreamed of his own obituary. It read that he had been charged with his own murder, which occurred outside his apartment. John, both the perpetrator and the victim, kept insisting to those who would listen that he wasn't guilty' (Guiliano, 2000, p. 71). The creative genius as both the perpetrator and the victim. Not guilty.

As without, so within

Opposites co-exist in physics. Heraclitus and Jung both used the concept of **enantiodromia**. Opposites turn into each other. 'The cycle is the experiential reconciliation of permanence and degeneration' (Guerrière, 1980, p. 88). In the great cycle of Life or lives, there are punctuation points that are the extreme and complete contradictions of each other. Life and death. Love and hate. The individual and the collective. Breathing in and breathing out. Eating and defecating. The belly receives the food, but is left with only the bran. The body of Christ is eaten and shat out.

The human being is born in faeces and blood. Babies do not find the smell offensive – disgust is a learned reaction. Indeed I am told that in some modern maternity hospitals the mother is not immediately disinfected since the smells of her body turned inside out are comforting to the neonate on her breast. The first creative activity of the infant is the production of shit. It's the miracle of taking in and giving out. And anyone who has seen a youngster proudly bring his potty to show his turds to the vicar at tea knows the exquisite delicacy of admiring them **and** sending the toddler away without shaming him. But few people, except parfumiers, know that the most precious perfumes in the world need to contain the ingredients indole or skatole – the essence of faeces.

The individual who takes in from the world and does not 'create' becomes psychologically constipated. The individual who 'expresses' it all is psychologically diarrhoeic. The faeces needs to be transformed into African houses, dried and used for cooking, eaten by the pigs bred for bacon, used to fertilize the earth as manure, to make money from sewage farms, to re-member Venice. A personal journal is only rarely a book, expressive art therapy is not art, the piano keys bashed wildly in emotion is not a symphony. Rank (1932) wrote about the neurotic as an artist who had failed life's active self-creative force. It is the act of creativity – the **auto-poiesis** of physis, which transforms the raw material into use, truth or beauty (Clarkson, 1997).

Why are so many people afraid of their own creativity? Why do some valuable papers not get offered to be published in the public sphere? Why are people afraid of speaking in public? Why do so many people feel that they can't write, can't sing, can't draw? Children, like dogs, like 'showing off' – that is until they get shamed for their 'productions' – their creativity. What is shame? The feeling that you are not worthy of being in relationship – outcast from the community, denied common humanity. Not one of 'us'.

> O they have banished Hermodorus, the ablest man among them, saying
> No one shall be the ablest of us;
> or if there be such, let him be it elsewhere and among others.
>
> (Guerrière, 1980, p. 123)

Outcast. Expelled. Ex-communicated. People die from lack of relationship – witness marasmus, solitary isolation, 'being sent to Coventry', the way human beings simply die from a hex or voodoo spell making them 'dead' as far as their community is concerned. We are relational beings from birth (see Costall et al., 1997). The denial of relationship is the primary cause of shame. Shame is the fear of death from lack of relationship – a more terrible death than dying.

When we risk our creativity in the world, we risk dying of shame. When the collective extrudes or de-humanizes the creative individual, their relationship with the collective dies. No wonder that there are so many suicides or other (apparently) self-inflicted ways of seeking death among the highly talented – witness Gross, Hemingway, Monroe, Maradona, Presley, Plath, Pollock, Shams, Semmelweis, Woolf – you can add to this list for a long, long time. The sensitive children bullied to death on the playground. Jung (1954): 'Great gifts are the fairest, and often the most dangerous, fruits on the tree of humanity. They hang on the weakest branches, which easily break' (par. 244). The greatest fame extracts the ultimate price – death. And we wonder why people so often don't meet deadlines?

'Polemos is the father of all things'

Heraclitus again: 'War is father of all and king of all' (Kahn, 1987, p. 67). Polemos means war, conflict, strife. Individuals at war with their own creativity inside and the collective at war with its own creative individuals outside. This situation is an existential given for which there is no cure. Can a peace be made?

No, because creativity is born from this conflict within and without. Heraclitus said: 'The counter-thrust brings together, and from tones at variance comes perfect attunement, and all things come to pass through conflict' (Kahn, 1979, p. 67). It is an eternal cycle, an enantiodromia that is never-ending. **Ananke**. Necessity. Another name for **physis**.

Without **physis** sex is just sex and death is just death. But from this pulsation of war and peace in ourselves and between us, **physis** transforms Eros and Thanatos into, for example, the wondrous works of the Greek tragedians and Shakespeare. They have no easy answers. Neither do they spare us, the audience, the contradictory opposites of freedom and destiny, of loyalty and betrayal, of love and hate – the Aristotelian catharsis of 'pity and terror' which the playwright-creator offers to the collective for their benefit – and without whom the creative individual could not exist.

So, there's not a lot one can do about it

True, but there are some consolations for lessening the pain and increasing the lessons. Consider the dammed-up creativity in your own heart when you diminish the achievements of others. Be gentle with yourself in your creativity as you are gentle with those who create. The muse is never 'broken in'. Creativity only happens at far from equilibrium conditions. Fertilize not only your own field, but also the furrows of others. Live bravely and die as well as you can, but love life. Enjoy the good times. Laugh a lot. Practise gratitude. Love your enemies – they are your most generous teachers. Accept that you cannot avoid benefiting them. Normalize conflict and learn to transform it – again and again and again. There are no innocent bystanders. Live with the opposites without falling (permanently) into the simplistic dualisms of good and bad, life and death, individual and 'other'. Everything passes into its opposite. Pain hurts. Weeping is the price we pay for the gift of love. This too shall pass. Commit arbitrary acts of kindness and random acts of beauty. Consider the cycles of life and death in the large and in the small scale. Do not seek meaning, make it. Never has there been a time when the world has needed our creative individual and collective **physis** more. 'The gifted ones are the torchbearers, chosen for that high office by nature [**physis**] herself' (Jung, 1943, par. 252). We are all part of the whole and the whole is us. Both perpetrator and victim. Not guilty.

References

Bohm D (1985) Wholeness and the Implicate Order. London: Ark Paperbacks. First published 1980.

Clarkson P (1995) The Therapeutic Relationship. London: Whurr.

Clarkson P (ed.) (1997) On the Sublime. London: Whurr.

Clarkson P (1998) The psychology of 'fame': implications for practice. In Clarkson P (ed.) Counselling Psychology. Integrating Theory, Research and Supervised Practice. London and New York: Routledge, pp. 308–23.

Costall A, Reddy V, Williams E, Draghi-Lorenz R (1997) Unexplaining Social Development. Poster presented at the 27th Annual Symposium of the Jean Piaget Society, June 19–21, Santa Monica, California.

Dielska M (1995) Hypatia of Alexandria (trans. Lyra F). Cambridge MA: Harvard University Press.

Guerrière D (1980) Physis, sophia and psyche. In Sallis J, Maky K (eds) Heraclitean Fragments: A Companion Volume to the Heidegger/Fink Seminar on Heraclitus. Alabama: University of Alabama Press.

Guiliano G (2000) The last torments of Lennon. Daily Mail 13 April, p. 71.

Grinberg L, Sor D, Tabak de Bianchedi E (1975) An Introduction to the work of Bion (trans. Hahn A). London: The Roland Harris Educational Trust.

Hinshelwood RD (1989) A Dictionary of Kleinian Thought. London: Free Association Books.

Holmes TH, Rahe RH (1967) The social readjustment rating scale. Journal of Psychosomatic Research 11: 213–18.

Jung CG (1943/1954) The Gifted Child. London: Routledge & Kegan Paul.

Kahn CH (1987) The Art and Thought of Heraclitus. Cambridge: Cambridge University Press.

Klein M (1984) Envy and gratitude. In Klein M, Envy and Gratitude and Other Works. London: Hogarth, pp. 176–235. First published in 1957.

Klossowski de Rola S (1973) Alchemy. London: Thames & Hudson.

Laplanche J, Pontalis J-B (1988) The Language of Psycho-Analysis (trans. Nicholson-Smith D). London: Karnac.

Lovelock J (1989) Gaia: A New Look at Life on Earth. Oxford: Oxford University Press. First published 1979.

Mandelbrot BB (1974) The Fractal Geometry of Nature. New York: Freeman.

Onions CT (ed.) (1986) The Shorter Oxford English Dictionary Vol. 1. Oxford: Clarendon Press.

Peitgen HO, Richter PH (1986) The Beauty of Fractals. Images of Complex Dynamical Systems. Berlin: Springer-Verlag.

Rank O (1932/1989) Art and Artist. New York/London: WW Norton & Company.

Woolgar S (1985) Why not a sociology of machines? The case of sociology and artificial intelligence. Sociology 19(4): 557–72.

Chapter 7
Supervision – including the Clarkson Invariant Action Sequence

Petrūska Clarkson

Introduction

This chapter presents an Intervention Priority Sequencing Model for clarification and decision making in counselling, psychotherapy, supervision and consultancy as well as in the training and supervision of practitioners in these fields.

The model can assist professionals to differentiate whether the focus for most urgent intervention in any part of the supervisory system primarily concerns areas of danger, confusion, conflict, deficit or development, and gives examples referring to health psychology and cultural diversity as well as providing some guidelines for application.

Context

Reviewing the vast literature on the practice and learning of supervision (for example, Watkins, 1997) one is impressed by the enormous volume of opinions, models, research studies, and studies of research studies on the one hand, and the comparatively sparse fruits from this decades-long endeavour for the participant, practitioner or teacher of supervision.

Ellis and Ladany (1997, p. 495) typically write:

> Conceivably, the most telling implication of this review [of research findings] is for practitioners to be extremely cautious and sceptical of the empirical literature we have reviewed. There are few practical implications of the research reviewed here. The research suggests that the quality of the supervisory relationship is paramount to successful supervision.

For **reviewing the values and vectors of the supervisory relationship** over a period of time, the Supervision Relationship Model might be the most suitable model drawn from my work. This is based on extensive qualitative research (Clarkson, 1990, 1995), which has resulted in the identification and use of five kinds of therapeutic relationship common across all the major approaches to psychotherapy. These are: the working alliance relationship, the transference/countertransference relationship, the reparative or developmentally needed relationship, the person-to-person relationship and the transpersonal relationship.

To become skilful in using (and, what is more, teaching or supervising) any of these or other models of supervision demands an in-depth study and extensive supervised practice and supervision of supervision. The preliminary point here is to validate using a variety of tools and models available to supervisors to create a professional world rich in variety, creativity and flexibility (Clarkson, 1995).

Furthermore, we should endeavour to match the model to the purpose. For example, my Bands of Supervision Model (Clarkson, 1992) is best suited for teaching supervision while my Supervision Assessment Model (Clarkson, 1992) is more useful for the assessment of supervision and learning how to assess one's own and others' supervision in a short space of time according to quite definite criteria.

Developing range and flexibility in using different models for different people at different times is perhaps a more inspiring objective than to adapt to the demands of one 'right' model. Whether or not the 'supervisory philosophy and structure' was appropriate can be judged by the demands of the situation rather than the precision of replicating one single 'right' model – whatever we may conceive that to be (Doherty, 1991). The most important quality in a trainer or a supervisor is probably the desire to continue learning rather than the achievement of 'being right' defined by only external criteria. The findings of my research with Aviram (Clarkson and Aviram, 1995) provide another empirically based conceptual model for comparison or integration.

The present purpose of this chapter is unashamedly utilitarian and practical. The priority sequence model presented here was developed from some 25 years' experience as a consultant supervisor and teacher of counselling, psychology and psychotherapy in multiple approaches and settings. The justification for presenting it rests solely on the numerous novice and experienced practitioners and supervisors who have found it extremely helpful in their everyday practice where the pressures of finding one's way through the multi-faceted complexities of the therapeutic relationship hone effectiveness in a very direct and phenomenologically proven way.

Prioritizing interventions in the supervisory field

The intervention prioritizing framework discussed here was specifically developed as a conceptual map to help both experienced and novice supervisees and supervisors in an immediate way. It is of particular value in locating where a problem is likely to be focused and how to direct the supervisory effort more effectively within the usually limited periods of time devoted to professional development, maintenance or support.

There is so much to comprehend – the conscious relationship between (at least) three pairs of people (patient/analyst, analyst/supervisor, supervisor/patient), the unconscious relationship between each of them, the diagonal relationships between them in terms of mutual awareness or otherwise of each other's unconscious material and motivations, the relationship of each one between the conscious and unconscious dimensions of their own contribution to the interaction and, of course, the interplay of all of these with the specific professional or training organization or institution on the one hand (Carr, 1995) and the larger forces of life and collective evolution on the other.

Counselling and psychotherapy supervision are such complex fields that the more one learns, the more options for action open up. Contemporary economic and professional conditions often demand that we all need to produce more in less time. One of the greatest challenges for novice and experienced supervisors is to quickly, efficiently, appropriately and helpfully prioritize for attention or action the complexity of material brought to the supervisory relationship.

Taking the next decision (of responding or not responding, questioning, supporting, challenging, clarifying, reflecting, facilitating, catalysing, modelling, structuring or interpreting) can become increasingly difficult for any supervisor. Often, the greater one's understanding of the complexity of the situations and – sometimes – of the life-and-death issues that are the daily bread of people in this profession, the greater the range of choices, decisions and understandings that inform the supervisory process. It used to be the case that supervision was considered a natural result of experience as an analyst, but recent developments have shown an increasing recognition of the role and value of training and supervision for supervisors.

As the field of supervision grows and develops it also becomes clear that there is only so much to which one can pay attention in any given period of time. Of all the many choices facing supervisors, one of the most strategically important is probably how to prioritize – what is most important in a specific situation, how to select what to do next, which factors to give most urgent attention. In a way, the operational imperative is which **figure** to select for attention from the dynamically fluctuating **background** of often competing and frequently conflicting possibilities. How can the greatest beneficial effect practically be attempted in the brief interludes of reflection on practice that is supervision?

The intervention priority sequencing model

To make the choices of where to focus most economically and efficiently for everyday bread-and-butter supervision, the Danger, Confusion, Conflict, Deficit and Development Model for deciding priorities for supervisory attention may be suitable and beneficial. It is also extremely effective for decision-making hierarchies in crisis intervention situations whether these be natural disasters or psychiatric emergencies occurring in the context of conferences.

In particular it is efficient and useful because its use can often prevent or reduce wastage of time and effort, thus increasing efficiency and effectiveness. Many counsellors and psychotherapists of course also use it for treatment planning and anticipating twistings and turnings along the therapeutic journey. It is also good for the training and supervision of supervisors, trainers and consultants. (See also Clarkson, 1992; Clarkson and Kellner, 1995, regarding applications.)

At any given moment the supervisory focus may involve any part of the supervisory system, ranging from the inner world of the client on the one hand to current events impacting the cultural assumptions of an organization on the other. Although detailed consideration of how any part of the supervisory system can be chosen to be the focus for an intervention is precluded here for reasons of space, for explanatory purposes it is possible to show some examples from a variety of situations. Specific applications are left to the individual reader and future publications.

Of course any diagrammatic representation of systems or subsystems involved in the supervisory field, such as in Figure 7.1, are never truly

Figure 7.1 Overlapping Supervisory Systems

independent. Each can represent the whole at certain epistemological, metaphysical or narrative levels. The notions of supervisory fractals (Clarkson, 1993) or parallel process (e.g. Searles, 1955) both indicate ways in which whatever part is detailed for attention or intervention, the effects will be system-wide. However, in this instance the signals are sorted into five categories, being primarily concerned with:

- danger (some threat in the system);
- confusion (some loss of focus in the system);
- conflict (some split, polarization or conflict in the system);
- deficit (some experience of need or deprivation or need for reparation);
- development (some requirement to increase depth, breadth or complexity).

When we think about supervision as a system, this framework suggests that any disturbance can be classified in at least these five major ways. The framework provides a way of thinking about the supervisory system that enables the psychotherapist and the supervisor jointly to explore, contract and evaluate interventions. The categories represent a sequence that can maximize effectiveness in making supervisory interventions.

The priority sequencing model has an underlying and invariable order if it is to be used successfully. Work needs to be done in this order if it is to be effective. Perhaps most of the impasses in therapy, consultancy and supervision can be traced to having skipped one or more of these sequential steps.

Danger

Where any part of the client/therapist system is in perceived danger, the conscious or unconscious preoccupation of the system is with survival issues. These will tend to bind or cathect the libidinal energy so as to make work with other themes ineffective. Therapeutic or supervisory issues concerning homicide, suicide, psychosis, risk to others, and ethical concerns almost always need to be dealt with first. Since the Tarasoff case (Thompson, 1990), psychotherapeutically involved professionals are even more aware of their duties to third parties and the other dangers constituted by their professions.

People cannot engage in learning, developing or healing effectively if they feel endangered at any level – and this includes moral endangerment as in collusion with crime, deceit or abuse. When the supervision is used for any other reason than to deal with this perceived danger or to develop plans, strategies and resources to cope with it, avoid it or transform it, the effort will probably be wasted, since the key issue for focal concern will have been missed. One can be working with a supervisee for quite a long while, getting nowhere, before it emerges, for example, that she is physically so afraid of a homicidal client that she could not think at all.

If safety is endangered (consciously or unconsciously) there is little energy left for anything but defensive behaviour to avoid collapse. Human biological needs, even in supervision, usually take priority. To the extent that these are denied or avoided, no significant other work can be accomplished in the therapy or the supervision. Sometimes danger can be overestimated, as in the example of the group psychotherapist who (as it transpired, falsely) felt that a group member was a spy for the totalitarian government and potentially endangering not only the work of the group but also the survival of that organization in that particular country. The fact is that until such danger issues are attended to, the work of the group cannot truly progress.

Whether supervisory issues are presented as **confusion** ('help me sort this out'), **conflict** ('help me resolve this conflict') or **deficit** ('give me x, y or z which I need') it is vital to separate out relevant **danger** issues and deal with them first. When there is the presence or potential for danger it is important to listen, to acknowledge the feelings, to explore the sources of the danger, assess their reality and deal with the nature of the danger as well as the potential for retrieving or developing resources to deal with it. These may in fact involve management issues such as admission to hospital, referral to another practitioner, calling the police.

There may sometimes be a temptation for the supervisor to teach when the people are not ready to learn, or to reassure when such reassurance would be false. A therapist may also attempt to draw the supervisor into 'rescuing' them – taking their responsibility away from them rather than enabling them to deal with the threats to their clinical, professional and/or organizational survival in a realistic way.

The survival issues may not always be as the therapist or supervisor perceives them. In counselling and therapy it is essential to question all our assumptions as culturally biased. For example, for many women from certain African cultures the fear of being rejected by marriageable men outweighs the dangers of contracting AIDS. For them, to be rejected as a result of their insisting on condom use is a more immediate and palpable danger than potential death from the disease (Airhihenbuwa, DiClemente, Wingood and Lowe, 1992).

To the inexperienced and economically dependent counsellor, financial danger regarding the mortgage and children's education may result in an ill-considered rejection of brief therapies, a refusal to confront ethical and professional misconduct in professionals making referrals to them and also in keeping on clients who actually need far more experienced or specialized care than they can actually provide.

Confusion

Issues to do with confusion and contamination need to be dealt with next. Unconscious transference, countertransference and projective identification phenomena can become pervasive and crippling. Learning and healing require confusion to be dispersed. Deconfusing the issues precedes work with conflict. The value of and means for separating out different universes of discourse have been discussed by authors such as Gilbert Ryle (1966) and also in my epistemological seven-level model (Clarkson, 1975).

Cultural assumptions can increase confusion and misdiagnosis. A black man was diagnosed as schizophrenic in a South African hospital on the basis of his 'hearing voices'. It was only when a young psychiatric registrar asked him what the voices were saying that it became clear that 'the voices' were the intercom calls for doctors and nurses to different wards: *'Calling Dr Smith, will Dr Smith please come to ward 6.'*

A supervisory system suffering from confusion has difficulty identifying priorities or achieving high focus. High focus is classically associated with higher likelihood of effectiveness of outcome. Where such confusion reigns, it may even be difficult to identify the problem. The supervisory system does not know what information is relevant. Prejudices about childhood history or theory are not examined or tested (McNamee and Gergen, 1992). In the confused supervisory system, feelings are often presented as facts. For example, a therapist may be convinced that because 'this person is a borderline' certain procedures will not be effective. The supervisor will notice these and many other signs of confusion.

When a supervisor is unclear about what the task is, or when the therapist is confused about client goals, there is a general sense of disorientation and lack of direction. This is obviously not a good time to deal with conflict or to provide input or teaching. Often the supervisor may feel that the therapist wants or needs this. The supervisor's task is to restrain premature action, and to help to clarify the issues, boundaries, roles and relationships, including authority and expertise issues. It is also important to provide interpretation, analysis, models and maps to facilitate exploration of options and choices, and consequent assessment of the impact of possible alternative interventions.

Engaging in conflict resolution when the supervisor/therapist system is unclear about the nature, consequences and significance of conflict is also a waste of time. It is vital that the supervisor finds some way of dealing with any danger experienced by the system first. They may then engage with clarifying confusion – without getting drawn into premature attempts to resolve conflict (this is bound to fail), or premature attempts to provide replenishing or corrective experiences (except those that help people clarify confusion). These are likely to be wasteful and not as effective as if the system had been adequately prepared to receive and use the resources which are provided.

When a supervisory system is in a confused state it is most important not to get sucked into that confusion. Most supervisors have experienced the rapidity and persuasiveness with which they can be drawn into sharing the feeling of confusion and an atmosphere of inability to sort it out which is characteristic of some therapist/client systems. At the same time there may be a temptation to over-simplify and reduce the confusion artificially by accepting only one frame of reference, or getting into an argument about the best way forward – thereby creating conflict before the system is ready to deal with it.

What may appear as accidental insulin mismanagement may in fact be masking a deep-seated suicidal intention – work devoted to confusion in the supervisory system may entirely miss the danger. Indeed it could as effectively preclude appropriate intervention. A counsellor who either through ignorance of the symptoms or nervousness about consulting 'the establishment doctors' about counselling patients may not notice severe and increasing signs indicating a neurological investigation – thus continuing in counselling while a massive brain tumour was wreaking irredeemable damage. Working with empathy, interpretation or dialogue on repetitive headaches, unusual visual disturbances and increasing loss of balance are examples of working with deficit, confusion or conflict as foci, and missing the danger.

Sometimes working with confusion alone can be sufficient to resolve a problem quickly and easily – for example, misunderstanding instructions about birth control, understanding and using a hospital's patient charter, the difference between psychiatrists and psychotherapists, or an interpretation that allows a lesbian woman to withdraw a projection on to her doctor of her authoritative father and question his misdiagnosis of her premenstrual tension as sexual frustration.

Conflict

Once clarification has been achieved, it is more probable that conflict resolution, mediation, integration or mutual respect for difference can be accomplished. Attempts to work with conflict before the previous stages have been done often fail. We need to be clear about the protagonists in a conflict and about which issues the conflict is actually being conducted. Much unnecessary blood has been spilled and lives ruined because of people or countries engaging in conflict or wars before clarifying what was at stake.

It is not too difficult to diagnose when the therapist/client system is in conflict. It is more difficult to ensure that such conflicts are clearly understood by all involved. Conflict issues tend to be characterized by splits, a great amount of energetic activity, categorically different positions, failure of all reasonable attempts to negotiate, an unwillingness to compromise, and some combination of active acting out or passive-aggressive behaviour by any or all parties.

If supervisors have satisfied themselves and, importantly, also the participants that there is no real danger in exploring, clarifying or engaging with the conflict, it is possible to begin to use it. The conflict can then become a source of enhanced creativity; anger, aggression and difference can enable everybody affected by the system more effectively and creatively.

There is often a myth that therapist/client systems are more successful when there is no conflict or even implicit disagreement. The existence – even the celebration – of conflict can be a profound spur to creativity, innovation and resilience. In therapy, 'empathetic failures' or 'therapeutic errors' can provide the points of breakthrough as much as breakdown (Safran, 1993). However, the genuine fruitful engagement with conflict can only happen if (a) there is no experience of danger – for example, if there are no damaging consequences of expressing and standing up for different views; and (b) if the system is not experiencing confusion – for example, if there is not widespread vagueness or incapacitating bewilderment about exactly what the issues or the subsystems involved are.

It may be important for the supervisor to learn the history of the conflict in order to discover for example whether it is primarily a personality type clash (for example, an extrovert therapist imposing his or her notions of mental health on an introverted intuitive) or whether the protagonists are genuinely interested in common values and the productive outcome to the benefit of all. To gain from the benefits of conflict, it is important that the supervisor models effective conflict handling – welcomes it, tries to understand it, and works towards resolution. The most important thing is to show how it can be productively used.

The supervisor can become a model and help the therapist/client system to understand conflict and transform it into effective and creative problem solving. Therapist/client systems are often in need of learning or improving their abilities to manage conflict. Providing an arena for the conflict to be surfaced, examined or rehearsed is most valuable. Then the space, the time and the safety in which to pursue difference can lead towards integrating or co-existence – or a celebration of diversity and variety.

It is a common supervisor error to pathologize conflict – the therapist who is in conflict or conflictful may already feel sick or wrong. This often arises from the supervisor's own fear or denial of his or her own aggression or past trauma. Ignoring or minimizing it reduces the possibility for learning from it and benefiting from the potential for enhanced creativity and better understanding which conflict brings in its wake. Neutrality is usually a good starting position as long as there is no danger of abuse by holding such neutrality. There are many situations where neutrality in fact is ill-disguised support for the aggressor – and the so-called helping professions are by no means exempt (Clarkson, 1995).

Common intrapsychic conflicts are the stuff of everyday life – and 'the psychopathology of everyday life' (Freud, *Standard Edition* 6). Wanting to give up smoking, but afraid that creativity will die in the process; working too hard with high blood pressure, but reluctant to sacrifice what is felt as the life-enhancing adrenaline rushes of risky futures ventures; knowing that exercise will help depression, yet too down to move away from the TV. Then there are conflicts at work, in the family, between friends and of course – disagreements about implicit or explicit values as these affect counselling and psychotherapy every minute of the 50-minute hour, the four-session managed care or the five minute home visit.

Conflicts can be overdiagnosed, tackled prematurely (before the previous stages), displaced, or appear within the WOT (way of talking – Farrell, 1979) of the therapy as 'resistance' whereas sometimes violations are taking place, the dangers of which are irretrievable dangers to identity, integrity, community. These are too often overlooked – particularly when working with anyone who is not West European, educated and middle class.

> Whatever their ideology the majority of 'talk therapists' will see their individual clients as the main 'problem' . . . patients may have to *learn* this world view gradually acquiring with each session a further understanding of the concepts, symbols and vocabulary that comprise it. This can be seen as a form of 'acculturation' whereby they acquire a new mythic world couched, for example, in terms of the Freudian, Jungian, Kleinian or Laingian models. This mythic world, shared eventually by patient and therapist, is often inaccessible to the patient's family or community, who in any case are excluded from the consultation.
>
> (Helman, 1994, p. 280)

Deficit

Issues to do with replenishment of lacks, reparenting, knowledge or skill deficits, and so forth, are most likely to be effective if the previous stages have been cleared. In the last instance the therapist/client system can primarily be characterized as needing something – being in 'deficit'. If it is information about a specific approach that is needed, the provision of such a system will tend to be satisfying, satisfactory and comparatively easily accomplished. Training or educational input that is provided to the therapist when the deficit is appropriately and accurately identified results in appropriate change in the client/therapist system.

However if helpful hints or useful strategies are brought in to give the therapist/client system something while the therapist/client system is still experiencing conflict, confusion or a sense of danger, it is more than likely that the anticipated outcome will not materialize and unpleasant disillusionment and cynical responses are to be expected.

On one occasion a request for teaching on developmental theory (apparently meeting a need) coincided with a sudden reduction in therapist income. In this context, the request may have been coming from a position of confusion, or it may have been an attempt to deal with conflict about whether the patient should be discouraged from termination. It is likely that the therapist was experiencing danger, possibly in value conflict, and confused about their own future. Without taking these issues into account in contracting and designing this work, the supervision would not have been effective.

Strategic priorities when meeting a deficit are first to establish what people **already** have as resources, skills, training, options before providing anything. It is also necessary to find out what worked before and, most importantly, to identify what went wrong before. This is to ensure that the consultant is not working fruitlessly within one of the three previous areas of danger, confusion or conflict.

When one is as certain as possible that there is actually a deficit need, it becomes reasonably simple to follow the classic instructions to start from where the supervisor/client system is, establish the needs and wants, and to provide and review the use of relevant input. It may be for the client to take the medication as prescribed or for the trainee to keep adequate records or for the supervisor to display better empathetic attunement.

A common mistake within this focus is to assume that there is a solution that can be provided by teaching. All the time-honoured admonishments against giving advice or information to clients or supervisees is grounded in the frequent and sometimes disastrous errors when deficit-filling interventions are delivered without having a sound enough working alliance and within a distorted and unresolved transference or countertransference reaction. '*I was assertive like you taught us, but when I hit the waiter over the head, they put me in prison*', or '*I did what you told me and the client had a terrible relapse.*'

Sometimes the deficit-focused intervention may result in a beneficial change, but not the desired improvement, because the intervention did not address the problems as experienced by the participants. Another common mistake is to 'do it' for the therapist/client system rather than enabling participants to find, use or discover their own resources.

However, on the other hand, to deprive clients or supervisees of information, guidance or advice when it is clear that they need it and likely that they will be able to use it well if carefully delivered, can be simply an unethical prolonging of ignorance and distress (Boadella, 1988). A married man needed only one session to relieve him of incapacitating guilt he felt for masturbating, by providing him with the statistical information available on how normal and ordinary it is for many married men to do this – even happily married men. For a supervisee worried about whether the client complaining of persecution was delusionally paranoid, a call to the GP and the local race relations office was all that was needed to confirm that there was vicious harassment on the housing estate.

Development

This supervisory focus concerns issues to do with increasing complexity, effectiveness, capacity and an increase in range and flexibility of understandings, sensibilities and behavioural repertoire. It is not meant only to refer to step-by-step hierarchical developmental models (as these are often culture bound), but may include those alongside more cyclic models of professional enhancement (Clarkson, 1994) or the sudden and apparently unpredictable shifts that characterize postmodern conceptualizations of evolutionary or quantum changes in complex systems. **It is moving our mutual universes of discourse from simplex to complex to multiplex** (Stewart, 1996).

Reviews of the research concerning supervisee development have, in any case, found it to be 'simplistic . . . not acceptably tested, and no tentative inferences from the data to the model seem justifiable given the inadequate rigor of the studies' (Ellis and Ladany, 1997, p. 483).

In terms of supervision the notion of development is here, for example, referring to the learning edge or developmental stretch for the therapist/supervisor system – those issues which are not nurtured through avoidance (such as cultural implications for example) or which are avoided because of ignorance or feeling overwhelmed and helpless (due to overpowering organizational forcefield influences) or even the blunting that comes from over-use and desensitization.

An example of the latter is the phase of 'unconscious incompetence', which, as Robinson (1974) showed, follows after the achievement of 'conscious competence'. This last sequel of achieved competency can, however, be transformed if the supervisor or supervisor's consultant repeatedly again involve themselves in a continuous cycle of continuing education, questioning and research – even with regard to the very assumptions on which they had based their practice and their teaching in the first place.

There is, of course, always the potential for development, but only rarely would it take priority over the previous foci in terms of importance or urgency – particularly as far as client need must take primacy. This is necessary and sometimes regrettable because these developmental edges may be the very sources of nourishment and creativity that keep a professional in these disciplines alive, questioning and vibrant. It is perhaps associated to the leisure in supervision, which can be a prerequirement for creative growth analogous to that for artistic development in a society.

When supervision is normally a rushed business, an attempt to cover too many patients in too little time, or to meet endless external 'requirements' rather than to burgeon as a professional in tune with the tides of a life in these disciplines, these aspects are pushed out and ignored at risk of the very joy, curiosity and creativity that often brought people to this work in the first place. Of course clients must come first. However, the care and nurture of the professional, whether novice or veteran, should accompany this priority if the supervisory system is not to become an empty hypocrisy.

When the supervisory system is in need of development (or when it is in need of the space/time to generate such development) the focus needs to be on learning what is generalizable to other situations, other clients, other supervisees. It may mean creating the space for new needs to emerge (Skevington, MacArthur and Somerset, 1997). It concerns metaphorically developing an aspirational arrow that is never satisfied with being good enough, but is always striving around questions such as 'What if this didn't work?' 'How would I know that something completely new for me might not be better?' 'What is the effect of this on the whole of society?' (bystander issues – see Clarkson, 1996) 'How can I bring beauty, poetry, soul into this work?' (Clarkson, 1997).

Application

Using this framework for using the subjective, feeling reality of the client/therapist system results in three sets of issues for supervisors:

- accurately diagnosing the supervisee's need as presented within the relevant subsystem;

- understanding that the presenting problem may be only an acceptable way of requesting help on a different underlying issue which the therapist may or may not be aware of; and
- choosing an appropriate intervention or intervention strategy aligned to the focussed psychological reality of the supervisor/therapist/client situation.

Accurate diagnosis relies on sensitive and accurate perception of relationships within the therapist/client system. This develops as the supervisor responds to the needs he or she perceives in the client, or experiences the therapist as having – this provides an initial diagnosis.

From an archetypal perspective, a place can be used as an illuminating metaphor for pointing to the different ambiences that can help differentiation and the efficacy of the work: (a) **danger**, the notion of the survival, communication and alliance issues of the tribal hunting grounds; for (b) **confusion**, the idea of the tensions and ambivalence of love and hate in the home or intimate community; (c) **conflict**, the imagination of the arena – place for combat and tests of strength and cunning; for (d) **deficit**, the leisurely discussions, lively arguments and Socratic dialogues of the olive groves of academia; and for (e) **development**, the sacred precincts of the Temple, the hermit's cave, the silence of the inner sanctum of the buildings or the inner sanctum of the soul. (See Clarkson, in press b, for a development of these themes in Jungian terms related to parallel process and synchronicity).

As is perhaps immediately apparent from the symbolic echoes of real life supervisory activity, the roles of the supervisor and the needs of the supervisee and patient may be quite different in the different domains. Tasks and goals may be quite different depending on what is required. In danger boundaries may be abrogated in an emergency (for example, an epileptic fit); in the deficit stage it would depend on what actually needed to be learnt – to keep boundaries or to become more flexible about them (for example, never ever to change appointment times or to respond to a considered and realistic request).

Of course there are always exceptions.

When we think about the supervisory relationship as a system, this framework suggests that any supervisory issue can be characterized as primarily concerned with at least one of five foci. These are macro-sorting capacities of course and may overlap, supersede or blend in with one another or others. Furthermore, identifying the type of issue in terms of content or dynamics may be a primary prerequisite to help the supervisee clarify or discover which of these are the most compelling or the most avoided aspects of the supervision.

However, necessary qualifications apart, the suggested framework can provide a useful way of thinking about the supervisory moment in such a way as to enable the supervisee and the supervisor jointly to explore, contract and evaluate interpretations, strategies and possibilities of relationship. The categories can then represent a sequence that can maximize effectiveness in selecting among the myriad of possibilities available to the supervisor.

This is only a map. In the training and supervision of supervisors, this imaginary exercise, of course, does not obviate the difficulties of choice, decision-making and responsibility. But it can perhaps expand the range and nature of the imaginary and effective realm of the supervisory venture.

References

Airhihenbuwa CO DiClemente RJ, Wingood GM, Lowe A (1992) HIV/AIDS education and prevention among African-Americans: A focus on culture. AIDS Education and Prevention 4: 267–76.

Boadella D (1988) Biosynthesis. In Rowan J and Dryden W (eds) Innovative Therapy in Britain. Buckingham: Open University Press, pp. 154–77.

Carr J (1995) A model of clinical supervision. In Kugler P (ed.) Jungian Perspectives on Clinical Supervision. Einsiedeln Daimon, pp. 233–9.

Clarkson P (1975) Seven-level model. Invitational paper delivered at the University of Pretoria, November.

Clarkson P (1990) A multiplicity of psychotherapeutic relationships. British Journal of Psychotherapy 7(2): 148–63.

Clarkson P (1992) Transactional Analysis Psychotherapy: An Integrated Approach. London: Routledge.

Clarkson P (1993) Two thousand five hundred years of Gestalt – from Heraclitus to the Big Bang. British Gestalt Journal 2(1): 4–9.

Clarkson P (1994) The Achilles Syndrome: The Secret Fear of Failure. Shaftesbury: Element.

Clarkson P (1995) The Therapeutic Relationship in Psychoanalysis, Counselling Psychology and Psychotherapy. London: Whurr.

Clarkson P (1996) The Bystander (An End to Innocence in Human Relationships?). London: Whurr.

Clarkson, P. (in press a) Conditions for excellence – the coincidentia oppositorum of the inferior function. In Clarkson P (ed.) On the Sublime (in Psyche's World). London: Whurr, pp. 219–43.

Clarkson P (in press b) The archetypal situatedness of supervision: parallel process in place. In Clarkson P (ed.) On the Sublime (in Psyche's World). London: Whurr, pp. 279–88.

Clarkson P, Aviram O (in press) Phenomenological research in supervision: supervisors reflect on 'being a supervisor'. In Clarkson P (ed.) Counselling Psychology: Integrating Theory, Research and Supervised Practice. London: Routledge.

Clarkson P, Kellner K (1995) Danger, confusion, conflict, and deficit: a framework for prioritizing organizational interventions. Organizations and People 2(4): 6–13.

Doherty WJ (1991) Family therapy goes postmodern. Family Therapy Networker 15(5): 37–42.

Ellis MV, Ladany N (1997) Inferences concerning supervisees and clients in clinical supervision: an integrative review. In Watkins CE Jr. (ed.) Handbook of Psychotherapy Supervision. New York: Wiley.

Farrell BA (1979) Work in small groups: some philosophical considerations. In Babington Smith B, Farrell BA (eds) Training in Small Groups: A Study of Five Groups. Oxford: Pergamon, pp. 103–15.

Freud S (1960) The psychopathology of everyday life. London: Hogarth Press and Institute of Psycho-Analysis.

Helman C (1994) Culture, Health and Illness. 3rd edn. Oxford: Butterworth, Heinemann.

McNamee S, Gergen KJ (1992) Therapy as Social Construction. London: Sage.

Robinson WL (1974) Conscious competency – the mark of a competent instructor. Personnel Journal 53: 538–9.

Ryle G (1966) Dilemmas: The Tarner Lectures. Cambridge: Cambridge University Press.

Safran JD (1993) The therapeutic alliance rupture as a transtheoretical phenomenon: definitional and conceptual issues. Journal of Psychotherapy Integration 3(1): 33–49.

Searles HF (1955) The informational value of the supervisor's emotional experiences. Psychiatry 18: 135–46. (Also in Searles HF (1986) Collected Papers on Schizophrenia and Related Subjects. London: Karnac.)

Skevington SM, MacArthur P, Somerset M (1997) Developing items for the WHOQOL: an investigation of contemporary beliefs about quality of life related to health in Britain. British Journal of Health Psychology 2: 55–72.

Stewart I (1996) Signing off. Tate Magazine (Winter): 80.

Thompson A (1990) Guide to Ethical Practice in Psychotherapy. Chichester: John Wiley.

Watkins CE Jr (1997) Handbook of Psychotherapy Supervision. New York: Wiley.

Chapter 8
Collegial Working Relationships – Ethics, Research and Good Practice

PETRŪSKA CLARKSON AND GEOFFREY LINDSAY

> The effectiveness of these [professional ethics] codes depends on four main factors: (1) the benefit that members perceive in retaining their membership; (2) the effectiveness of the association in communicating the code and a sense of its importance to its members; (3) the willingness of members to monitor the behaviour of fellow members and to apply the sanctions when appropriate; and (4) the efforts by the profession to educate the public as to what constitutes competent and ethical behaviour by its members and to support any legitimate complaints about such behaviour by members.
>
> (Thompson, 1990, p. 130)

> *The greatest dilemma is whether or not to remain belonging to UKCP and ensure my status is safe, for future (e.g. legislation), whilst at the same time believing it is creating a false position and status for its members (of safety and effectiveness) in the eyes of the public, that they generally don't deserve based on any objective evidence and are in fact simply creating a closed shop under the banner of protecting the public. P.S. This is true of many of my colleagues.*
>
> (extract from 'Response in UKCP ethics research on ethical dilemmas' by Clarkson and Lindsay, in Clarkson, 2000)

> To ignore an ethical violation is an ethical violation in itself . . . (Bernard and Jara, 1995 p. 67) but – *[I have difficulty reconciling] . . . my own moral standards with that of the organisation I'm involved in at any given time and my need . . . to earn a living . . . I feel that the counselling and supervision network is quite a small network . . . therefore in order to pay myself OK I need to be on reasonable terms with most people who might . . . refer clients to me.*
>
> (extract from 'Response in research on ethical dilemmas in supervision' by Clarkson and Lindsay, in preparation)

What should you do if you hear that a colleague, as result of some 'impairment', is too mentally and/or physically unwell (in your judgement) to work effectively with clients on a temporary or a permanent basis?

What should you do if a client tells you confidentially that he was one of several boys who had been sexually abused by a school counsellor, but despite knowing that he had the right to complain, he did not want any complaint made?

What should you do if a colleague who is benefiting from the increase in referrals tells you that their working relationship with an eminent colleague has so 'broken down' that her name has been deleted from the organization's lists and that therefore clients and supervisees are no longer to be referred to her?

These are only three examples of the kinds of dilemmas about collegial conduct many of us face or may face in our professional lives. (Some answers to these dilemmas are imbedded in this Chapter. You could check them again at the end to see if your view has changed.) That ethical dilemmas are complex and imbedded in our socio-legal cultural context is taken for granted. The available literature on this covers much ground that cannot be discussed in this one chapter. Here we wish to focus on only one aspect that has a way, notwithstanding all efforts to circumscribe it, of permeating all of our ethics codes, moral awareness and standards of practice anyway – **our working relationship with our colleagues**.

All professional ethics codes contain items regarding collegial working relationships and most have procedures for dealing with breaches of such principles of ethical practice (British Association for Counselling, 1992; British Psychological Society, 1995; United Kingdom Council for Psychotherapy, 1995-6).

Yet as Freidson (1970, pp. 186–7) pointed out, a code of ethics 'has no necessary relationship to the actual behaviour of members of the occupation . . . In this sense a code of ethics may be seen as one of many methods an occupation may use to induce general belief in the ethicity of its members, without necessarily bearing directly on individual ethicality.'

It remains one of the most fraught areas of our professional theory and practice of ethics and calls into question complex foundational moral questions of integrity and responsibility towards the professional organizations one belongs to, the clients' or students' interests we claim to be protecting and one's own survival issues as a professional with a livelihood to make in these professions.

This chapter will briefly review, in a preliminary way, some early findings from research into ethics in terms of collegial working relationships, offering some guidance from the literature and from experience for reminders of good practice. Quotations from respondents in this and other stages of the study will be used to highlight qualitative aspects of these ethical concerns.

Background to this analysis of ethical dilemmas concerning collegial conduct

Following on North American (Pope and Vetter, 1992) and British research studies (Lindsay and Colley, 1995) of ethical dilemmas of psychologists, a joint survey was undertaken into the ethical dilemmas as experienced by a random sample of 1000 UKCP psychotherapists (Clarkson and Lindsay, in press). This sample was posted a simple survey form with pre-paid reply envelopes asked for a response to the following question: 'Describe in a few words, or more detail, an incident that you or a colleague have faced in the past year or two that was ethically troubling to you.' In this preliminary report we will highlight only some findings.

Of UKCP psychotherapists who replied, 73.2% reported experiencing ethical dilemmas, 22.1% reported that they had experienced no dilemmas and 4.7% wrote that they were unable to comment for various reasons. In the opinion of the researchers such a high proportion of practitioners grappling with ethical dilemmas indicates a serious commitment to engaging with such issues in our professions. As we believe that there is hardly any clinical or supervisory event at all without its ethical or moral dimensions we would hope that, in time, with increased education and professional awareness, this figure will rise to 100%. This research and this chapter are an attempt to increase appreciation and exploration of this dimension of our work in all its guises.

The most frequently reported troubling ethical dilemmas for UKCP psychotherapists included in the first Lindsay and Clarkson survey (accepted for publication 1998) were: confidentiality (29.2%), followed by colleagues' conduct (13.5%), then dual relationships (11.8%), then sexual issues (8%), then academic training issues (5.6%) and then issues of competence (4.9%). Other issues were proportionally somewhat less significant.

The fact that colleagues' conduct emerged as the second highest source of ethical dilemmas for UK psychotherapists seemed to warrant much further and deeper investigation. A detailed secondary analysis of all respondents' comments specifically mentioning colleagues conduct were thus made to facilitate such consideration. This is a qualitative study, so it is not suggested that these results are necessarily representative of the profession of psychotherapy, or counselling for that matter, but merely that they are a starting point for exploration and discussion. (The BACP does not differentiate between counselling and psychotherapy and, although we do not know how many responding UKCP members are also BACP members in this survey, counselling was frequently mentioned. We are thus assuming, until further research proves otherwise, that for the purposes of education, exploration and practice improvement, the issues regarding ethics for counsellors and psychotherapists are substantially the same.)

So the overall theme is our working alliances or working relationships with our colleagues. Paraphrasing the definition in Clarkson (1995c), a working alliance or relationship is defined as: 'That part of a colleague–colleague relationship which enables them to work together even when either of them experiences some desires to the contrary' (p. 41). As professionals we are required to work together for the benefit of our clients, our students and members of the public and also for the sake of the profession as long as we are members of these professions. There are many times when we have to work effectively together with people with whom we disagree or don't like or with whom we may not want to be 'close friends'.

As long as people remain members of the same professions they are highly likely to serve on committees or research projects together; they may be involved with different members of the same family or with students from the same organization, and they will hopefully be joined in the common purpose of competent and ethical service to clients, students, colleagues and members of the public, notwithstanding their own personal foibles, preferences or fears. Therefore members of the professions are required to maintain such working relationships in order to fulfil the code items regarding not bringing the profession into disrepute.

Professions exist on the public trust (MacDonald, 1995) so that the good of the students, the clients and the public will prevail and that mutually effective working relationships will be developed, maintained and secured. The maintenance of effective working relationships – particularly when there are conflicting desires or potential difficulties – is thus of the greatest and most crucial value to the profession of psychotherapy in its claim to be protecting and serving the interests of the public.

Some respondents in our study also argued that there was not sufficient guidance about collegial relationships. *'This shows up a general lack in the profession of laid down criteria/ethical code guidance for collegial relationships within our organizations and procedures for the breach of them.'* We, to the contrary, think that the guidance does exist, but is not frequently taught or questioned.

The relevant item from the British Association for Counselling reads as follows: 'B.2.4 To other Counsellors: 2.4.1 Counsellors should not conduct themselves in their counselling-related activities in ways which undermine public confidence in either their role as a counsellor or in the work of other counsellors. (see B.9)' (BAC Code of Ethics and Practice, 1992, p. 4). The UKCP code, under item 2.11, 'detrimental behaviour', states: '2.11 (I) Psychotherapists are required to refrain from any behaviour that may be detrimental to the profession, to colleagues or to trainees' (p. 1).

It has been suggested (for example, Bernard and Jara, 1995) that a primary reason for the comparative neglect of teaching and education about responsible collegial behaviour is that all kinds of 'unwritten protection laws' have proliferated along with fear, justifiable or not, of the destructive consequences of becoming responsibly involved. Some of our respondents had experienced this: '*The organization was furious when we made the complaint . . . a colleague lost her job without due notice.*' (Quotations from respondents used in this chapter will be largely accurate except where changed for sense or the protection of identifying details.)

On the other hand, several respondents expressed regret of some kind for not acting appropriately in cases where they had grave cause for concern: '*Sadly this seemed to me to indicate some confirmation of my own fears and I regret that I did not take more strong action at the time the trainee was still seeing me.*'

Others were reasonably clear about personal responsibility for choices along the continuum from bystanding to responsible involvement. It is the problem of being aware that, '*some other practitioner is working with what I see as an incompetence that is culpable and damaging. I may understand well why but since I'm not being approached by them for supervision, I feel uncomfortably powerless, but when it's close to home and I feel obliged to act then ultimately it has to be about recognizing abuse and not tolerating it.*'

Research results

Eighty-one specific ethical dilemmas (with two coded in two instances) regarding collegial conduct were mentioned in this part of the research project and a category analysis revealed the following results in terms of rank order for type of reported dilemma. The 83 code items are broken down in Table 8.1.

Here follows some discussion with examples and brief commentary on these issues, taking into account the limitations of our study on the one hand and the space available for discussion in this format on the other. It is envisaged that any one of these types of dilemmas could benefit from a paper, a chapter or even one or more books written about them. Hopefully this initial attempt will encourage colleagues to join us in the

Table 8.1 The types of ethical dilemmas concerning collegial conduct

1	a	Serious concerns about colleagues' competence	29 responses
2	b	Sexual misconduct with clients or students	19 responses
3	c	Attacks by colleagues on professional reputation	8 responses
4	d	Boundary breaks	7 responses
5	e	Financial exploitation of clients and students	7 responses
6	f	General misconduct	4 responses
7	g	Issues to do with moral competence including lying about qualifications	4 responses
8	h	Issues to do with discrimination of various kinds	2 responses
9	i	Issues to do with the abuse of power over clients or students or members	2 responses
10	j	Mismanagement of colleague's death – effect on clients	1 response

endeavour of finding more information and more questions about these very complex dimensions of being a responsible professional living and working with integrity in the confusing, uncertain and rapidly changing world of our current time. Of course this is not a spurious demand for perfection, but a serious call to accountability and responsibility. We know only too well, as Bauman (1993, p. 245) put it:

> What the postmodern mind is aware of is that there are problems in human and social life with no good solutions, twisted trajectories than cannot be straightened up, ambivalences that are more than linguistic blunders yelling to be corrected, doubts which cannot be legislated out of existence, moral agonies which no reason-dictated recipes can soothe, let alone cure.

Serious concerns about colleagues' competence

This was the largest subcategory, including concerns about both trainee and qualified colleagues. Due to the open-endedness of our question it is not possible to quantify this properly: given the fact that some North American studies found that 50% of psychotherapists have admitted to practising while incompetent one can see why this is such a serious issue. The dilemma for the supervisor is how to help supervisees admit that they need to actively challenge their clients and at the same time to contain the supervision group split between collusion and alarm. It feels as if some speedy action is advised, intervention rather than exploration, as the client's welfare and that of others is at stake.

The issue of client welfare is, of course, of overriding concern and the very foundation of claims to being a profession. The dilemmas reported in this study often concern how to inform the organization and prevent or

stop the abuse while not breaking codes of confidentiality that are interpreted to mean that 'nothing can be done'.

This leaves members of the public at risk of abusive and damaging
professionals while other members of the profession know of this, but feel
they cannot act. '*I am afraid that she might eventually be a very
damaging counsellor, but I don't seem able to let anybody know this,
even in the vaguest of terms, because I have no contact with her course
tutors. Am I right in thinking there's nothing I can do?*'

It seems to us that the rules requiring us to confront a colleague when
in doubt well cover these issues of competency. It appears as if the differentiation between trainee and qualified colleagues often made is either
spurious in these cases, or misunderstood because where the psychotherapist or counsellor suspect abuse or damage as a result of competency
issues, both the client and the practitioner can best be served by some
direct, personal and compassionate intervention.

Only after respectful discussion with the colleague concerned (always
on the assumptions that one may be wrong) can one make a reasonable
professional estimate of risk to clients. If such a discussion with the
colleague does not resolve the issue satisfactorily (for example, with a
clarification, explanation or commitment to get help of a particular kind),
then it is usually an ethical requirement that client welfare take prece-
dence over protecting the confidentiality of the practitioner and either
their supervisor, training organization or relevant professional organization be appropriately involved, with only those breaches of confidence
strictly necessary to deal ethically with the case.

Sexual misconduct with clients or students

The second largest group of responses about collegial conduct concerned
sexual misconduct with clients or students. A practitioner expressed
'grave concern' about a sexually abusing colleague who is still practising
sexual misconduct, but since the client will not complain has 'not checked
whether this organization takes third party complaints'.

The disruptive effect of sexual relationships between trainers and
students was another cause for distress. '*Issue for the organization in
terms of interpreting ethics – and unreconciled conflicts between organization and wider community.*'

Attacks by colleagues on professional reputation

'*I found that what I had heard seriously damaged my confidence in my
colleague's integrity as a psychotherapist. Yet there seemed to be no*

appropriate place to take my concerns, especially as the source of my information was so informal.'

'The main consequence of the distinction between the two forms of action [libel and slander] is that in libel the law presumes damage has been suffered and the plaintiff is not required to prove any loss. In slander however the plaintiff will have to satisfy the court that he or she has suffered financial damage arising from the defamatory statement'. There are exceptions to this rule which include slanderous statements which

'disparage a person in his or her business, calling or profession'. In fact, it does not require any great amount of special knowledge or skill to identify defamatory statements or acts. Most people know when a statement exposes someone to 'hatred, ridicule or contempt' or lowers him 'in the estimation of right-thinking members of [a] society generally'.

(Crone, 1991)

(Note: This is unchanged by the new Defamation Act of 1996)

Financial exploitation of clients and students

I find this troubling because, as therapists, our trust and integrity is carried in our word – our agreements. The BPS differentiates between disagreeing with views or methods or opinions as different from attacks on the person or the professional reputation of a colleague. 'For instance, two counsellors engaged in a heated public debate would not fall into this category [of undermining public confidence in counselling] unless either party became personally abusive and defamed the other or violence resulted' (Bond, 1993, p. 148). That gives quite a leeway.

Defamation is quite simple to establish in professional situations – where no financial damage needs to be proved: Therefore the deletion of a professional's name from referral registers for any other reason except proven malpractice or incompetence is defamatory. It can also be shown that the removal of any person's name from a professional list for reasons not related to their ethics or competence as professionals is in itself an illegitimate and unjust action. Such a removal or deletion is a damaging and defamatory comment on the individual's competence by virtue of the declared purpose of keeping and publishing such professional lists or registers. The very reason for maintaining a list of the names of professionals is for the distinction to be made in respect of the services provided by those professionals.

There is in addition to this the common perception of the import of such lists and the removal of a practitioner's name from such a list (i.e. that the practitioner has been proved incompetent or unethical). Accordingly any removal or deletion of name from a list of professionals is bound to cause serious damage to the livelihood of the person concerned, or cause them to be shunned, whatever the stated reason is for such a removal or deletion. Such damage would amount to a legal wrong and in terms of defamation would be able to meet the criteria for defamation without having to show special financial damage.

(Keter, 1998, p. 7)

Action taken

Filing ethics complaints

'The injunction to do no harm [non-malificence] can be construed to include the mandate not to remain passively acquiescent when fellow professionals are violating ethical principles and standards of practice' (Pope, Tabachnick and Keith-Spiegel, 1995, p. 78).

Respondents specifically mentioned filing ethics complaints, some feeling others (such as a boss) should have done 'something'. This is compared with one quarter (plus 9.3%) of respondents in a North American study who have filed an ethics complaint against a colleague. If only some 10% of colleagues were willing to act on information about colleagues' violation of ethics codes, this means that perhaps 90% will, through their unethical acts of omission, condone and thus collude with collegial misconduct and the continuing abuse of clients and trainees.

Although the research question was phrased in a very open way, not asking for this kind of information at all, it was also possible to make a very indicative subanalysis of responses in terms of what kind of action was considered or taken and what the outcome of the mentioned issue was. These results, so spontaneously mentioned, are definitely not to be generalized, but again provide fruitful food for thought. They may also indicate the depth and quality of the respondents' appreciation of and engagement with the complexity of the problem raised by the ethical dilemma in each instance. Another study could research this in much more depth. So, just because no action or reflection or outcome was mentioned in a particular response, we cannot assume that much more thought, consideration and a definite outcome did not actually follow in cases where these were **not** included in responses.

Yet the need to act is enshrined in our codes of ethics – indeed BPS, the BACP and UKCP publish this to the profession and the public, thus fostering the expectation that professionals are ethically obliged to act in cases where they have reason to be concerned about their colleagues' unethical behaviour. As clients are most likely to be disadvantaged by such behaviour, and they are usually least informed and least resourced in acting on their own behalf in such situations, if the professionals – who are most likely to hear about abuses from such clients – abrogate their responsibilities to and for each other as well, these are very empty promises.

The UKCP code (UKCP, 1995–6, p. 1) states:

> 2.11 (ii) Psychotherapists are required to take appropriate action in accordance with Clause 5.8 [initiate the relevant complaints procedure] with regard to the behaviour of a colleague which may be detrimental to the profession, to colleagues or to trainees.

The relevant item from the British Association for Counselling reads as follows:

> B. 2.4.2 If a counsellor suspects misconduct by another counsellor which cannot be resolved or remedied after discussion with the counsellor concerned, they should implement the Complaints Procedure, doing so without breaches of confidentiality other than those necessary for investigating the complaint (see B.9).
>
> (BAC Code of Ethics and Practice, p. 4)

Not acting in cases of concern

If a paractitioner therefore does not do this it is in itself a breach of ethics. No one in this study mentioned these specific ethical code items obliging all professionals to act in cases where they have reason to suspect misconduct. It may be possible that everyone knows these and acts on it so automatically that it is taken for granted.

On the other hand, it may be that there is the kind of complicity referred to in the quotation above that privileges a closing of ranks with our friends and colleagues against the interests of the public. Szasz, for example, challenged at the 1997 University's Psychotherapy Association Conference whether professional psychotherapy organizations don't really exist in order to protect the professionals from the public.

Yet this is a fundamental undertaking, published to the public in most of our ethics codes, thus leading members of the public to believe that professionals would intervene with their own colleagues – on behalf of those we serve at least – in cases where there were grounds for thinking that a collegial situation needed investigation or correction or regulation.

Thompson (1990, p. 129) wrote:

> This desire for power and identity [of professional associations] may or may not be accompanied by a strong desire to serve the public and to do so in more effective ways, even though the profession espouses such goals. The immediate, often tangible, benefits of protecting and enhancing one's prestige and one's political and economic status may often be more powerful incentives than those of good service to the public. Should the two conflict, or appear to conflict, the latter is apt to give way.

It is our moral and ethical responsibility to each other and to our clients, students and members of the public to take action with proper confidentiality preserved, after appropriate and timely consultation and without malice, but yet a professional may be wrong, deliberately or accidentally falsely informed, misled, or simply making a mistake. These additional concerns may prevent professionals from acting appropriately. The code items usually specify words like 'where there is reason to suspect', 'where there is ground to believe' – the codes do not require that the complaint be **proved** true or valid before it is formally made. It does imply a requirement to make an informed professional judgement about the seriousness of the charge and the urgency of confronting the colleague or calling for an investigation.

It is important for colleagues seeking such redress of harm to clients or colleagues, for example, to be aware that if they have taken proper consultation to avoid malice or breaches of confidentiality they may still be wrong about such assessment of probabilities without incurring the risk of being sued for defamation. In normal circumstances libel, slander and defamation tort would apply, but in professional circumstances there is the defence of qualified privilege which extends precisely this protection to responsible professionals for taking such risks, since it is actually their ethical duty to do so.

> The defence that a statement cannot be made the subject of an action for defamation because it was made on a privileged occasion and was not made maliciously, for an improper motive. Qualified privilege covers statements made fairly in situations in which there is a legal or moral obligation to give the information and the person to whom it is given has a corresponding duty or interest to receive it and when someone is acting in defence of his own property or reputation. Qualified privilege also covers fair and accurate reports of public meetings and various other public proceedings. The privilege attaching to professional communications between solicitor and client is probably qualified, rather than absolute.
>
> (Martin, 1997)

Recommendations

The willingness to monitor and correct unethical and incompetent behaviour by colleagues is difficult to instil or to encourage. Yet without such willingness the entire structure collapses. Many, if not most of the ethical violations by professionals come to the attention of fellow professionals when clients seek them out, sometimes to remedy the wrong that was committed, but more often because their original problem was not satisfactorily resolved. The clients [or students] may not even be aware that they were mistreated because they lack the requisite knowledge of professional standards [or accurate information]. Their current therapists can choose to ignore the matter, actively persuade the clients [or students] that no real wrong or harm was done, pursue the matter themselves (normally with the client's permission), or support their client's efforts to do so. Which course of action is chosen is crucial in the aggregate, in determining the effectiveness of the profession's self-policing.

(Thompson, 1990, p. 133)

A good working relationship between colleagues is fundamentally based on shared care for clients, other colleagues (including particularly clients, students and supervisees) as members of the public. To this end disagreements of policy, values and practice should be made explicit within an atmosphere of mutual respect for the persons involved so that difficulties can be addressed, mediated and resolved through ongoing dialogue and cooperation with or without the assistance of dispute facilitators or mediators, where there is reason to believe that a colleague (whether novice, peer or senior) is contravening items in an ethical code. The principles of a good working alliance require that such hearsay or suspicions be checked with the practitioner in question (or the person who reports this be encouraged to deal with it directly, personally and privately in the first instance).

The colleague may have been misunderstood or misreported, or may even welcome the opportunity to correct either a misperception or a misconduct. (This is the 'do as you would be done by' rule.) When appropriate, a concerned third party should offer to act as a mediator and refer the client (or gossiping colleague) to an impartial mediator or specially appointed dispute resolution or ethics consultant. It should not be assumed that bad intent is always the motivation – often it is lack of education and even lack of intellectual ability to understand the complexities of ethical consequences and moral choices in our world.

If this is not successful, it is the practitioner's ethical duty to report it, particularly in cases where detriment to others, self or the profession is concerned. Such reporting needs to be done with strict confidentiality, ensuring as far as possible the psychological safety for all concerned. If complainants are penalized, this demonstrates by example that complaints will not be welcomed and is more likely to encourage abuse and drive collegial ethical concerns underground.

Philosophy for psychology and psychotherapy

Stone (1984) recommended referral of clients who have been victimized by a colleague to consult a third party, an 'administrator', to reduce the dual role conflict of being both client's advocate and client's therapist. If the client agrees and the consultation takes place, from that point on the consultant takes on the responsibility of working with the client to further any legitimate complaint, including obtaining any necessary waivers of confidentiality.

Good collegial working relationships involve assisting with the research studies

Some respondents specifically asked that certain stories not be published yet were willing to share them in collated form: gratitude towards researchers, service on ethics committees, suggestions for improved practice, deep concern about one's own and others' conduct and the principles of our work, and care for our profession.

Gawthop and Uhleman (1992) showed that the recognition of ethical dilemmas and the ability to resolve them improves with training. Most of the studies done indicate that the teaching of ethics by osmosis, 'add ons' or the compliant introjection of 'rules' or group 'norms' without ongoing critical reflection or constant grappling with the complexities of ethical and moral decisions, is not enough.

In addition it has been argued that philosophical training is essential. I would add that a 'learning by enquiry' research-minded attitude to ethics and professional practice is more likely to keep us all questing and questioning than to lead to either 'conformist obedience' or cavalier carelessness.

> This is a good enough reason to make training in standards and ethics a formal part of every counselling course. There will be gains to clients in a greater sense of personal safety. Counsellors will also benefit because a sound understanding of standards and ethics is something which can unite counsellors from many different orientations.
>
> (Bond, 1993, p. 208)

The results of subsequent stages of this ongoing research into ethics (relating to supervision, organizational and research issues) will be reported on in forthcoming papers, and data regarding collegial conduct from these and the qualitative interviews will be added in future.

Anyone reading this who would like to be confidentially interviewed about their experience of ethical dilemmas or their experience of complaints procedures ethics investigations or any related issues should contact the author, who is doing the qualitative interviews.

In this way concerns about our professional ethics can be considered, communicated, addressed and perhaps improved without the painful personalization and fear or experience of retaliation, which is sometimes the result of responsible involvement according to our ethical duties. In this way the ethical principle of beneficence can also be served.

Any initial comments on this part of the project will be welcomed. We would also like to express our grateful thanks to all respondents who completed our questionnaire, thus helping to further research information and education in this vitally important underpinning of all our work. Without their willingness to share problems, uncertainties and experiences, there would be no progress in this most delicate and painful area of our work. Our grateful thanks also to the University of Surrey and PHYSIS for financial support for part of this work.

We would like to end on a quotation from Hannah Arendt (1964, pp. 294, 295) who demanded that

> human beings be capable of telling right from wrong even when all they have to guide them is their own judgment, which, moreover, happens to be completely at odds with what they must regard as the unanimous opinion of all those around them . . . These few who were still able to tell right from wrong went really only by their own judgments [during the Holocaust], and they did so freely; there were no rules to be abided by . . . because no rules existed for the unprecedented.

We may yet face many unprecedented events and currents in the ethics and morals of our professional worlds of psychotherapy and counselling.

References

Arendt H (1964) Eichmann in Jerusalem: A Report on the Banality of Evil. New York: Viking Press.

Bauman Z (1993) Postmodern Ethics. Oxford: Blackwell.

Bernard JL, Jara CS (1995) The failure of clinical psychology graduate students to apply understood ethical principles. In Bersoff DN (ed.) Ethical Conflicts in Psychology. Washington DC: American Psychological Association, pp. 67–71.

Bond T (1993) Standards and Ethics for Counselling in Action. London: Sage.

British Association for Counselling (1992) Code of Ethics and Practice for Counsellors. Rugby: British Association for Counselling.

British Psychological Society (1995) Division of Clinical Psychology, Professional Practice Guidelines. Leicester: BPS.

Clarkson P (1994) Ethics for the counselling office. Counselling 5(4): 282–3.

Clarkson P (1995a) Values in counselling and psychotherapy. Changes 13(4): 299–306. (Presented at 'What is Human?' Conference. Keele University, August 1994.)

Clarkson P (1995b) Training, supervision, and ethical issues. In Clarkson P, The Therapeutic Relationship. London: Whurr, pp. 276–324.

Clarkson P (1995c) The Therapeutic Relationship. London: Whurr.

Clarkson P (1996) The Bystander: An End to Innocence in Human Relationships? London: Whurr.

Clarkson P, Aveline M (1996) Oaths and codes of ethics and practice. The Psychotherapist 7: 12.

Clarkson P, Lindsay G (2000) In Clarkson P (ed.) Ethics – Working with Ethical and Moral Dilemmas in Psychotherapy. London: Whurr.

Clarkson P, Lindsay G (in press) Ethical Dilemmas of UKCP Psychotherapists. The Psychotherapist (UKCP Publications).

Crone T (1991) Law and the Media. 2nd edn. Oxford: Butterworth-Heinemann.

Freidson E (1970) Profession of Medicine: A Study of the Sociology of Applied Knowledge. New York: Dodd, Mead & Co.

Gawthorp JC, Uhleman MR (1992) Effects of the problem-solving approach to ethics training. Professional Psychology: Research and Training 23(1): 38–42.

Keter V (1998) Report for UKCP Council re Restrictive Practice. Unpublished manuscript.

Lindsay G, Colley A (1995) Ethical dilemmas of the Society. The Psychologist: Bulletin of the British Psychological Society 8: 214–217.

MacDonald KM (1995) The Sociology of the Professions. London: Sage.

Martin EA (ed.) (1997) A Dictionary of Law. 4th edn. Oxford: Oxford University Press.

Pope KS, Vetter VA (1992) Ethical dilemmas encountered by members of the American Psychological Association. American Psychologist 47: 397–411.

Pope KS, Tabachnick BG, Keith-Spiegel P (1995) Ethics of practice: the beliefs and behaviors of psychologists as therapists. In Bersoff DN (ed.) Ethical Conflicts in Psychology. Washington DC: American Psychological Association, pp. 72–84.

Popper K (1992) In Search of a Better World. London: Routledge & Kegan Paul.

Price D (1997) Defamation: Law, Procedure and Practice. London: Sweet & Maxwell.

Robertson C (1993) Dysfunction in training organisations. Self and Society 21(4): pp. 31–5.

Scott-Bayfield JS (1996) Defamation: Law and Practice. 1st edn. London: FT Law & Tax.

Stone AA (1984) Law, Psychiatry, and Morality. Washington, DC: American Psychiatric Press (Cambridge University Press, 1986).

Thompson A (1990) Guide to Ethical Practice in Psychotherapy. Chichester: John Wiley.

United Kingdom Council for Psychotherapy (1995–6) Ethical guidelines of the UKCP. In National Register of Psychotherapists. London: Routledge.

Chapter 9
The Sublime in Psychoanalysis and Archetypal Psychotherapy

PETRŪSKA CLARKSON

This is Frederico Garcia Lorca speaking about duende:

> In all Arabic music, either dance, song, or elegy, the duende's arrival is greeted with energetic cries of Allah! Allah! which is so close to the Olé of the bullfight that who knows if it is not the same thing? And in all the songs of the south of Spain the duende is greeted with sincere cries of Viva Dios! – deep and tender human cry of communication with God through the five senses, thanks to the duende, who shakes the body and voice of the dancer . . . The duende does not come at all unless he sees that death is possible . . . With idea, sound or gesture, the duende enjoys fighting the creator on the very rim of the well. Angel and muse escape with violin and compass; the duende wounds. In the dealing of that wound, which never closes, lies the invented, strange qualities of a man's work.[1] [And a woman's work too]

> Years ago, an eighty-year-old woman won first prize at a dance contest in Jerez de la Frontera. She was competing against beautiful women and young girls with waists as supple as water, but all she did was raise her arms, throw back her head, and stamp her foot on the floor. In that gathering of muses and angels, beautiful forms and beautiful smiles, who could have won but her moribund duende, sweeping the ground with its wings of rusty knives.[2]

The sublime enters into psychotherapy and psychoanalysis in a similar way. In some particular moment some communicative relationship is established that celebrates life and death in beauty, in awe and in reverence. Longinus said that without the sublime, the body is left without soul.[3] The sublime lifts up the soul in 'joy and vaunting';[4] gladness and boastfulness; in exultation. 'As though it had itself produced what it has heard.'[5] In this moment there is no 'other'. Creator and created are one, audience and artist vibrate to the same hummingbird's wing. The space between breaths becomes one soul. Whenever we speak of the soul, we

speak of the sublime. **Peri Hypsous**. Concerning the sublime. The eleva-
tion. The height.

And a young woman came to see me because she wanted to be a high
tincture – to attain 'whiteness and brilliance in Venus and Luna',[6] divinely
virgin, to be pure like a distilled Madonna lily, like brilliantly polished
silver, sanctified, resurrected, purified and made white, so that 'all the
uncleanliness of the blackness, all death, hell, curse, wrath, and all poison
would depart'.[7] But what she forgot in her Romantic sublime was the
necessary manifold work of circulating the tincture through the endless
distillations 'in and out of the forms and qualities of nature'[8] – 'the water
. . . and heavenly dew',[9] but the blood and the rage – and the mud. For
ever and ever.

Longinus also said that the sublime must be referred to **physis**
(nature), for it is by physis 'that man is a being gifted with speech'.[10] So,
whenever we speak of the sublime, we speak of **physis** – 'the original and
vital underlying principle'.[11] Inadequately translated as 'Nature' by the
Romans, **physis** is the very life force itself, the **élan vital**. The soul of the
world and the soul of the word. **Physis** is also the root word for physicist,
physician, physic – as in medicine. Perhaps the medicine for the injured
soul **inextricably** embodied. Heidegger thinks that **physis** as logos is the
poesis of **physis** – 'the ultimate source of thought as well as of language
and poetry. The human **logos**, as it shows itself in language and poetry, is
merely a response to the **logos** of **physis**'.[12]

'The Greeks did not learn what **physis** is through natural phenomena,
but the other way around; it was through a fundamental poetic . . . experience of being that they discovered what they had to call **physis**'.[13] **Physis**
is growing, becoming, coming into being, healing, creativity, evolution,
very nature. Heraclitus bears witness that '**physis** loves to hide'.[14] It represents the eternal cycle. The 'experiential reconciliation of permanence
and degeneration'.[15] That means always the opposites of coming into
being and being destroyed. **Enantiodromia** for ever and ever. From the
fullness of one, its opposite. Breathing in and breathing out, living and
dying. Endlessly. *Et saecula et saecula*.

Of course *logos* is not only words. The sublime also speaks in the
silence. 'The silence of Ajax in the Underworld is great and more Sublime
than words'.[16] Thus spoke Longinus. Approximately 1,900 years later
Weiskel says that 'the sublime moment establishes **depth** because the
presentation of unattainability is phenomenologically a negation, a falling
away from what might be seized, perceived, known. As an image, it is the
abyss.'[17] It is the void. 'It is a terrible thing to fall into the hand of the living
God, but it is a much more terrible thing to fall out of them.'[18] A poet
speaks the poesis of despair. My patient says: I have always dreamed that

there is nobody on the other end of the phone when I call. It just rings and rings and rings as if in an empty house because all the people have moved on to another place. Lawrence again:

> Are you willing to be sponged out, erased,
> cancelled,
> made nothing?
> Are you willing to be made nothing?
> dipped into oblivion?
> If not, you will never really change.[19]

Without the sublime, the human is bereft of soul, abandoned to a pedestrian existence on crowded and dusty hot sidewalks. Without the sublime, the world soul is emptied of awe, of mystery – but also of the possibility of nuclear extinction, or obliteration by cyclone, or armies of jeeps hunting tigers, robbed of its particular perilous grandeur. In denial of the sublime, Freud can say that Leonardo's drawings of fountains and the wondrously chaotic movements of water are simply to do with his childhood enuresis, and his translucent Madonnas the sublimation of his incestuous love for his mother.

> The how of the telling has more eternity than the what. The wine-dark sea or the woods of Dunsinane.
> The keening against the silhouettes of mosques in torture or the worksongs bled out in painblinded endurance
> and diamondbright brilliant exuberance in a field of cocoa, or tea or innocent sunpolished poppies.
> There was a man who believed the whole world could be put in one part of one story – the middle part – and that was a life.
> He told the story well and many believed him, but many did not.[20]

Freud's views on the oceanic, the merging, the religious, the spiritual and the artist are well known. Without the sublime, we have to practise a therapy of the psyche which reduces the sublime to diagrams of 'the positive sublime' and 'the negative sublime'.[21] This is the *reductio*. Creativity has become just the result of our sublimation of sexual and aggressive drives. For Mrs Klein even the pleasure of learning becomes just epistemophilia – the thirst of knowledge regarded as either a derivative of scopophilia, i.e. as an extension of sexual curiosity, or as a sublimation of oral drives.[22] (The better known spelling 'scoptophilia' dates from a mistake made by Freud's first translators.)[23] 'Klein's first psychoanalytic writings demonstrated the close link between sadism and the desire to know.'[24] Thirst for knowledge becomes a sublimation of the pleasure of looking at shit. Scopophilia and the love of learning – practically the same thing. What is sublimity now?

[The] process postulated by Freud to account for human activities which have
no apparent connection with sexuality but which are assumed to be motivated
by the force of the sexual instinct. The main types of activity described by Freud
as sublimated are artistic creation and intellectual inquiry.[25]

Freud's own gifts were great. Sex is numinous indeed, and death
compelling. But – $E = MC^2$, the Sistine ceiling, the poignant hope of a
bruised Madame Butterfly thrilling into 'one fine day', a lapis and gold
icon burnished with faith and miracles, the ironwork tracery in Islamic
courtyards, the benzene ouroborous, the plastic heart valve, the dirty
saucer left by the cleaning maid put to service against pestilence, the
smoky sacredness of patchouli incense drifting over the Ganges, the
pyramids gloating against the onslaught of eternity. For better sex lives –
merely the end of art and science! A poetic injustice? But, to use Blake's
protesting words: 'You shall not bring me down to believe such fitting and
fitted I know better and please your Lordship.'[26]

Jung said it this way: 'Freud invented the idea of sublimation to save us
from the imaginary claws of the unconscious. ['Nature, red in tooth and
claw'?[27]] But what is real, what actually exists, cannot be alchemically
sublimated, and if anything is apparently sublimated it never was what a
false interpretation took it to be . . . it is a view that springs from fear of
nature.'[28] Physis phobia? He also said, 'Sublimation means nothing less
than the alchemist's trick of turning the base into the noble, the bad into
the good, and the useless into the useful. Anyone who knew how to do
that would be certain of immortal fame.'[29] And the poesis of physis reveals
and conceals itself inevitably always already in the telling of the tale, the
ordering even of unlovely words, the hesitant invocation of the presencing
of the sublime and the insistent lamentation for its loss.

It has been said of Jung that he also 'defended himself through
technical analysis against feeling the aesthetic response' to Picasso's
work.[30] Bleakley goes on to say that 'art is more powerful than
psychotherapy, and prior to it.' I would say that **physis** is more powerful
than Eros and Thanatos, and prior to both. If not present, it may be merely
concealing itself in the background of the Gestalt – the whole. Until the
images are made and the songs are sung

Until the stories are told, there is only the thing itself without its history,
without its cast, without its incidental music.
Until the vitality of its life is distilled in the telling the construction of a bridge
across a gorge cannot become the bones of a life.
Until a heartbreak is fashioned into pearls of remembrance, there is only the
heartbreak.[31]

I would say that Jung was the man who opened his arms to the whole feast of stories, the myths, the legends, the ancient woodcuts. He welcomed them into the healing rooms, he made his heart hospitable for them and their puzzles and their furies. He honoured and flowered the signs and symbols and signifiers and souls and stones and signals. He and his dog, in Aesklepian partnership, attended the dreams, the distractions, the disappointments, the despairs. Not just one story, but all of them, all the time, in their fullness. And he described the numinosum, the self and the mystery of the **sublimatio**. And if he quaked and shuddered and transgressed, so much more to the story and so much more to learn. He writes like this:

> Through scientific understanding, our world has become dehumanized. Man feels himself isolated in the cosmos. He is no longer involved in nature and has lost his emotional participation in natural events, which hitherto had a symbolic meaning for him. Thunder is no longer the voice of god, nor is lightning his avenging missile. No river contains a spirit, no tree means a man's life, no snake is the embodiment of wisdom, and no mountain still harbours a great demon. Neither do things speak to him nor can he speak to things, like stones, springs, plants and animals. He no longer has a bush-soul identifying him with a wild animal. His immediate communication with nature is gone for ever, and the emotional energy it generated has sunk into the unconscious.[32]

Then therapy is the restoration of relationship between the microcosmos and the macrocosmos, the alchemical meaning and the spiritual magic, man and nature. In the words of Heraclitus – the way up and down is one and the same.[33] Jung knows that 'there is a god hidden in matter',[34] and that it is God who cures. Meier reminds us that how **psyche** acts on **physis** and how **physis** acts upon **psyche** is an enigma.[35] At the roots of nature lies the soul energizing the will to recover. Without this

> *spontaneous healing tendency of Nature* . . . skill is of no avail, either in the somatic or in the psychic sphere. The dexterity of the surgeon creates nothing but destruction, and the skill of the psychologist is reduced to a dangerous experiment of the sorcerer's apprentice.[36]

A man dreams that he bleeds from a wound in his thigh made by his father's sword. Emerald drops form a snake curling into a chalice of rubies, salted by a memory of killing a stag one day driving impatiently along a highway going to a city meeting and his soul just won't rest until he plants a tree to mark the spot of his guilt. 'How can the all-embracing logic which mirrors the world use such special catches and manipulations? Only because all these are connected into an infinitely fine network, to the great mirror.'[37] And the scientists also teach that human blood is the identical twin of chlorophyll – but for the molecule of iron at the centre.[38] And whose self is it then? Mine – or the world's?

Self can stand for many things. That which is not my ego, my day time self. That which is both my centre and my circumference, or that which is my Self as archetype of the supreme soul – and of course therefore not myself. Jung's notion of the self as totality archetype represents an organized wholeness of the personality expressed in symbolic experience which is transpersonal and transcends the incompatible opposites psychically and physically which apparently constitute the human being – psyche and soma, ego and non-ego, inner and outer.

> The matter at issue in Heraclitus is physis . . . And correlative to the matter is a self-experience, which is as deep as physis is comprehensive. The experience of physis is an experience of self for two reasons: (1) physis comprehends (encompasses) the self as it does everything else; and (2) the self is the locus where (for the human self) physis comprehends (understands) itself. Human experience is, in terms of physis, the self-experience of physis.[39]

Yet Jung at other times almost recoils from **physis**: 'Man's connection with physis, with the material world and its demands, is the cause of his anomalous position; on the one hand he has the capacity for enlightenment, on the other he is in thrall to the Lord of this world'.[40] The medieval alchemist sees the work as *contra naturam* – against nature. The function of the sublimatio is to separate the physical from the psychical, spirit from matter, 'for the purpose of purifying away the *mali odores*, the *foetor sepulcrorum*, and the clinging darkness of the beginning'.[41] What is this smell that he smells? Perhaps it is not totally surprising that '*meretrix* the whore is a synonym for the *prima materia*, the *corpus imperfectum* which is sunk in darkness, like the man who wanders in darkness, unconscious and unredeemed. This idea is foreshadowed in the Gnostic image of Physis, who with passionate arms draws the Nous down from heaven and wraps him in her dark embrace'[42] in the stinking waters . . . 'where he assumes the chthonic form of the serpent'.[43] But which serpent? And whose stink?

> And even as man seeks to rise higher and higher – in his knowledge too – so the ground fractures more and more beneath his feet. 'Nature' is forever dodging his projects of representation, of reproduction. And his grasp. That this resistance should all too often take the form of rivalry within the hom(m)ologous, of a death struggle between two consciousnesses, does not alter the fact that at stake here somewhere, ever more insistent in its deathly hauteur, is the risk that the subject (as) self will crumble away.[44]

Hillman too has this ambivalent relationship with the anima mundi[45] who gives soul 'with each thing, God-given things of nature and man-made things of the street'[46] and he acknowledges that 'the human psyche is one of the great forces of nature'.[47] At other times he waxes vociferous against these very 'man-made things' – the subway, the organization of the workplace, the ugly, the neurotic, the noxious, 'the hysterical theatrics of baroque altars; in the anorexic emptiness of high, glass-enclosed atriums; in the oppressive claustrophobia of low-ceilinged, overstuffed trailers; in gaudy escape through the slot machine casino and provincial red-light district'.[48] Would it be different if it was a **cosmopolitan** red-light district?

Once there was a client or a patient (and why would it matter if it were a man or a woman?) who wandered into a park in central Paris. Languishing on a wooden bench, with collar turned up against the autumn breeze, suddenly hearing the gentle and penetrating song of a bird. Recognizing the nightingale's voice, there was marvelling at its beauty, the particular miracle of its out-of-season exuberance, the gentle magic of a moment of awe and mystery. Soul nourished, the wanderer stepped out on to the path where a noticeboard politely thanked the Paris Municipality (or such) for the provision of the electronic equipment. The nightingale's song had been mechanically reproduced from another place, another time – was its sublime pleasure thus diminished or thus enhanced?

Tacey said:

> The task ahead is to free ourselves from Jung's dualism, to realise that psychic depth and meaning can be found both in ourselves *and* in the so-called external word. Having withdrawn psyche from the world to experience our own souls, we must now break this artificial dualism and grant the world again its soul dimension, while remaining aware of soul within.[49]

The physicist used to live in a world where a clear distinction existed 'between spirit and matter, **physis** and **psyche**'.[50] But to the dream stranger (as the quantum physicist Pauli told it to Von Franz), there is no distinction between the physical and the psychical. Contrary to the deep rift in Pauli's personality, 'as the spirit of matter, he embodies a unity of **physis** and psyche which cannot be comprehended rationally'.[51] 'But the image is of a cosmos very different from the one we have known up to now in our era. This yet to be is the image of a PSYCHOPHYSICAL COSMOS'.[52] But of course it is also a very old one. Skatole is a necessary ingredient of all the most refined perfumes in the world.[53] Without the smell of faeces, there is no jasmine for the *Fedeli de Amore*.[54]

'The myth of the omnimorphic soul [imagines the world soul in such a way as it] includes all of experience, all situations, all happenings, without exception.'[55] There can be no separation of the self. There is nothing that lacks soul. Nothing. There is only

> the ongoing movements and happenings of psychological life, in the adventures, interactions, and fates of fantasies, images and experiences. In this way of imagining, soul qualities are inherent to all psychological life, and can never be absent or lost from it.[56]

Neither can it be lost from the world. No matter what. When we take this view of the 'world' soul, there is no 'war with monotheism, because polytheism and monotheism exist in two different dimensions of imaginal life'.[57] The normative and the transpersonal. Levels 4 and 7.[58] And this is the view of the later more Taoist Jung. Tao is defined as:

> The Way; principle; cosmic order; nature. [Again] 'the Tao that can be expressed in words is not the eternal Tao.' It is 'vague and eluding,' 'deep and obscure,' but 'there is in the form' and 'the essence'. Its 'standard is the natural' (Lao Tsu).[59, 60]

So how will the therapist, the alchemist, the patient be different from 'that of an animal fulfilling the will of God unreservedly?' The only difference I can see is that I am conscious of, and reflect on, what I am doing. 'If thou knowest what thou art doing, thou art blessed'.[61] Jung continues, 'Life then becomes a dangerous adventure, because I surrender to a power beyond the opposites, to a superior or divine factor, without argument'.[62]

> And if, in the unforeseeable future, she happened to unleash some nameless potency, it would not be up to her to judge whether or not this unpredictable event had occurred. *She* would not concern the sudden unchecked appearance of the *physis* as a monstrosity, and aberration in the essence of plant life . . . And if, through some impossible – in the aristotelian meaning of that word – realization of some as yet unknown essence, matter were to supplant or at least question the ontological development of man himself, overturning the premises that ensure his logic, then it seems likely that discourse would set out to prove that she was malformed.[63]

Hillman says, 'Therapy has to be sublime. Terror has to be included in its beauty.'[64]

And fate-ful Hekate of the sun and of the moon, guardian of thresholds, fecund goddess of the life-force, ensouler of the world, **physis** herself, birther and destroyer, the very earliest **anima mundi**, queen of the dream-world, primordial matter or mater, with nature on her back enters on the world stage ablaze with terror and glory, with city walls for a crown, and screaming at the crossroads, her angels and demons and dogs barking over the sewers of the world, straddling ocean and heaven and hell with the source of the virtues faith, truth and love boiling from one hip, and the source of souls from the other gushing forth in abundance from the other, the serpent coiling about her thighs irradiating healing, Leo viridis in attendance, presiding over the Katharsia at the crossroads, the opposites finally reconciled. The beginning and the end. 'How does the force of life manifest as the force of death?'[65] How else could it be? This is Nature conforming to her own laws. Sublime. Some say she is even older than the Father of the gods.[66] She heals sick limbs and raging souls, and guides the weary to the haven of piety with her winds. She trashes cemeteries and eats the dead. She also rules chaos.

Longinus (or perhaps he was only a pseudo-Longinus) ended his treatise concerning The Sublime thus: 'Such are the decisions to which we have felt bound to come with regard to the questions proposed, but let every man cherish the view which pleases him best'.[67]

Notes

[1] Garcia Lorca F (1980) Deep Song and Other Prose. Ed. and trans Maurer C. London: Marion Boyars, p. 46 and pp. 49–50.

[2] Ibid., p. 46.

[3] Longinus (1899) Longinus on the Sublime. Ed. and trans. Rhys Roberts W. Cambridge: Cambridge University Press, XI, 21.

[4] Ibid. VII, 23.

[5] Ibid. VII, 23–4.

[6] Jung CG, CW 16, 2nd edition, para 515.

[7] Ibid.

[8] Ibid.

[9] Ibid.

[10] Longinus (1899) Longinus on the Sublime. Ed. and trans Rhys Roberts W. Cambridge: Cambridge University Press, XXXVI, 18.

[11] Ibid. II, 5.

[12] Avens R (1984) The New Gnosis: Heidegger, Hillman and Angels. Dallas TX: Spring Publications, p. 70.

[13] Heidegger M (1959) An Introduction to Metaphysics (R. Manheim, trans.). New Haven: Yale University Press, p. 14.

[14] Kahn CH (1981) The Art and Thought of Heraclitus: An Edition of the Fragments with Translation and Commentary. Cambridge: Cambridge University Press, p. 33.

[15] Guerrière D (1980) Physis, Sophia, Psyche. In Sallis J and Maly K (eds) Heraclitean Fragments: A Companion Volume to the Heidegger/Fink Seminar on Heraclitus. Alabama: University of Alabama Press, p. 88.

[16] Longinus (1899) Longinus on the Sublime. Ed. and trans Rhys Roberts W. Cambridge: Cambridge University Press, IX.

[17] Weiskel T (1976) The Romantic Sublime: Studies in the Structure and Psychology of Transcendence. Baltimore, Maryland: Johns Hopkins University Press, pp. 24–5. (My emphasis.)

[18] Lawrence DH (1971) The Complete Works of D.H. Lawrence. New York.

[19] Ibid., p. 728

[20] Clarkson P (1995) Story as medicine, narrative to sing for the world. In Clarkson P, The Therapeutic Relationship: In Psychoanalysis, Counselling Psychology and Psychotherapy, pp. 105–7. London: Whurr, pp. 106–7.

[21] Weiskel T (1976) The Romantic Sublime: Studies in the Structure and Psychology of Transcendence. Baltimore, Maryland: Johns Hopkins University Press, pp. 152 and 106.

[22] Rycroft C (1972) A Critical Dictionary of Psychoanalysis. Harmondsworth: Penguin, p. 45.

[23] Hinshelwood RD (1989) A Dictionary of Kleinian Thought. London: Free Association Books, p. 148.

[24] Ibid., p. 292.

[25] Laplanche J, Pontalis JB (1988) The Language of Psychoanalysis. London: Karnac, p. 431.

[26] Blake W (1965) Annotations to Wordsworth's Preface to The Excusion. In Erdman DE (ed.) The Poetry and Prose of William Blake. Garden City, NY, pp. 655–6.

[27] Tennyson, In Memoriam, lvi. Ross RH (ed.) In Memoriam. New York: WW Norton, 1973.

[28] Jung CG, CW 16, 2nd edition, para 328.

[29] Jung CG, CW 15, para 53.

[30] Bleakley A (1994) Psychotherapy Stinks! – or, Hekate Rising (by what light shall we read symptoms when the oil runs out?). Unpublished manuscript.

[31] Clarkson P (1995) Story as medicine, narrative to sing for the world. In Clarkson P, The Therapeutic Relationship: In Psychoanalysis, Counselling Psychology and Psychotherapy. London: Whurr, pp. 105–6.

[32] Jung CG, CW 18, para 585.

[33] Kahn CH (1981) The Art and Thought of Heraclitus: An Edition of the Fragments with Translation and Commentary. Cambridge: Cambridge University Press, p. 75.

[34] Jung CG, CW 13, para 138.

[35] Meier CA (1986) Soul and Body: Essays on the Theories of Jung CG. Santa Monica, CA: The Lapis Press, p. 176.

[36] Ibid., p. 30.

[37] Wittgenstein L (1922) Tractatus Logico-Philosophicus. Trans. Ogden CK. London: Routledge & Kegan Paul.

[38] Fox M (1983) Original Blessing. Santa Fe, New Mexico: Bear & Company, p. 352.

[39] Guerrière D (1980) Physis, Sophia, Psyche. In Sallis J, Maly K (eds) Heraclitean Fragments: A Companion Volume to the Heidegger/Fink Seminar on Heraclitus. Alabama: University of Alabama Press, pp. 129–30.

[40] Jung CG, CW 11, 2nd edition, para 263.

[41] Jung CG, CW 16, 2nd edition, para 403.

[42] Jung CG, CW 11, 2nd edition, para 312.

[43] Ibid., para. 380.

[44] Irigaray L (1985) Speculum of the Other Woman. Trans Gill GC. Ithaca NY: Cornell University Press. Originally published, 1974, p. 135.

[45] Garufi B (1993) Anima Mundi and Anima Mater: A Reply to James Hillman's talk: 'Beyond the narcissism of psychology'. Sphinx 5: 266–77.

[46] Hillman J (1982) Anima Mundi: the return of the soul to the world. Spring, p. 77.

[47] Hillman J, Ventura M (1992) We've had a Hundred Years of Psychotherapy – and the World's Getting Worse. San Francisco CA: Harper Collins, p. 123.

[48] Ibid., p. 128.

[49] Tacey DJ (1993) Jung's ambivalence toward the world-soul. Sphinx 5, pp. 278–87.

[50] Erkelens H. van (1991) Pauli's Dialogue with the Spirit of Matter. Psychological Perspectives 24: 34–53, p. 41.

[51] Ibid., p. 41.

[52] Holms D (1992) Synchronicity and Science. Fourth Jung Studies Forum: Synchronicity, pp. 6–9. University of Kent at Canterbury, p. 6.

[53] Toller S van, Dodd GH (eds) (1991) Perfumery: The Psychology and Biology of Fragrances. London: Chapman & Hall.

[54] Corbin H (1990) Jasmine of the Fedeli d'Amore: a discourse on R°zbeh,n Baqli of ShÓr,z (522/1128-606/1209). Sphinx 3: 189–223.

[55] Wheeler C (1993) The lost Atlantis: a myth of soul in the modern world. Sphinx 5: 287–302, p. 290.

[56] Ibid., p. 291.

[57] Ibid.

[58] Clarkson P (1995) The transpersonal relationship. In Clarkson P, The Therapeutic Relationship: In Psychoanalysis, Counselling Psychology and Psychotherapy. London: Whurr, pp. 181–221.

[59] Lao Tsu, Tao Te Ching. Trans. Feng G-F and J. New York: Vintage.

[60] Runes DD (1966) Dictionary of Philosophy. Totawa NJ: Littlefield, Adams & Co, p. 312.

[61] Jung CG, CW 18, para. 1628.

[62] Ibid., para. 1628.

[63] Irigaray L (1985) Speculum of the Other Woman. Trans. Gill GC. Ithaca NY: Cornell University Press, p. 163. First published 1974.

[64] Hillman J, Ventura M (1992) We've had a Hundred Years of Psychotherapy – and the World's Getting Worse. San Francisco CA: Harper Collins, p. 127.

[65] Ronan S (1992) Chaldean Hekate. In Ronan S (ed.) The Goddess Hekate, pp. 79–139.

[66] Kroll W (1894) De oraculis chaldaicis. Breslau, pp. 29–31.

[67] Longinus (1899) Longinus on the Sublime. Ed. and trans. Rhys Roberts W. Cambridge: Cambridge University Press, XXXVI, 27.

Chapter 10
The Clarkson Seven-Level Model – Developing Epistemological Consciousness about Psychotherapy

PETRŪSKA CLARKSON

Introduction

This chapter describes a tool for thinking and developing consciousness about the epistemology contained and revealed in our discourse and practice about psychoanalysis and psychotherapy. It is concerned with knowledge, with how we can know and with how we can sensibly speak about knowing – **and** what we do with our knowing **and** our unknowing in the work of psychological healing.

There is one vital caveat before you decide whether to continue reading this chapter. If you think there is one truth in psychotherapy which is the whole truth and nothing but the truth (as far as other people or approaches to other disciplines are concerned) you should skip it.

This chapter is strictly for people who grapple with the experience of multiple co-existing kind of 'truths'. Experience has shown that the seven-level model is a kind of answer which is only useful if you've asked a certain kind of question. It is like a key which can unlock a particular door. However, if someone is not interested in unlocking that particular door, the key would obviously be useless to them.

The conceptual model of what originally was originally called the seven epistemological levels was first taught in 1975 in order to help students who were grappling with the wide variety of models of psychology or orders of human experience so that the similarities, differences and

146

contradictions of the existing models could be clarified and clear communication enhanced. Although it may appear deceptively simple, it is a tool designed to deal with **complexity** – that all-pervasive quality of postmodern science and culture as well as the 21st century psyche.

It is therefore a philosophically grounded way of effectively tackling difficult experiential and intellectual problems. It is a particularly useful tool for dealing with issues such as how apparent contradictions can co-exist and even sometimes be all true, but in different worlds of 'talk'. In this book's Chapter 4 I have already begun to show in a preliminary way how clinically useful the model is when engaging with the fraught subject of 'recovered memories' of abuse.

The seven-level model implicitly or explicitly permeates all my life and work since 1975. It has previously been described in Clarkson (1992) in terms of training psychotherapists and also in terms of applying it to psychotherapeutic formulations and 'treatment planning' (Clarkson and Lapworth in Clarkson, 1992). It is used in the *Therapeutic Relationship* (1995), my *Bystander* book (Clarkson, 1996) and in Clarkson (2000) *Ethics – Working with Ethical and Moral Dilemmas in Psychotherapy*.

It is simply the best tool I have found to conceptually and experientially hold a multiplicity of discourses and human experiences in order to attempt *phronein* – thinking and acting well – as Heraclitus (in Kahn, 1981) advised.

Characteristics

Contrary to Wilber's (1980) levels, this model is not hierarchical nor developmental in the sense of moving from one level to another so that one is in any sense seen as being 'higher', better or 'more developed' than another. It follows the phenomenological rules of 'epoch' description and 'equalization' (Spinelli, 1989). The levels of descriptions in this model co-exist as descriptions of equal value which may even be mutually contradictory at the same time.

The model is not intended to express any values in itself and it sets no hierarchies of value either. Originally, the model offered simply a category sorting tool for thinking of the implications and ramifications of each level in terms of clarifying and preventing the kind of logical fallacies which the Oxford philosopher Ryle (1960) identified as **category errors**. It is most useful in clarifying **discourse**, i.e. defined as text and talk in psychotherapy.

Essentially the seven-level model is **phenomenological** in the sense that it makes provision for the description of differentiated domains of discourse while avoiding common category errors. Discourse analysis applied to psychotherapy is not so much a tool to get at positivistically defined empirical truths but rather a different way of conceptualizing talk – 'a new perspective' (Silverman, 1992) – although it **includes** such truths.

The model provides a simultaneous implication of different domains of human existence alongside the different modes of discourse used and the different narratives involved. It is a kind of conceptual container grid for all experience and knowledge. It is a kind of taxonomy – a phenomeno-graphic classification or categorization tool.

Phenomenography is the empirical study of the limited number of qualitatively different ways in which we experience, conceptualize, under-stand, perceive, apprehend etc. various phenomena in and aspects of the world around us. These differing experiences, understandings etc. are characterized in terms of categories of description, logically related to each other, and forming hierarchies according to given criteria (Marton, 1992).

In this sense the seven-level model is a **phenomenographic** tool as in the phenomenological nominative domain of discourse. It is not intended as a 'theory' (level 6) or as a 'fact' (level 5). As the poet Rilke (1964) asked, 'Are we, perhaps, *here* just for saying: House, Bridge, Fountain, Gate, Jug, Fruit tree, Window, – possibly: Pillar, Tower?.... but for **Saying**, remember, oh, for such saying as never the things themselves hoped so intensely to be' (p. 64).

For level-3 descriptions, opinions or values are temporarily 'bracketed off' – as is required in the practice of the discipline of phenomenology. The levels or **domains** (as Matura in a personal communication prefers that I call them) could equally well be numbered in the opposite way (from the top down) – or not numbered at all. According to Peat (1996),

> Bohr's complementarity states that a single consistent description will never exhaust the meaning of what is happening at the quantum **level**. Rather, what is required are a number of complementary, mutually contradictory descriptions. An electron is described as both delocalized and wavelike, but also localized and particlelike.
>
> (p. 264, my emphasis.)

If the diagram reproduced here has a hierarchical appearance, it is simply because one cannot say everything at once in the one-dimensional space of a page. Also because there are different logical criteria – different *kinds* of 'truth values' for each domain (see Copi, 1961). This means that different kinds of knowledge are evaluated by different means.

It is best not to imagine the seven-level model as a kind of ladder, but rather as a sheet of paper folded into a circular tube shape where level 1

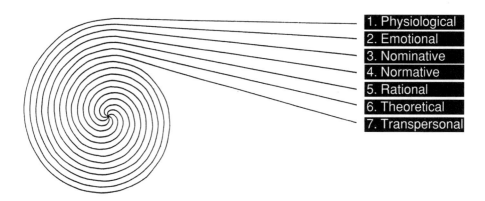

Figure 10.1 Diagrammatic representation of the seven-level model.

and level 7 touch each other. Using it this way could change your perspective on the world.

This model does **not** intend to be normative in any way. Its application should be judged solely by bearing in mind the potential usefulness for perception and developing of an epistemological consciousness in the various fields to which it is applied. (It will soon be obvious to readers familiar with developmental and/or evolutionary backgrounds that there is an ontogenetic and phylogenetic, unfolding across the domains.)

However, it should be stressed that in my view all of these levels co-exist right from wherever we wish to start talking about 'the beginning' – otherwise known as 'initial conditions'. Any notion that one domain is 'higher' or 'better' than another would show a misunderstanding of its purpose. However, different domains may be better for different purposes when applying it in practice or in analysing certain discourses.

The particular question which is at the heart of our work is: 'how does healing happen?' or 'how do we know that healing happens?'. In order to understand this we read the literature, we learn from our teachers and supervisors as well as from our own experiences and that of the people who seek us out for such healing. In particular the seven-level model can help to clarify the truth values appropriate to each epistemological domain – thus potentially preventing category errors, improper conflations and unnecessary confusions, as well as many avoidable miscommunications.

The model is both **ontological** (in that it is concerned with **existence**) or being as well as **epistemological** (in that it is concerned with **knowledge**, what and how we can know, and the methodologies we use in distinguishing varieties of truth values between different domains). It has thus a double aspect.

Ontologically it reflects our experience of 'being' (**physis**). This is our experience of ourselves. For example, in answer to the question 'How are you?' there is rarely a simple answer which reflects the whole of our experience. We usually politely say 'fine'. But a friend – or a therapist – may genuinely want a fuller, truer answer, even if it is more complex and potentially contradictory.

In natural everyday occurring talk it is commonplace to say: 'at one level this, at another level that...' (This apparently unconscious use of the device of distinguishing different levels (or domains) is also surprisingly frequent in academic, theoretical and scientific writing and discourse.)

So perhaps it's true that overall I'm sort of 'fine'. Like I'm not physically ill. But I am physically somewhat under par, I'm also extremely worried about my friend who is very ill, at one level I am pre-occupied about what a colleague really meant when they recently jokingly referred to my working class accent, I am at the same time confused about what to do about my guilt feelings for cheating on my wife, at another level I am also excited about learning how useful understanding philosophy can be in my psychotherapy practice, I am furthermore concerned about the meaning of my life now that my children have left home or I am facing ageing and retirement, at yet another level I am truly fine – I have moments of inexpressible peace in my garden.

Our experience of our own being-ness is often like this. Multi-vocal – having many voices 'inside' our self – or selves. Only rarely does a human being feel 'all of a piece'. 'Fine' all the way through at all levels. Many workers in our field have tried to organize these different 'voices' or different experiences of our multiple co-existing selves by offering us concepts such as 'id, ego and superego'; 'good' and 'bad' internal objects; complexes and archetypes; sub-personalities; competing 'schemas' etc. etc.

Whatever we do and whatever we choose to call these different voices or self experiences, their continuing co-existence seems to be a fact – an existential given of human experience. It seems to me that the more the psychotherapist can tolerate or welcome the multiplicity of their own experience of being human, the more that psychotherapists can tolerate, welcome and be effective in helping the other to become more fully healthy – more fully human. The seven-level model offers us what has been found to be a very valuable tool in terms of sorting these ontological experiences into manageable categories. We can think of this in a way as the 'inner' aspect of organizing human experience – thus ontology.

Epistemology concerns our relationship to external knowledge in addition to our inner knowing. When we face outward towards the world, we are again confronted with a multiplicity of co-existing discourses about knowledge – many different 'voices' often saying (or writing) things which make sense in one context and nonsense in another.

Almost everyone who has ever sincerely engaged with more than one good theoretical explanation of how it is that human beings experience psychological distress has had the experience of being – for some time at least – totally convinced by the one and then **also** totally convinced by another psychotherapeutic narrative – even though these different 'stories' may appear totally contradictory.

As a 'scientific' psychology student the overriding importance of conditioning and learnt behaviour as an explanation for pathology seemed totally and completing convincing to me. Yet, somehow it did not answer all my questions. However, neither did I fail to be entirely persuaded by the eloquence of Freud, for example in reading his *Interpretation of Dreams*. Now I read that there is conclusive evidence of animals dreaming. Do animals have super-egos? Do I?

In 1975 when I was a young university lecturer sincerely and enthusiastically teaching all the major – very different – models of personality my students got equally confused. That was the birthing ground of the seven-level model. It helped us then and has helped many others since. Personally, at times of the most profound personal distress it has been a truly profound compass and support.

Different 'worlds' of experience

When the therapist says something like: 'I wonder if, perhaps, there is some way you can take some personal responsibility for your cancer, rather than just handing it over to the medical professionals', the client may feel this as a statement of truth that they have 'brought the cancer upon themselves'.

Or the therapist may say something like 'Your dreams seems to indicate your unconscious desire to murder your mother, so that you can have exclusive sexual possession of your father'. That may be experienced as devastating and completely different from the way the therapist meant the interpretation. Another way of saying this is that they were in **different universes of discourse**.

Their 'talk' was from different worlds of meaning. For each of the individuals in these examples, their words might have been genuine, sincere and well-meant within their own 'world of talk'. It makes perfect sense within the one person's world of talk. However, the other person is hearing and talking from another world of meaning and experience which is perhaps also genuine, sincere and well-meant, but completely different from the other person's.

As Derrida (1992) says: 'No, that which is other is what is never inventable and will never have waited for your invention. The call of the other is a call to come, and that happens only in multiple voices' (p. 342).

Unless they both (or all in the group) know (or explore quite precisely and deeply what their differences of meaning are and are willing to acknowledge their different meaning universes) and can create a common world (in Heidegger's German – a *mitwelt*), there is little hope for restoring the integrity of the working alliance and developing the relationship further. Then it might just flounder on the rocks of mutual misunderstanding and confusion. We have probably all been in relationships or attended meetings where we could see this happening and felt helpless to sort it out.

So one client could give quite a full answer, for example, *'Well, my health is quite good, but at an emotional level I am still grieving very much for the loss of my home, my family and for having to leave my country during the current Fascist regime. I wake up during the night and scream and scream. At the same time I also feel good about having done the right thing in working here now with other refugees. It is good and important work and I feel I am doing something for other people who have gone through similar experiences. I have worked at the trauma clinic for 6 months now and have seen some two dozen clients for psychotherapy.*

I am myself in therapy and supervision on a weekly basis. I still have tremendous difficulty in making any sense of it all. The meaning of my life is shattered. I try to find comfort from reading the ancient books of wisdom of my culture and sometimes I think that the doctrine of reincarnation can help me find my way through this terrible tragedy – perhaps we are just here to learn in the Great Cycle of Being. Sometimes during my meditations, for brief moments, I even have a sense of peacefulness amid it all. It is almost as if there is a riverbed that is still and solid and a kind of container for the great river of life. There may be calm periods as well as rapids, crocodiles and dangerous waterfalls. But they are also part of life. When I can contact the riverbed – which is not often – it helps me. Perhaps it's about eternity in a way. It's about God and not about God. I don't really have words for it. It's just a feeling, but without those moments, my life would not be worth anything to me now.'

To the question, 'how are you really?' from an interested other person such as a supervisor, this man is distinguishing seven 'levels' of experience. These levels of talk are all co-existing at the same moment – and sometimes quite contradictory.

The seven-level model is especially useful for distinguishing between what philosophers call different kinds or categories for talking about the 'truth values' of statements and what psychoanalysts and psychotherapists may call different levels of experience, as I shall show later in this chapter.

Many individuals and several communities of knowledge and practice are effectively using this seven-level model to clarify their thinking and their communication. In my view, it is an implicit ordering principle of all clear-thinking discourse whether or not the speaker or reader is conscious of it.

For example, an eminent psychoanalytic writer/practitioner such as Eigen, interviewed by Molino (1997), demonstrates his awareness of the 'primacy of multiplicity' by writing: 'Rather than have war between all these different dimensions of experience, it's much more fruitful to keep open the possibility that each has a voice, that each has say in the play of voices, and to see what happens . . . '.

Not all writers and thinkers are so clear about the multifacetedness of experience and universes of discourse. However, Eigen does not specifically name them – such an effort might illumine his exposition in a very helpful way. In other cases the seven-level model could be used to clarify the potential confusions and misunderstandings when we try to constrain discourse or experience to only one or two levels instead of their multifaceted multiplicity.

'Psychoanalytic theory often appears to have a disadvantage through being formulated in such a descriptive way that the observational and the theoretical levels seems confused, at the same level of abstraction' (Bion in Grinberg et al., 1975). In my opinion the confusion of levels is ubiquitous in psychotherapy and psychoanalysis generally right across all the approaches, thus conveying our confusion to our clients too. Yet there are examples of clarity in almost every major psycho-language.

To illustrate the seven-level model as a multivocal expression of human transpersonal experiences, here follows a transcript of an interview with Eigen demonstrating his awareness of the 'primacy of multiplicity'. As far as I know he has never heard of the Clarkson seven-level model, yet he spontaneously in this interview distinguishes between co-existing domains of experience in relation to what we have called 'the transpersonal'.

I include the relevant extract from Molino with some comments in square brackets in order to demonstrate how this psychoanalyst differentiates between his subjective levels of 'the transpersonal' dimension of his experience of being human.

What is faith for Michael Eigen?
Different things at different times. I guess there's spiritual faith and there's natural faith. I place a great deal of weight on natural faith. I've nothing against spiritual or mystical faith, . . . but there's an awful lot of faith that springs simply from sensory experience, from how good it feels to be able to walk down a street and move one's limbs and not be in prison . . . It brings up a feeling inside

that, while it might be stretching things to call 'faith', I really do have to call it that . . . It makes one feel good to be alive, it makes one feel that life is good . . . The body seems to have this faith . . . Very often I've been astonished by how a dying animal seems to not know it's dying, by how it acts in the face of death, and seems to live, to be moving or trying to move or live to the last ounce... It just keeps going to the end . . . Or even when it stops moving and gets into a dying position, it doesn't seem to be angry or yelling about its imminent end. Somehow there seems to be an acquiescence, a simple ebbing of energy in the direction of death. It's a kind of body faith, a faith the body has.

[Here Eigen is describing the feeling of physis – life energy – at the physiological animal body level whether it is the energy of just being alive or the energy 'ebbing in the direction of death'. Refer to the earlier Heidegger quotation where he wrote that 'dying can be the highest act of living'. Of course the very act of description already removes it from the direct sensory experience of the body – domain one. He seems to be aware of this in drawing the analogy with animals who cannot speak but can only be observed, and with referring to a faith of the body. Quite naturally he goes on to the second or affective domain by using exclamations of emotional expression:]

I suppose one could talk about an affective faith or an emotional faith: the 'ouch!' and 'Yum!' of things . . . 'Ouch! That hurt!' . . . or 'Yum! That was worth it!' So it's more than pleasure and pain, I think. When one talks about a pleasure or pain principle, one's de-animated it [de-animation = stripped of animation, vitality or liveliness] because A's not simply bad or good [as at sensory physiological level 1] it's heavenly, it's heavenly . . . It's wonderful! . . . it feels yummy all through . . . You know, one would have to be totally mad not to have a secular or ironical self and see the limits of things,

[showing awareness of the irrationality of the emotional realm – thus not the domain of reasoned discourse which he refers to earlier in this interview as 'scientific ground'(p. 108) or domain 5 which is subject to the 'animosity' of some other analysts, but also the critique of self-reflection and self-parody – and stressing the *feeling, liking* and *sense* which dominates]

but I rather like siding with this feeling of 'good to the last drop in psychoanalysis . . . like a bug that never stops moving . . . There's just a sense of never giving up . . . never giving up on a case . . . not giving up on anyone . . . Who knows better? . . .

[The interviewer, introducing the nominative or third level potentially present where things and experiences are **named** (given a name instead of a sensation or a feeling) in any such discourse about faith, asks:]

All this begs another question. What does Michael Eigen mean by God?
God only knows!

[I speculate that this is an emotional exclamation, but he quickly moves to the commonly understood discourse which provides the **narrative** (domain 6) for 'faith' in his **normative** cultural grouping (domain 4) – presumably similar or understood and shared by his interlocutor.]

I think I have to be honest to say I mean a biblical God, the God of Abraham, Isaac and Jacob . . . But having said that I can step back [move perspective] and say: 'Hey well what I mean by God could be anything, because I don't know . . .

[Eigen can be read to express his awareness that 'knowing' about the God of

Abraham, Isaac and Jacob is not the kind of 'knowledge' which can be proven at a rational objective level.]

In a sense God is a total unknown

[the sense in which at level 5 God's existence has not been conclusively proved, but Eigen says there is a 'sense' of being 'tied' or in a relationship to God which is closer than his relationship to himself] and yet in others

[other senses or varieties of meaning]

the very notion ties the so-called biblical, personal God closer to me than I am to myself . . . . And then there are times one can just lift up one's hands and say, 'Wow, all this out of nothingness' . . . which feels wonderful . . . [the 2nd or emotional domain] to blank oneself out and be totally open [the epoche of phenomenology at level 3]

to whatever currents pulse this way or that ... whether you're into body [1], or emotions [2] . . . Taoist or Buddhist

[different narratives or stories or ancient explanatory theories]

whatever, it feels good. You know, in the Kabala [another domain 6 story for which there is no 'hard evidence]

God has . . . is . . . goes beyond names . . . the Ein Sof, the infinite of infinites, the great unknown, the 'I-itself' . . . By the time God gets named! . . .

(or undergirds or interpenetrates) all experience. [The interviewer then comments: Then a loss of words and silence. This is a rather exquisitely direct expression of the domain which I have called the 'transpersonal' characterized by the fact that it is wordless and cannot really be articulated – it can only be pointed at or experienced. Of course Christianity, Islam and Buddhism (especially in their mystical traditions) and Taoism all acknowledge the essential inarticulability of God **in one of several dimensions** of the experience of faith. The Tao which can be spoken is not the Tao. The God which can be named is not the God-experience which transcends.]

I had a patient once who, in the midst of a fierce negative transference, blurted out loud: 'I am that I am', without any apparent sense of the phrase's biblical echo.

[God's words and very similar to the Hindu Tat Swam Asi.] *The woman was stating her difference and uniqueness in a rather commonsensical sort of way, [!] but the sheer power of her words was unmistakable.*

[A person in so-called negative transference using God's words in relationship with her analyst.]

That's wonderful. I think Ben, in my book *Coming through the Whirlwind*, does something like that at one point. It's what we're doing all the time: we're 'am'ing . . . and we're 'am'-ing each other too . . . we're enabling each other *to am* [Here the power of '**am'-ing** in relationship with each other. See Heidegger (1989) about Physis as **Being**. It may be helpful to compare Eigen's spontaneous separation of the universes of discourse about faith with my intentional analysis of the seven kinds of discourses about the transpersonal in Chapter 10 of *The Transpersonal Relationship in Psychotherapy* – the hidden curriculum of spirituality, which is in press.]

Psychoanalytic theory is replete with dichotomies, intrapsychic/interpersonal, drive/relational, fixation/regression, deficit/conflict, even the hoariest of all, nature/nurture. One is always tempted to say, 'Why not see and use both perspectives?' But there are not different perspectives on the same reality: they are different realities, entirely different pervasive sets about what reality is. They are opposing philosophies of life. Therapists who talk about character and character disorders see patients, psychotherapeutic devices, and outcomes differently from therapists who talk about personality. Just because we are using the same words, we are not using them in the same way. We talk to each other, we must begin with the assumption of difference. I believe that our particular Tower of Babel is built on the paradoxical illusion that we are all speaking the same Tongue . . . Any reader, not totally committed to one ideology or another, cannot fail to be impressed – and one might hope, dismayed – by the total conviction with which prominent analysts proclaim diametrically opposed clinical strategies for what they diagnose as the very same characterological category. (Levenson,1991, p. 244.)

In summary, in this interview Eigen distinguishes the seven levels (without specifically naming or numbering them as I have done). He differentiates;

1. 'a **natural faith of the body**' which is like that of animals and includes 'a simple ebbing of energy in the direction of death' (ebbing has the connotation of life's rhythms);
2. an **affective or emotional faith** expressed – 'the Ouch and Yum of things';
3. a **biblical God with specific names** – the God of Abraham, Isaac and Jacob;
4. a **realm with moral implications** – 'never giving up on a case', 'not giving up – not giving up on anyone';
5. an **acknowledgement of the rational/scientic realm** (where he says what many scientists have said before): 'One would have to be totally mad not to have a secular or ironical self and see the limits of things . . . ';
6. the **realm of experience where different narratives (or perspectives)** can be used to refer to the transpersonal – Kabbalism, Taoist, Buddhist; and then
7. the **experiential realm** where words simply fail: where one can just lift up one's hands and say: 'Wow, all this out of nothingness . . . blank oneself out and be totally open to whatever currents pulse this way or that . . . ' – the region beyond names.

This example of the natural **emergence** of seven ways of engaging with the transpersonal experience in the spontaneous discourse of someone I have never met leads me to conclude (not for the first time) that the seven different ways of **being** (ontology) and **knowing** (epistemology) constitute an embedded phenomenological shape (fractal) of human experience and human discourse.

What I think I have done is to recognize a naturally occurring phenomenon, not to construct another cognitively preconceived 'model' that **has** to be learnt in order to be applied. People who have seriously grappled with the sometimes mutually contradictory but yet **co-existing** realms of human experience or human search for 'what can be known and how we can know it' seem to use it spontaneously. Learning to **recognize** this implicit pattern, however, can facilitate self-understanding, communication and philosophical clarity, and hopefully also the human condition.

BY WAY OF A REMINDER, THE **FIVE RELATIONAL FRAMEWORK** IS CONCERNED WITH THE **PROCESS** OF HUMAN RELATIONSHIPS; **THE SEVEN-LEVELS** ARE CONCERNED WITH THE CONTENT.

Experience/talk and truth values appropriate to the different levels/domains

Descriptions of the seven domains can be applied (a) ontologically – to our human **experience** or (b) epistemologically – to **knowledge** and its uses. For practical purposes the word 'level' seems more natural when we are speaking about phenomenology or subjective experience. The word 'domain' (for which I thank Maturana's personal interest in this model) seems to be more precisely applicable when discussing episte-mological concerns or issues to do with other kinds of 'knowledge'.

For want of better one, I currently use the term 'discourse' to mean both 'internal experience' **and** 'external sources of knowing' . However, it is important to note that there are at least three experiential levels and epistemological domains (1,2&7) which may be word-less.

It is important to notice from the start that (a) different epistemological levels may or may not contradict each other (e.g. parents may be loved and hated as well as honoured or acknowledged by the use of their surname); (b) that different domains of discourse or experience of 'knowing' co-exist (e.g. to believe that abortion is a morally wrong murder of a foetus and yet to assist such an abortion when it is the result of rape of an eleven-year old girl); and that (c) it is possible to differentiate between the different domains when we differentiate the criteria for evaluating what kind of 'knowledge' or logical 'truth value' can be assigned to the different domains.

Domain 1: The physiological/perceptual

Description of kinds of discourse appropriate to this level/domain

This is the realm of sensory experience, the part of our experienced world that functions in time before language manifests. The sources of knowledge on this level are the objects and events perceived through our senses and also the proprioceptive experience of phenomena within our bodies. It concerns body processes such as sleep arousal, psychophysiology, natural sleep rhythms, physical conditions of disease, the physical manifestation of anxiety and general sensory awareness.

Epistemological truth value/methodology

Physiological processes can be 'measured' in some instances such as brain wave patterns on an EEG, but – as philosophers over centuries have been at pains to show – it is probably impossible to ever know whether another person's sensation of the colour red is similar or different from one's own. Perception, like pain, is irretrievably subjective and embodied.

Domain 2: The affective/emotional

Description of talk appropriate to this domain

This level comprises the feelings that we have in common with infants and animals – fear, pain, joy, anger etc. Emotions and subjective feelings pervade our existence, and even the smallest possible segments of our perceptions carry an 'emotional colour'. Emotions are the subjective feelings which arise as a response to one or another stimulus event.

This domain involves a pre-verbal area of experience and activity. It concerns those psychophysiological states or electro-chemical muscular changes in our bodies we talk about as feelings, affect and/or emotion in psychology. What one person experiences as distress in the vertiginous post-modern condition, another may experience as pleasurable excitement at the unfolding of creative potentials of chaos. It has been convincingly demonstrated and argued that there is always an emotional layer or sub-text to any communication – even if it is the acknowledgement of the other person.

Epistemological truth value/methodology

Emotions are essentially subjective, experiential and felt states, whereas our knowledge about them seems to be existential, phenomenological and unique. Whatever a client feels is **their truth** – whether or not we can feel the same or think that it is reasonable to feel like that. Sometimes we are puzzled by our own 'unreasonable emotions'. Many people, for example, are shocked by the rage they experience at a beloved who has died. The bereavement counsellor can often normalize the co-existence of contradictory and 'unreasonable' emotions.

Domain 3: The nominative

Description

This level comprises naming through words, a process that rests on division into classes and categories and precedes complex abstract thinking. (This model is a level 3 discourse itself.) This is the area of objective nominalism, when objects are placed together on the basis of certain resemblances. Linguistic identity is established through the repetition of a unique sound that supports the development of an objective reality outside the self.

Name-giving implies reflective shared experience, the basis of human culture. Within any common set of language rules the fact that certain kinds of words are known to stand for certain kinds of objects can be agreed, debated or disputed. Philosophically it represents the realm that the phenomenologists such as Merleau-Ponty posited as a third way between idealism and positivism.

It is **not** in the same universe of discourse as voice. The psychoanalyst McDougall (in Molino, 1997) is describing level 1 – sensory – experience and differentiating it from the domain of words – the nominative domain, when she says:

> I've thought a lot about it: 'In the beginning was the word.' But no, in the beginning was the voice .... the way the mother is feeling, all her emotional states are transmitted to her baby through her voice, her skin and her smell .... I'm thinking in terms of an infraverbal language .... While an infant is born into a speaking environment, socioculturally determined and so forth, at the same time there's another language being transmitted. A language absorbed by the child as a body language.' (p. 82)

Epistemological truth value/methodology

In this realm of discourse there can be some agreement or disagreement within or between groups, within dialect or language or disciplinary groups, e.g. 'what things are called'. Within any common set of language rules the fact that certain kinds of words are known to stand for certain kinds of objects or phenomena can be agreed, debated or disputed.

Without clarity of definition (or discourse about such definitions), words such as 'self', 'ego state', 'psychotherapy' or 'transference' and 'effectiveness' are far too often used idiosyncratically, whimsically or arbitrarily. In this way it leads to endless needless disputes, misunderstandings and unnecessary relational damage, not only between client and psychotherapist – but sadly between psychotherapists themselves.

Domain 4: The normative

Brief description

The normative level comprises the various aspects of the individual encountering the norms and values of the group, the tribe, the family, the professional association, the culture, etc. This level of discourse tends to deal with the knowledge of attributes and practices regarding people as 'cultural beings'. It deals with values, norms, collective belief systems, stereotypes of gender or race or 'pathology', for example, and also societal or organizational expectations.

Epistemological truth value/methodology

Values, morals, ethics are not always subject to logical tests of truth or statistical rationality – it is a different realm of questioning and knowing. Norms, ethics, laws provide containment and limitation, security and meaning, a sense of belonging or exclusion. Our values, our ethics, our professional codes of conduct, our personal *Weltanschauung* (world view) is never the same **kind** of knowing as in the next domain – that of objectively provable truth (5)

Domain 5: The rational, logical

Indicative description

This is the level of facts, the logical-rational dimension of testable state-ments, where causal relations can be clearly established. The rational permits clear positivistic principles of verification, it operates with that which can be objectively identified, defined and proved – for **that** time and **that** culture. The discipline of psychology prides itself on its record – quite rightly – of establishing scientific evidence about many human experiences.

Psychotherapy generally, by contrast, is impoverished in this area and perhaps overrich in theories to explain (or explain away) psychologically proven facts.

Facts in this realm exist not as subjective feelings, mere words or shared beliefs, but as rational conclusions derived in a repeatable form from a body of well established empirical data. This layer of knowledge and activity includes thinking, making sense of things, examination of cause and effect, working with facts and information of the time and place. It covers science, logic, statistical probabilities, provable facts, verifiability according to Popper, established 'truth' statements and consensually observable phenomena.

Epistemological truth value/methodology

It is characteristic of all level 5 discourse that it is possible to establish truth values by consensual practices of that time and that culture. That is, it is the **only** realm of discourse where dispute can be settled by reference to external tests resembling what is commonly understood as the modern scientific method – or the 'gold standard' of objectively proven evidence. If there is disagreement about a 'fact' within a particular knowledge community, it is a misnomer and does not belong within this realm of discourse, but in one of the others.

Domain 6: The theoretical/metaphorical

Indicative description

The theoretical level attends to explanations, metaphors, the stories that are told to show how things have come about, narratives and metaphors. They are the means by which we make sense of the world; they do not establish the 'Truth' but remain some of the possible versions that, when verified or negated, pass from theory to the factual domain (5). Within the sixth domain there are the hypotheses, explanations, metaphors, narratives and stories that humans have created in order to explain why things are the way they are and why humans behave in a certain way. Psychotherapeutic theory which is not underpinned by the rationality of domain 5 tends to over-rely on the belief structures of level 4 – if these are even logically differentiated at all.

Almost all psychotherapy and psychoanalytic approaches, 'stories', 'narratives' and 'theories' fall into this category, basically trying to explain all the other domains of experience and knowledge not necessarily by using 'facts', but by offering explanatory paradigms which can help the psychotherapist learn and understand his or her work more effectively. For many years now in all my 'beyond schoolism' work, I have argued against the notion that any of these 'theories' can be said to be 'true' in the same way that some facts of science such as gravity can be true.

If theories of personality or psychoanalytic theories were 'true' in a level 5 sense, they would no longer be 'theories', but consensually agreed facts – and thus indisputable by sane people of the same culture. It is an obvious but frequently overlooked logical error to use the (sometimes useful) explanatory myth of the Oedipus complex as a truth of the same kind as the temperature at which water boils.

I would suggest that the bulk of the problems attendant on finding 'hard evidence' for the efficacy of psychotherapy, and in particular the apparently intractable problems in psychotherapy, outcome research, stem from similar conceptual confusions between different kinds of 'evidence' appropriate to different levels of human experience.

Epistemological truth value/methodology

When a theory, narrative or hypothesis is 'proved' true, it belongs to the domains of facts and logical or statistical probabilities. Until this becomes the case, such explanatory notions belong to the narrative or theoretical ontological and epistemological domain.

However, there are criteria for judging whether a particular theory is better or worse. Such criteria help us to choose or prefer some psychological theories or explanations or hypotheses over others. The criteria for evaluating such theories or narratives usually include dimensions such as validity, reliability, coherence, lack of internal contradictions, elegance, utility, economy of explanation (e.g. Occam's razor), 'fit' with surrounding theories and already proven facts.

Domain 7: The transpersonal or currently inexplicable

Indicative description

The transpersonal level is the category assigned to the unexplained areas of human interaction and experience. This domain refers to the epistemological area or universe of discourse which transcends words. It makes space for 'the uncanny', the inexplicable, the inexpressible kinds of knowing. It is beyond level 5 rationality, facts and theories and concerns the paradoxical, the unpredictable and the inexplicable. It is a region of unknowability, a horizon that has to be left open for the development of future areas of discourse and reference for these currently unknown conditions.

Epistemological truth value/methodology

It is characteristic of experience in this domain that people are convinced by 'direct experience' which feels impossible to articulate or effectively communicate to others who have not shared similar direct experience – or who come to do so. It is in the region of what Jung called 'synchronicity', the knowledge of the mystic, the 'peak experience' or the quantum physicist who marvels at the beauty of our universe and concludes that 'God does not play dice'. Or it is simply those experiences or discourses which we cannot 'prove' at level 5, nor explain satisfactorily at level 6.

Category errors between different domains in psychotherapeutic discourses

Common category errors in psychoanalytical and psychotherapeutic speech and writing occur for example when different epistemological categories (or domains of discourse) are confused, contaminate each other, when it is assumed that different categories of knowledge can't co-exist despite apparent contradictions and when there is cross-level displacement.

So the first communication and philosophical problem is when discussants, writers and practitioners confuse these universes of discourse, do not distinguish between them, conflate them or overemphasize one at the expense of the other. For example Brierley (1942) pointed out that: 'We must distinguish between the patients' language (describing their phantasies) and scientific language – between living experience and our theoretical inferences' (p. 110).

Although he succeeds in separating out the universe of discourse from 'living experience', unfortunately it seems as if Brierley himself here is mistakenly equating 'scientific language' with 'our theoretical inferences'. These discursive domains are not the same and cannot be judged by the same criteria or logical 'truth values'.

Domain confusion

A form of category confusion indicating a wrong identification of domains, for example, is when a statement that expresses a group norm is taken to be rational definition or fact. Statements like 'because we think it is good therapy to believe our clients, what they say must be true' or 'All psychotherapy should be evidence based' demonstrate philosophical domain confusion.

Other examples of domain confusion occur when a theoretical hypothesis or possible explanation is treated as a proven fact, as in the following examples from Freud: 'only those children are predisposed to fear whose sexual instinct is excessively or prematurely developed, or who are exigent in manner as a result of pampering' (p. 616).

> One says rightly that the Oedipus complex is the nuclear complex of the neuroses, that it represents the essential part in the content of the neuroses. It is the culminating point of infantile sexuality, which through its after-effects decisively influences the sexuality of the adult. The task before each new human being is to master the Oedipus complex; one who cannot do this falls into a neurosis. (p. 617)

Taking the metaphorical phrase 'the body doesn't lie' literally or concretely is another form of confusion between different universes of discourse. If what is meant by the statement is to pay attention to the language of the body in therapy as having its own kind of visceral truth – it is good clinical advice. When it is taken to mean that the traces of our experiences are accurately laid down in our physiology to correspond with the actual events of observable reality, it is nonsense.

Bodies do lie – they respond physically, vicariously attuned with the emotions of others, as anyone who has been to a rock concert or the funeral of a public figure could testify. Bodies show blisters when they have not been burnt under hypnosis. Bodies register physical trauma when only a word or a look has passed. In some parts of the world, people die from no known physical cause when they are 'hexed' by their communities.

According to Hinshelwood (1989), for example, Kleinians use the terms 'introjection' and 'projection' to refer to the subjective experiences of their patients, yet the terms were originally developed to refer to psychological features and processes objectively described in a scientific manner – i.e. Freudian 'metapsychology' (p. 425). (He is emphasizing that Freud used a scientific manner to describe his theories; he is not saying that Freudian metapsychology is a **science**.) Introjection is thus, for example, **not** an 'objective scientific term'; it is a technical name given to an hypothesized psychological process.

Imprecise language and lack of definitions support many domain confusions.

Domain contamination

Domain contamination also happens when one or more domains is impaired by the controlling influence of another domain. One example would be: 'If the effectiveness of psychotherapy cannot be proved by double-blind random controlled trials like psychotropic drugs, it is useless.' This suggests that one domain (that of current consensual reality proven by laboratory-type trials) is the only way of establishing or 'knowing' the effectiveness of psychotherapy.

There are several other domains by which people claim that psychotherapy has been effective for themselves judged by their own criteria (cf. Seligman, 1999). It may currently be the favoured 'objective' way of achieving scientific results – but quantum physics for example shows alternative 'objective' facts such as the fact that objects are somehow interrelated even though there is no evidence of any causal connection between them.

Furthermore this kind of statement needs to be read in the context of what has been 'proven' about psychotropic medication – for example that the placebo rate for commonly used anti-depressants has been 'proved' by such laboratory criteria to be between 25 and 35% (Professor Laden of the Maudsley, 1999, personal communication).

Domain conflict

Domain conflict exists when one or more levels are experienced in opposition. An indication would be a phrase like: 'I should not feel anger because my spouse died. I know it wasn't their intention to abandon me, but I also know how I feel.' Extensive studies of bereavement substantiate that some kind of anger toward the dead person is felt alongside **knowing** that such a feeling is 'unreasonable'.

At the extremes the same can be said by most people suffering from obsessive compulsive disorders or phobias, but anecdotal evidence (and some self-reflection) will probably support the notion that there are very few human beings whose feelings and thoughts are always in accord, e.g. new year's resolutions, getting up on a cold winter's morning, only being sexually attracted to socially approved or suitable partners. Too often, at a phenomenological or experiential subjective level people find that: 'the spirit is willing, but the flesh is weak' or patients say: 'I know one thing in my head, but my heart (or guts) just can't accept it'.

Conflict between epistemological domains also exists when one or more levels of language are in opposition – and in fact, they usually are. There is a world of difference between a client saying 'daddy was just messing around' and 'daddy raped me'. Another indication from a psychotherapist would be a phrase like: 'Because my physiological countertransference indicates that the client is telling the truth, I will testify that the event actually happened.'

That is taking 'knowledge' from my own body – which is a kind of physiological/emotional knowledge and equating that with the kind of knowledge (or truth) that judges and police officers are trained to evaluate. It is a different kind of truth and the domains (the court, the consulting room, the imagination, the dream) where these truth values can be enacted are different.

It is argued that rigorous definition of terms and conscientious specification of domains of discourse would be of inestimable help to clinical and supervisory practice, the courts, our profession and particularly our patients who already suffer from enough confusions of feeling and thinking, moral values and fact, fantasy and phantasy, observation and trance induction, truth and lies. It is also held that this thesis requires this kind of epistemological clarity in order to achieve its task.

At the metaphorical heart of much of the confusion and conflicts in the field of psychoanalysis and psychotherapy lies the unresolved mind–body problematique. If a dual world is posited in which 'a ghost in a machine' pulls the levers of the body (to use Ryle's famous phrase) it becomes logically impossible to make valid 'scientific' statements about the psyche.

Psychotherapists often write or speak as if we can observe someone objectively and as if we can also sample their subjective experience through our own psycho-physiological and symbolic experiences through empathic identification with their subjectivity. There is a major problem with the notion of objectivity and a minor one with the notion of subjectivity.

The minor problem is the assumption that we can ever know another person's world subjectively through empathy. In this regard it is salutary to read Abrams, Self-attention and the ego-centric assumption of shared perspective, which was published in the Journal of Experimental Social Psychology in 1993. What kind of knowledge is based on empathic attunement and how could we ever know if their experience of being burnt with cigarettes is the same as mine – or what I imagine theirs to be?

Also, we usually assume that the 'attunement is one-way' – but intensive countertransference studies have other narratives which are highly persuasive and have clearly been used to conduct effective therapy in many cases (Searles, 1975; Casement, 1985; Langs, 1976). Few exponents of the current panacea of empathic attunement take into account the possibility that that very attunement can be iatrogenic (cf. Illich, 1975).

If attunement is good and non-attunement is bad, then it follows that bad attunement could be disastrous. Yet some world-famous psychotherapists such as Albert Ellis (e.g. in the well-known Gloria film) hardly display empathic attunement – and yet appear by consensual evidence to be successful in many cases.

Some theorist-clinicians for example consider that a story of being raped as a child told to the therapist encodes the patient's experience of being psychologically raped by, for example, over-intrusive interpretations or breaks in the analytic frame (Smith, 1991). This may be 'true knowledge' at the symbolic narrative level of discourse – verifiable by the verbal or physiological response to the interpretation.

But what if the patients are intentionally deceiving themselves (Mollon, 1999); you as the therapist are being hypnotized (e.g. projective identification); or the client is manifesting what is commonly called 'multiple personality disorders' or dissociation as a result of abusive trauma?

> In these states of dissociative pathology, where the unity of consciousness (always illusory) is sharply breached, we are faced with another puzzling question. Who is remembering? Who has forgotten? Is it a matter of memory at all? One state of consciousness seems to know something (or fantasise something) which another part does not know. Perhaps it is better to think of this as a kind of epistemological pathology. (Mollon, 1996, p. 198)

And might the pathology lie in our professionals and the expressions of our professional thinking itself? The major epistemological problem with the notion of objectivity (the idea that randomized control studies can provide evidence of effectiveness) is that there are a very large number of scientific studies which question the possibility of there ever being a neutral or objective observer. Experimenter effects have for example even been observed in rats learning mazes. They have also been observed in the famous Elkin (e.g. 1995) studies.

Furthermore, the arch-scientists, the physicists, have already (albeit reluctantly) come to the inescapable conclusion that the observer is **always** part of the field, i.e. 'objective observation' as is commonly understood is scientifically impossible. (Of course constructionists and constructivists have always had their philosophical doubts about it too.)

If this is a fact in the consensually accepted domain (and it appears that it is) classical notions of self and other, objective and subjective, individual and group, inside and outside, the very nature of psychological knowledge and what we as psychotherapists think we do with it, need to come under very serious review.

Yet psychology and some enclaves of psychotherapy outcome researchers still try to model their work on 19th century scientific paradigms by longing for the conclusive positivistically scientific evidence – like Freud tried to do – and then they wonder why their research so consistently and repeatedly fails to reach such a 'gold standard'.

It is not that some dimensions of human experience cannot reach this standard – some kinds of measurements like heart rate can be made and results shown. It is that this **kind** of measurement is not appropriate for other psychotherapeutically significant dimensions of human experience. The leading scientists of our time have for decades, now, known this about their field.

Quantum Entanglement, for example, indicates that scientifically self and other are inseparable, i.e. at some levels we exist in interrelationship – affecting each other – forever. Isham (1995):

> Ordinarily, we regard separate objects as independent of one another. They live on their own terms, and anything tying them together has to be forged by some tangible mechanism. Not so in the quantum world. If a particle interacts with some object – another particle, perhaps – then the two can be inextricably linked, or entangled.... In a sense, they simply cease to be independent things, and one can only describe them in relation to each other. (p. 27)

'In 1935 Einstein recognised that if two particles were entangled, doing something to one could immediately affect the other, even at a great distance. As a result, Einstein doubted that entanglement could be real. But since then, experiments have provided strong evidence that this "non-local" linking of distinct parts of the world really happens' (Crown, 1999, p. 26).

Might this explain how clients sometimes arrive at the next session quite improved after the psychotherapist has had some good supervision or a particularly fruitful turning point in their personal therapy?

Cross-level displacement

Cross-level displacement occurs when a condition pertaining to one level cannot find expression on that level and manifests on another level in symbolic form, perhaps as a symptom. An example of that kind is when, for example, notions such as ego or id or 'the unconscious' are reified – treated as a factual entity or place instead of a theoretical construct or names given by certain communities of discourse to refer to common meanings shared by definition by members of that community, e.g. all Freudians, all Jungians, all Aboriginals.

The reality of my feelings is no less real than the reality of the fact that this glass will fall if I drop it, and no less real than the fact that this chair upon which I sit is a whirlpool of molecules in motion – yet they are **different kinds of realities** – to be judged or eveluted by different means and measures. It is no good discarding apples because they do not meet the criteria for aeroplanes – it is epistemologically appropriate to use different criteria for different kinds of knowing.

McDougall (in Molino, 1997) for example displays, in my opinion, a conflation of universes of discourse when she writes: 'I said in my paper that we never know, nor ever will know, what is the actual cause of psychic change. So many things happen in the analytic relationship that are never put into words..... Our interpretations may have some effect on the changes that occur, but I think it's relatively minor' (p. 87). Just because some things about it cannot be put into words and we don't currently know why positive change occurs in psychoanalysis, does not automatically mean 'We will never know'.

Domain conflation

The commonest form of logical category error in terms of universes of discourse is domain conflation. This involves simply the denial of different kinds of co-existing realities or discourses. It frequently takes the form (along the whole continuum from conscious to unconscious) of trying to fit the complexities of our experience of being and our talk about our world in **a simplistic monistic 'one-truth must be true for everybody all the time'**.

A rather typical example is when people say, 'yes, it's all very well that we are energy fields of sub-atomic structures existing in relationship, but you can't deny that when I drop this glass it will fall on the floor!' (As if that proves anything but that different experiences and different kinds of knowledge are present simultaneously in our world.)

Another classic is the simplistically interpreted adage: 'Nobody can "make" you feel something'. Well, let someone kick you very hard on the shin, and if they can't make you feel the pain, you should probably very quickly consult a doctor. If someone has that degree of numbness in their body (or their heart) their body has lost one of its most important protective alarm systems.

Another frequently occurring logical category error in terms of domain conflation in the talk and text of psychotherapeutic discourse is the adoption of a **simplistic dualistic paradigm**, i.e. body/mind; male/female, true/false etc. etc. I am proposing that we consider at least a *heptuality* (seven-sidedness) of co-existing experiential and discursive realities. It seems a far better fit with the complexity of human beingness and human knowing.

Conclusion

According to Wittgenstein philosophy itself is a medicine (physic). He sees philosophy as the discipline of thinking about thinking. 'The object of philosophy is the logical clarification of thoughts. Philosophy is not a theory, but an activity. The theory of knowledge is the **philosophy of psychology**' (Wittgenstein, 1922, p.77) (my emphasis).

The basis and sine qua non for all disciplined thinking and acting is the avoidance of logical fallacies (e.g. Copi, 1961), spurious conclusions (e.g. Aristotle) and category errors (e.g. Ryle, 1960)

This chapter has specifically engaged with taking this kind of medicine for the dis-eases of our psychotherapeutic talk and text. It is not an easy endeavour, not can it be accomplished in one – or several – readings without serious study and supervised practice over an extensive period of time. Yet, it may hold the hope for psychotherapy to become well again.

At the 1998 UNESCO Symposium it was

> recognized how the nature of reality itself, with its inherent complexity and multiform character, but at the same time with its deep unity, requires transcending the boundaries of single disciplines. It was also observed that the probable reason for these global issues to necessitate a transdisciplinary approach is that they tend to reveal, more than others, the underlying complexity of reality. (p. 8) . . . Consequently, the shift of transdisciplinarity is from a parallel analysis of problems to the establishment of a common

dialogue, which would address complex issues on the basis of shared approaches and methods. (p. 12)

If leading thinker-practitioners engaging with global human issues are admitting that a transdisciplinary approach is more likely to reveal the underlying complexity of reality and pleading for transdisciplinarity of a common dialogue, how can psychotherapists still with any kind of integrity maintain the unquestioned superiority of any one single schoolist approach (as I described in Chapter 1) instead of seeking dialogue, a common transdisciplinary language to learn from and with each other – and to enquire together?

The way to attain an integrated concept and practice of knowledge, and consequently to address many crucial issues of our age through a transdisciplinary approach, does not lie in applying ready-made, 'mechanical' procedures based on automatic, stereotyped formulas and standardized recipes (UNESCO report, 1998, p. 7).

Are the complex issues of the human soul less important than the complex issues of our globe? Can we effectively engage with the one and not the other?

References

Abrams D (1993) Self-attention and the ego-centric assumption of shared perspective. Journal of Experimental Social Psychology 29: 287–303.

Brierley M (1942) Internal objects and theory. International Journal of Psycho-Analysis 23:107–20.

Casement P (1985) On Learning from the Patient. London: Tavistock.

Clarkson P (1992) Systemic Integrative Psychotherapy Training. In Dryden W (ed.) Integrative and Eclectic Therapy: A Handbook. pp.269–95. Milton Keynes: Open University Press.

Clarkson P (1995) The Therapeutic Relationship in Psychoanalysis. Counselling Psychology and Psychotherapy. London: Whurr.

Clarkson P (1996) The Bystander: An End to Innocence in Human Relationships? London: Whurr.

Clarkson P (2000) Ethics – Working with Ethical and Moral Dilemmas in Psychotherapy. London: Whurr.

Clarkson P, Lapworth P (1992) Systemic integrative psychotherapy. In Dryden W (ed.) Integrative and Eclectic Therapy: A Handbook. Buckingham: Open University Press, pp.41–83.

Copi IM (1961) (2nd edn) Introduction to Logic. New York: MacMillan.

Crown M (2000) Random reality. New Scientist Vol 165, issue 2227: (26 February).

Derrida J (1992) Acts of Literature (D. Attridge, ed.). New York & London: Routledge.

Eigen M (1997) In A. Molino (ed.) Freely Associated, pp. 93–126. London: Free Association Books.

Elkin L (1995) The NIMH treatment of depression collaborative research program: major results and clinical implications. Changes 13(3): 178–85.

Freud S (1938) The Basic Writings of Sigmund Freud. Translated and edited, with an introduction by Dr. A.A. Brill. New York: The Modern Library.

Gawthorp JC, Uhleman MR (1992) Effects of the problem–solving approach to ethics training. Professional Psychology: Research and Training 23(1): 38–42.

Geertz C (1973) The Interpretation of Cultures. New York: Basic Books.

Grinberg L, Sor D, Tabak de Bianchedi E (1975) Introduction to the Work of Bion. Strath Tay: Clunie Press.

Heidegger M (1987) An Introduction to Metaphysics (R. Manheim, trans.). New Haven: Yale University Press. (First published 1959)

Hinshelwood RD (1989) A Dictionary of Kleinian Thought. London: Free Association Books.

Illich L (1975) Medical Nemesis: The Expropriation of Health. London: Calder & Boyars.

Isham C J (1995) Lectures on Quantum Theory – Mathematical and Structural Foundations. London: Imperial College Press.

Kahn CH (1981) The Art and Thought of Heraclitus: An Edition of the Fragments with Translation and Commentary. Cambridge: Cambridge University Press.

Langs R (1976) The Bipersonal Field. New York: Jason Aronson.

Lepper G (1996) Between science and hermeneutics: Towards a contemporary empirical approach to the study of interpretation in analytical psychotherapy. British Journal of Psychotherapy 13(2): 219–31.

Levenson EA (1991) in Feiner AH (ed.) The Purloined Self: Interpersonal Perspectives in Psychoanalysis. New York: William Allison White Institute.

Lindsay G, Colley A (1995) Ethical dilemmas of members of the Society. The Psychologist: Bulletin of the British Psychological Society 8: 214–17.

McDougall J (1997) in Molino A (ed.) Freely Associated, pp. 53–92. London: Free Association Books.

Marton F (1992) Phenomenography and 'the art of teaching all things to all men'. Qualitative Studies in Education 5: 253–67.

Molino A (ed.)(1997) Freely Associated – Encounters in Psychoanalysis. London: Free Association Books.

Mollon P (1999) Memories are made of-what? In Greenberg S (ed.) Mindfield. The Therapy Issue, pp. 89–94. London: Camden Press.

Peat D (1996) Blackfoot Physics. London: Fourth Estate.

Rilke RM (1964) Selected Poems (J. B. Leishman, trans.). London: Penguin.

Ryle G (1960) Dilemmas: The Tarner Lectures. Cambridge: Cambridge University Press.

Schoenewolf G (1990) Turning Points in Analytic Therapy: The Classic Cases. Northvale, NJ: Jason Aronson.

Searles HF (1975) The patient as therapist to his analyst. In Giovacchini PL (ed.) Tactics and Techniques in Psychoanalytic Therapy Vol II, pp. 94–151. New York: Aronson.

Seligman MEP (1995) The effectiveness of psychotherapy. American Psychologist 50(12): 965–74.

Silverman D (1992) Interpreting Qualitative Data: Methods of Analysing Talk, Text and Interaction. London: Sage.

Smith D (1991) Hidden Conversations: An Introduction to Communicative Psychoanalysis. London: Routledge.

Spinelli E (1989) The Interpreted World: An Introduction to Phenomenological Psychology. London: Sage.

Thompson A (1990) Guide to Ethical Practice in Psychotherapy. Chichester: John Wiley.

UNESCO (1998) International Symposium of Transdisciplinarity – Towards Integrative Process and Integrated Knowledge, pp. 1–12. New York: United Nations.

Wilber K (1980) The Atman Project: A Transpersonal View of Human Development. Wheaton, Ill.: Theosophical Publishing House.

Wittgenstein L (1980) Remarks on the Philosophy of Psychology. Vol. 1 (GEM Anscombe, trans.), Oxford: Blackwell.

Wolman BB (ed.) (1965) Handbook of Clinical Psychology. New York: McGrawHill.

Wolman BB, Ullman M (eds) (1986) Handbook of States of Consciousness, pp. 133–58. New York: Van Nostrand Reinhold.

Woodmansey AC (1988) Are psychotherapists out of touch? British Journal of Psychotherapy 5: 57–65.

Index